D0555979

ASTRONOMY

THE DEFINITIVE GUIDE TO THE UNIVERSE

ASTRONOMY

THE DEFINITIVE GUIDE TO THE UNIVERSE

Duncan John

p

This is a Parragon Publishing Book
First published in 2006

Parragon Publishing
Queen Street House
4 Queen Street
Bath, BA1 1HE, UK

Produced by Atlantic Publishing

Photographs courtesy of Science Photo Library
Text © Parragon Books Ltd 2006

ISBN 1-40546-314-7

Printed in China

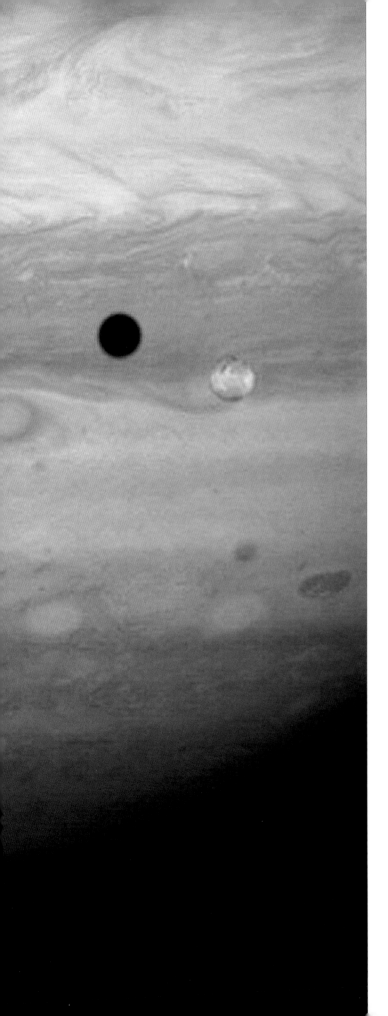

CONTENTS

INTRODUCTION   7

EARLY ASTRONOMY   8

THE COPERNICAN
REVOLUTION   14

THE SPACE AGE   20

THE SOLAR SYSTEM   30

THE SUN   38

MERCURY   50

VENUS   60

EARTH   72

MOON   84

MARS   100

JUPITER   118

SATURN   128

URANUS   142

NEPTUNE   152

PLUTO   164

ASTEROIDS, METEORS
AND COMETS   172

STARS   184

CONSTELLATIONS   196

NEBULAE   206

THE MILKY WAY   214

GALAXIES   220

THE UNIVERSE   230

APPENDICES   236

INDEX   252

ACKNOWLEDGEMENTS   256

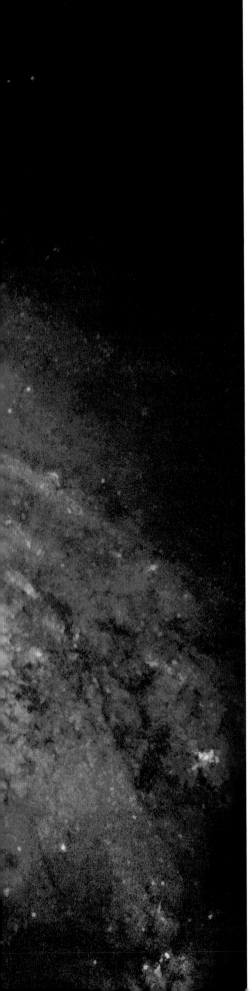

INTRODUCTION

The night skies and astronomical bodies have been a source of wonder and speculation since the development of the earliest civilizations. The sun, with its life-giving energy, was deified, its daily journey across the skies imbued with religious significance. The Ancient Egyptians calculated the length of the solar year, adding five days to their original 360-day calendar, a margin of error of just six hours. Where myth and mysticism led, scientific discovery quickly followed.

5000 years on, our knowledge of the solar system and what lies beyond may be considerable, yet the sense of awe is hardly less than that experienced by the earliest observers.

This book takes us on a journey of discovery, from a detailed study of the planets in our solar system to the far-distant galaxies and outermost reaches of the universe. All the spectacular cosmic phenomena are featured, including comets, asteroids, meteors and nebulae. Some may be less familiar, such as quasars, remote galaxies whose extraordinary luminosity and energy make our sun appear like a 40-watt bulb in an unlit cathedral; dark matter, which forms some 90 percent of the universe even though it cannot be detected directly; and black holes, superdense matter with a gravitational pull so strong that not even light can escape.

The canvas of space and time is vast: 15 billion years since the Big Bang, when the entire universe occupied the space of a sub-atomic particle; 5 billion years since a cloud of gas and dust collapsed to form the star which sustains life on Earth. To study an object in deep space is to see hundreds of millions of years into the past, such are the mind-boggling distances that light has to travel.

Whether you're an inveterate star-gazer or a new student of astronomy, this lavishly illustrated book will enhance your knowledge and understanding of the universe. It includes the most recent images from the Hubble Telescope and Cassini probe, and thus provides an authoritative but accessible overview of the latest exciting developments in space research.

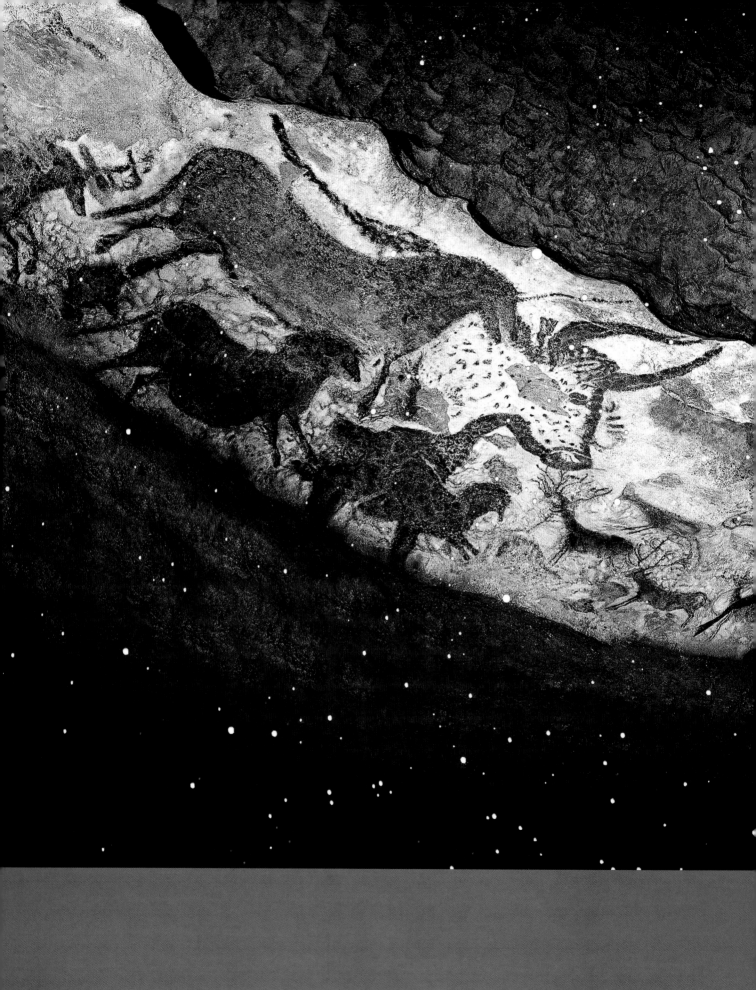

EARLY ASTRONOMY

The term astronomy derives from the Ancient Greek phrase meaning the laws or science governing the stars. However, astronomy is not just the study of the stars; rather it is the study of all celestial phenomena. It combines all the other Earth sciences and applies them to the study of all the matter existing outside our own planet, making it the widest ranging science.

In short, astronomy is the science of understanding everything that goes on beyond Earth's boundaries. Astronomy is also one of the oldest of sciences. Every civilization, through antiquity to the recent past, had stunning views of the stars night after night, as sightings of the cosmos would not have been hampered by light pollution and an indoor lifestyle, both of which hide much of the heavens from observers today. All over the world some sort of understanding of the celestial sphere was an integral part of civilization, whether or not they opted for scientific explanations of the observed phenomena.

Mesopotamia

The Babylonians, an ancient Mesopotamian people who flourished between the Tigris and Euphrates rivers, in the area of modern-day Iraq, were one of the earliest civilizations known to have adopted a scientific outlook towards the stars and planets. Pre-Mesopotamian civilizations had usually linked the celestial objects to spirits, but records still exist which show that, as early as 3000 B.C., the Babylonians recorded some constellations and mapped the recurrence of astronomical events.

One of the oldest surviving astronomical documents is the Venus Tablet of Ammisaduqa, which was discovered in the remains of a Babylonian library at Nineveh. The tablet is thought to date back to 1700 B.C., and shows records of the times at which Venus appeared and disappeared in the morning and evening sky. Records of the movements of Mercury have also been found, detailing the times when it could be seen and when it passed in front of or behind the sun, hiding it from view.

Chinese dragons

Ancient Chinese civilization paid close attention to the night sky because an important part of the culture's philosophy was the idea of harmony between man and nature. As a result Chinese astronomers correctly calculated the eclipse cycle; it is likely that this was the first civilization to have determined that there were 365 days in a year, by calculating the movement of the sun against the background stars. These great leaps forward came at a price; it is reputed that the Emperor would execute astronomers who made incorrect predictions.

Chinese mythology held that an eclipse occurred when a dragon was eating the sun and that the only way to defeat the dragon was to make as much noise as possible. In the event of an eclipse, people would make a mighty racket, which would scare the dragon off, and, naturally, the sun would return.

Pythagoras' globe

The Ancient Greeks greatly advanced the scientific study of astronomy by placing an emphasis upon observation and data collection. In 240 B.C., Eratosthenes, a Greek mathematician, successfully calculated the circumference of the Earth, and Anaximander was the first to suggest that the Earth floated freely in space, rather than being suspended like a ball on a chain.

Another Greek, Hipparchus, invented the astrolabe, an instrument which could predict the position of the stars and the sun among several of its functions, and the famous Pythagoras was the first to assert that the Earth was a globe rather than a cylinder as had been widely believed beforehand.

Greek scientists can also be credited with establishing the geocentric theory – the idea that the Earth lies at the center of the universe. Although this has turned out to be incorrect, it was the dominant belief in Europe and the Middle East for many centuries.

Above: Sunrise at Stonehenge. This megalithic stone circle is on Salisbury Plain near Amesbury in Wiltshire, England. The alignment of the stones is thought to have been used to make predictions about certain astronomical events such as solstices and lunar and solar eclipses. For instance, on the longest day of the year (the summer solstice) an observer at the center of the circle sees the sun rise directly over a distant pillar called the heel stone. Construction of this prehistoric monument began over 5000 years ago. The largest stones weigh over 40 tonnes and stand nearly 7 meters high. Stonehenge is a United Nations World Heritage Site.

Opposite: Satellite image of the three pyramids at Giza, in northern Egypt. The pyramids are thought to have been built between 2600 and 2500 B.C. as tombs and monuments for members of the ruling dynasties of ancient Egypt. They seem to be aligned with Orion's Belt, so as to guide the dead Pharaoh to the stars of the belt, which were associated with the god of death, Osiris.

Previous Page: Cave paintings in the Lascaux caves in France. They are around 17,000 years old. The superimposed dots of light are the stars as seen in the sky 17,000 years ago. This is illustrating a theory that the positioning of the paintings demonstrates ancient knowledge and use of astronomy.

Mayan pyramids

The Maya, in Central America, reached similar conclusions to their European counterparts, despite there being no known exchanges of information between them. They developed a solar calendar more sophisticated than the Julian calendar, without ever having knowledge of the Romans, the civilization which devised the idea of the Leap Year to allow for the fact the sun does not fit neatly into a 365-day orbit.

The sun, the moon and Venus held religious significance for the Maya. They aligned their pyramids, religious statues and temples with the points at which these three objects set and rose at various times in the year. The religious emphasis placed by the Maya on the planet Venus meant that they were ahead of their time in understanding Earth's nearest neighbor. They recognized that the morning and evening appearances of Venus were not separate entities as the Greeks had thought, but they were in fact one. Documents show that the Maya had also calculated the movement of Venus several years in advance and had even worked out Venus's synodic period – the time elapsed between successive conjunctions of the planet.

Celestial alignment

Archaeologists who specialize in investigating astronomical ruins are called archaeo-astronomers. They have discovered that many ancient monuments are celestially aligned. For example, in the neolithic structure, Stonehenge, found in Wiltshire, England, the stone pillars are arranged so as to trace the positions of the sun and the moon during solstices. Some archaeo-astronomers believe that Stonehenge might even be an ancient observatory. Others argue that Stonehenge is not meant to be celestially aligned at all and if this is the case, its position is an exceptional coincidence.

Most ancient megaliths were erected according to the positions of celestial bodies. Younger civilizations, including the Maya and the Egyptians, also celestially aligned civic structures. The Great Pyramid of Giza seems to be aligned with Orion's belt, so as to guide the dead Pharaoh to the stars of the belt, which were associated with the god of death, Osiris.

Astrology

Astrology stems from the belief that the position and movements of celestial bodies have a direct influence on our lives here on Earth, and that that influence can be divined by "reading" signs in the skies. In essence, space is employed to tell fortunes. The practice of astrology dates back to the ancient Babylonians who believed the movements of the five known planets indicated the will of five of their gods. Astrology has been around ever since, with different civilizations adopting different forms, but in effect, all track the movements of celestial bodies against the background of seemingly fixed stars.

Many religious societies believed, like the Babylonians, that movements in the heavens indicated the will of their gods. The ancient Chinese and the ancient Maya arrived at astrological interpretations of space independently of the Babylonians. But it was through the Babylonians that astrology made its way to ancient Greece and Rome, which in turn influenced the use of astrology in Christian and Arab cultures during the medieval era.

In Western Europe in the Middle Ages, while the scientific study of the stars was at a low ebb, astrology was one of the main means of interpreting the universe. Astrologers were influential in the courts of European monarchs and astrology became an integral part of the practice of medicine. The Black Death, a great plague which struck Europe in the fourteenth century, was often blamed upon an unfortunate alignment of the planets.

More recently, new technologies have scientifically explained the movement of these heavenly bodies, but many people today continue to prefer to interpret these movements through astrology, and horoscopes can be widely found in magazines and newspapers.

Islamic astronomers

During the Middle Ages, in Western Europe the scientific development of astronomy stagnated. Most scientists, thinkers and ordinary people were content to support many of the ideas propounded by ancient Greek astronomy, especially as it usually had the firm backing of the Church, with the result that to question the orthodox view was considered heresy. Nevertheless, observations of stars, eclipses, planetary movements and comets were still recorded.

While the advance of astronomy lost momentum in Western Europe, it accelerated in the Islamic empire which spanned a vast area and population, from the Middle East, through north Africa and into Spain and south-eastern Europe. Many of the works by Greek astronomers were translated into Arabic and developed by Islamic scholars, ensuring the details of the ancients' observations were not lost to the world.

Above: Portrait of the Portuguese navigator Ferdinand Magellan (c.1480-1521), whose ship was the first to circumnavigate the world. After passing through the stormy Strait of Magellan in South America the fleet struck out across a vast, tranquil ocean, which Magellan called the Pacific because of its calmness. It was not until this epic voyage that Europeans could observe the night sky of the southern hemisphere.

Opposite: Optical image of the Large Magellanic Cloud, a satellite galaxy of our Milky Way, in the constellation Dorado, the swordfish. This galaxy is the nearest to the Milky Way, around 170,000 light years away.

Knowledge of astronomy was useful in Islamic rituals, which interpreted the heavens as a guide to ensure prayer five times a day, to date religious festivals correctly, and also to accurately locate Mecca. Islamic scholars contributed widely to astronomy. Al Battani calculated that the sun's apogee – the point during orbit at which the Earth is farthest from the sun – is variable. This meant that the Earth's orbit of the sun was discovered not to be a perfect circle (or the sun's orbit of the Earth was not a perfect circle, which was the way it was looked upon by Islamic scholars at the time). Al Sufi was the first to record seeing the Large Magellanic Cloud in the tenth century. It is now known to be a galaxy outside our own, and was not discovered by Europeans until Ferdinand Magellan embarked upon his great voyage five centuries later, because it is only visible at southern latitudes.

THE COPERNICAN REVOLUTION

The Ancient Greek philosopher Aristotle believed that the Earth was at the center of the universe, and all the bodies in the sky orbited the Earth in eternal circles with perfect motion. This is known as the geocentric theory, as opposed to the heliocentric theory which places the sun at the center.

Aristotle was held in deep regard and his model was readily accepted.

However, upon closer inspection, Aristotle's idea of "perfect circles" seemed to be flawed. Some planets, Mars in particular, seemed to briefly switch into retrograde orbits – as if they were temporarily doubling back upon themselves. Moreover, the brightness of the planets appeared to vary as they orbited the Earth. This all seemed to contradict Aristotle, so Greek philosophers set about reconciling his theory to these anomalies. An answer, proposed by

Claudius Ptolemy, was held as truth for centuries; he continued to advocate a geocentric system, arguing that the varying brightness and the apparent, brief retrograde rotations were a result of epicycles. He claimed that the planets themselves do not orbit the Earth, instead they follow an epicycle, a circular pathway, rather like a mini orbit, on the plane of the much larger, circular orbit of the Earth.

Belief in the Ptolemaic system endured for a long period of time because Greek texts were translated into

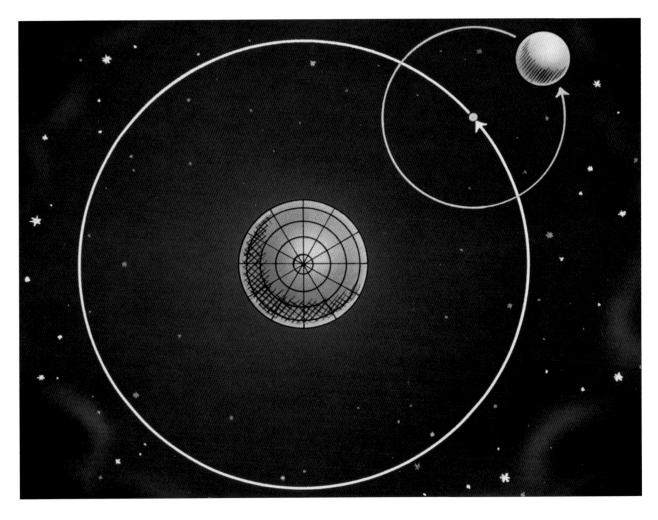

Arabic and became highly influential in the Islamic Empire at the end of the first millennium A.D. It was the Islamic Empire that kept the torch of astronomy burning during this period, but all of the discoveries and theories of Islamic astronomers were made with the background assumption that the Earth was at the center of the universe. In Western Europe too, Ptolemaic theory went unchallenged because the Catholic Church believed that a geocentric model was in keeping with the belief that God had created the universe and would have placed the Earth at its center. In fact, it suited most people because geocentrism placed emphasis on humanity as the central fact in the universe. Nevertheless, supporters of a sun-centered system had been around since the time of the Ancient Greeks. Shortly after the death of Aristotle, Aristarchus proposed a heliocentric theory of the universe, but this was unpopular among the Greeks. Thus, during the Middle Ages in Western Europe, the geocentric model, supported by the Church, had become sacrosanct.

The Copernican Revolution

Nicolaus Copernicus was born in the Polish town of Torun in 1473 just as the Middle Ages were giving way to the Renaissance era, which saw an emphasis placed upon careful, scientific observation in astronomy. Copernicus believed that the Ptolemaic system did not properly account for what he observed in the heavens. The reality seemed far more complicated, and many of the challenges that had faced Ptolemy could be overcome simply by placing the sun, rather than the Earth, at the center of the known universe. For example, Mars's temporary retrograde orbit could be explained as an optical illusion, caused by the fact that the Earth is orbiting the sun faster than Mars, and so, from Earth, Mars only appears to double back on itself.

Copernicus became the first to realize the true order of the planets in the solar system; Earth was demoted from the center of the universe to third rock from the sun. He published his findings in the book, *De Revolutionibus Orbium Coelestium*, which was published in 1543, the year of his death, although he had come to his heliocentric conclusion many years beforehand.

The Church was not too bothered by such heresy. Copernicus died before he could be challenged and, moreover, he had asserted that the planets orbited the sun in perfect circles. However, observational evidence suggested this was not the case. It fell to another scientist, Johannes Kepler, to make sense of these problems. Using the observational data compiled by the Danish astronomer, Tycho Brahe, he first suggested that the orbits of the planets were ellipses rather than circles. Brahe, reputedly rather

Above: Artwork showing the apparent retrograde motion of Mars in the sky. The orbits of the Earth (blue) and Mars (red) around the sun are seen at the bottom. Mars is generally seen from the Earth moving in an eastward direction (from right to left); when the Earth overtakes it Mars appears to slow to a stop and to move westward in a retrograde motion. As the Earth draws ahead of Mars, Mars resumes its eastward motion against the background stars. Because the orbits of the Earth and Mars do not lie in precisely the same plane the eastward motion of Mars does not resume in the same original path. This causes the loop-shaped feature (top center) seen in the trajectory of Mars.

Opposite: Artwork of a planet orbiting the Earth in the complex Ptolemaic system. This system, invented by Ptolemy in the second century A.D., placed the Earth (grey/blue) at the center of the universe, with every other body orbiting it. This alone did not explain the motions of the planets, however, as some occasionally showed "retrograde motion" (moved backwards for a short time). It is now known that this is due to the Earth overtaking them in their orbits of the sun. Ptolemy held that each body (for example, the yellow planet at upper right) moved in small circles (epicycles, yellow ring) around a point in its orbit (yellow dot). The system remained popular until the 1600s.

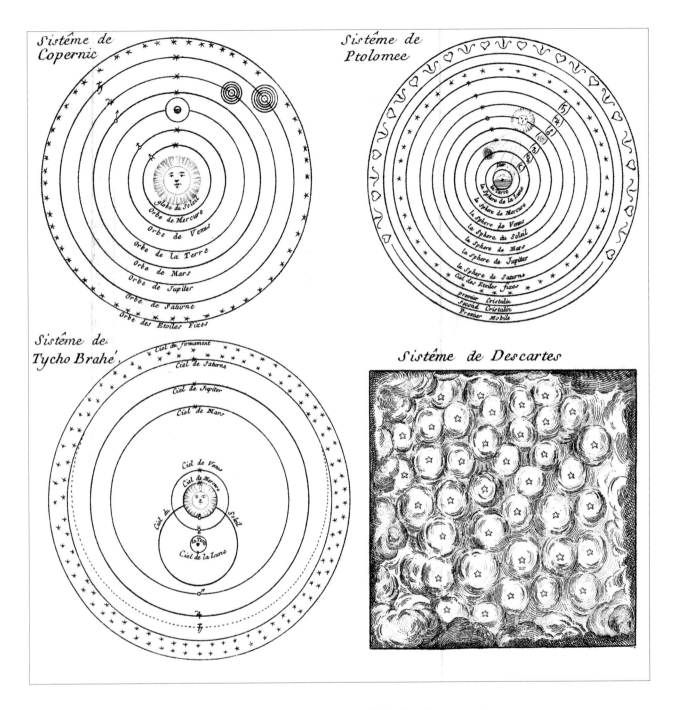

Sistéme de Copernic

Sistéme de Ptolomee

Sistéme de Tycho Brahé

Sistéme de Descartes

arrogant, did not accept Kepler's findings at first, instead preferring his own model. Named the Tychonian system, Brahe's postulation suggested that all the other planets orbited the sun, which in turn orbited the Earth. When Brahe fell out of favor with the Danish monarchy, he moved to Prague where Kepler became his assistant. The men were great rivals, but Kepler's theory and Brahe's observations made for a fruitful collaboration as Kepler was able to use the observational data to prove the elliptical orbits of the planets.

Galileo's observations

This new wave of astronomical thinking did not arouse the interest of the Church too much until it reached the Italian peninsula at the beginning of the seventeenth century. Galileo Galilei was unwilling to commit to a heliocentric model until there was sufficient observational evidence to prove it. To gather such evidence, Galileo pioneered the use of a telescope in astronomy by advancing the new Dutch invention for studying the heavens.

Many of the things he saw through his telescope

seemed to rule against a geocentric universe. He identified four moons, Ganymede, Callisto, Europa and Io, orbiting Jupiter rather than the Earth. He also identified changes in the appearance of Venus, which could only be explained if the planet were orbiting the sun. Furthermore, the moon and the sun, far from being perfect spheres, appeared to be covered in uneven terrain and sunspots respectively.

Galileo published arguments in favor of the Copernican system, angering the Church; following a papal warning, Galileo had little option but to relinquish public support for Copernicus. But events took a brief turn in his favor with the death of the pope who had condemned Galileo's support for the Copernican theory. The new pope, Urban VIII, was one of Galileo's friends, and, while he did not allow Galileo to publicly advocate the Copernican model, he permitted the publication of Galileo's *Dialogue Concerning the two Chief World Systems*. This treatise objectively analyzed both the Ptolemaic and Copernican theories. However, the Church charged that his account was biased towards the Copernican system, and he was tried for heresy by the Inquisition. He was found guilty and placed under house arrest for the remaining years of his life. While his book was blacklisted in many areas of Roman Catholic Europe, he managed to have it published in the Netherlands in 1638, with the consequence that his work was not lost to the world.

Sir Isaac Newton

Although Johannes Kepler had described how planets orbit the sun, he never managed to explain why they do so in such a fashion. That was an unknown for over half a century until the English physicist, Isaac Newton, established his three Laws of Motion, and a Law of Universal Gravitation, each outlined in his book, *Principia*, published in 1687.

Allegedly, while he was sitting under an apple tree, an apple fell to the ground and Newton realized that every object exerts a small force of attraction over every other object. He named this force gravity, after the Latin word for "weight". He argued that gravity is dependent upon the mass of an object; a body with a larger mass will draw a body with a smaller mass towards itself. Therefore the Earth pulls the apple towards its center of gravity, but the apple also attracts the Earth towards its center of gravity. On Earth this process is hard to detect; while two people standing next to one another are exerting a force of gravity over one another, the force is imperceptible because the objects do not have much mass. However, when this idea is applied to celestial bodies, it becomes much easier to understand. The sun is the most massive object in the solar system, therefore the nine known planets, all of which have

Above: Johannes Kepler (1571-1630), German astronomer who devised the three fundamental laws of planetary motion. These laws were based on detailed observations of the planets made by Tycho Brahe and himself. Kepler's first law states that the planets orbit the sun in elliptical paths, with the sun at one focus of the ellipse. The second law states that the closer a planet comes to the sun, the faster it moves. Kepler's third law states that the ratio of the cube of a planet's mean distance from the sun to the square of its orbital period is a constant. Newton used these ideas to formulate his theory of gravity.

Opposite: Historical cosmologies. Artwork of four historical models of planetary orbits. Ptolemy's geocentric (Earth-centered) model (upper right) dominated astronomy for over 1000 years. Copernicus published his heliocentric (sun-centered) model (upper left) in 1543. It was eventually recognized that the Earth orbited the sun, but Tycho Brahe's post-Copernican model (lower left) tried to keep the sun orbiting a stationary Earth. Theories of planetary motions included gravity (1687). Diagram published in Paris in 1777, four years before the discovery of Uranus.

smaller masses than the sun, are held in their orbits by gravity. While the sun draws the planets in, the planets also exert a gravitational pull on the sun. Newton also argued that the greater the distance between two objects the weaker gravitational attraction is. This concept supports Kepler's theory concerning elliptical orbits. As a planet nears the sun it experiences a stronger gravitational force, pulling it in closer, creating an elliptical orbit.

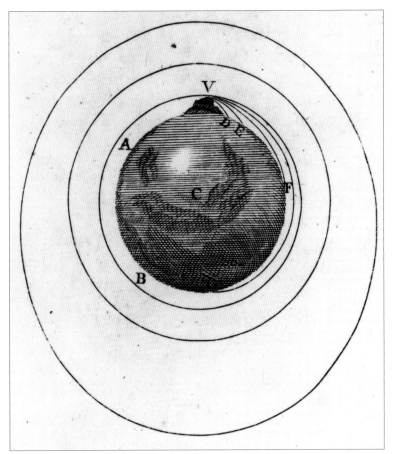

Above: Newton's gravity map showing the Earth and the paths of a projectile around it, depicting gravity. The projectile is launched horizontally from a "very tall" mountain (at upper center). The velocity of the launch determines the path of the projectile. At low velocities, the projectile travels short distances (D, E, F, G) before gravity forces it to strike the Earth. At high velocity the projectile escapes gravity to orbit the Earth. Engraving published in Newton's *A Treatise of the System of the World* (1728).

Opposite: Albert Einstein (1879-1955), German-born physicist. His famous mass-energy equation resulted from his 1905 paper on Special Relativity. This paper, with his 1915 General Theory of Relativity, replaced the previously unshakeable Newtonian world view, rewriting the concepts of gravity, space and time. Early work on the photoelectric effect won him the 1921 Nobel Prize for Physics. Emigrating to the USA in 1933, he encouraged the atomic bomb project. In later years he campaigned for nuclear disarmament.

Albert Einstein

Newton's ideas were groundbreaking. They were celebrated and revered for over two centuries, explaining how the Earth could be spinning, yet people did not fall off. His reasoning also showed why an apple fell to the ground, as well as explaining why the planets were held in orbit around the sun.

However, Newton's theory of gravity did not account for every eventuality; the orbit of Mercury was proving particularly troublesome. The planet's perihelion, its closest point to the sun, was not static, instead it was shifting by a fraction of a degree during every orbit. This infinitesimal movement means that it takes Mercury more than one million orbits to return to its starting point. Newton's theory of gravity could not account for these shifts. Urbain Le Verrier, the co-discoverer of Neptune, calculated that the combined gravitational pull of the sun and the other seven known planets was not sufficient to explain the advancing perihelion of Mercury. Scientists, in a time when Newtonian gravity was sacrosanct, assumed that the gravitational pull of a yet unknown planet was responsible. The planet, referred to as "Vulcan", would need to be sizeable to have the necessary force to explain the phenomenon of Mercury's orbit. The puzzle was not solved until a young German-born physicist, Albert Einstein, established a new theory of gravity.

In 1905, while working as a desk clerk for a Swiss patent office, Einstein had published his Special Theory of Relativity, expanding upon work that Galileo had pioneered. Essentially, Einstein had proved that, in a vacuum, light always travels at a constant speed, just under 300,000 km/s, relative to an observer. His theory also states that the velocity of light in a vacuum is the fastest speed attainable in the universe. One basic premise of this theory, in view of the calculation that speed is equal to distance multiplied by time, was that if the speed of light was constant, time and distance must be variable.

The Special Theory of Relativity provided Einstein with an important base upon which to structure his General Theory of Relativity, published in 1915, which contained a new interpretation of gravity. The Special Theory had shown that distance as well as time was variable. That meant that the three dimensions of space – height, width and depth – were also flexible.

In General Relativity, Einstein adopted the view,

first pioneered by a German mathematician, Hermann Minkowski, that space and time are linked in one four-dimensional unit called "spacetime". Einstein's General Theory of Relativity holds that mass distorts spacetime. It is the distortion of spacetime by mass rather than the mass of an object itself that is responsible for gravitational attraction. While Newton's apple fell to Earth because the more massive Earth is pulling it towards its center of gravity, in General Relativity, the apple is falling into a chasm in spacetime created by the mass of the Earth. The American physicist, John Wheeler, put it best when he said "Matter tells space(time) how to bend, space(time) tells matter how to move".

Four-dimensional spacetime is extremely difficult to comprehend, so a popular, two-dimensional example has arisen: imagine a cannon ball sitting in the middle of a taut sheet. The cannon ball makes a large dent. The cannon ball represents the sun, which makes a large "dent" in the fabric of spacetime. If a tennis ball is rolled, with adequate velocity, into the indentation created by the cannon ball, it can be launched into orbit, just as a planet orbits the sun. The tennis ball also creates a small indentation of its own, into which an even smaller ball (representing a moon) could be sent into orbit.

Proving Einstein's theory

Einstein had worked out the mathematics behind General Relativity, and to his delight, it even accounted for the advancing perihelion of Mercury. This showed General Relativity to be all-encompassing, something the oddity of Mercury's orbit meant Newtonian gravity could not claim to be. The scientific community was understandably skeptical; General Relativity would present a complete revolution in our understanding of the universe, and would require all scientists to restructure their methods of teaching and experimentation.

To counteract sceptical opinion, what Einstein needed was further evidence that his theory worked in practice. He needed to find a mass sufficiently large enough to show decisively that spacetime was being distorted. The distortion created by the mass of the sun would mean that light from stars directly behind the sun should be curved around the sun, and would, hence, still be visible. However, the sun is too bright to allow us to see this phenomenon occurring, and Einstein believed the most massive planet, Jupiter, would not show light being bent to a degree sufficient to prove General Relativity. Thus scientist were left with a focus on the sun, overcoming the issue of brightness by looking at the positions of stars during an eclipse, when the sunlight was briefly extinguished, allowing nearby stars to appear.

After a German expedition, supported by Einstein, to view an eclipse in the Crimea in 1914 was interrupted by the First World War, responsibility fell to two British initiatives, working independently of Einstein. Observers were dispatched to two locations, one in South America and one in Africa, where an eclipse was due in May 1919 – two locations reduced the risk of views being obscured by cloud. The result of the observations showed that the actual position of stars behind the sun did not match their apparent position, because light emanating from these stars could be seen during the eclipse. Such an occurrence could only be explained by General Relativity: the sun was distorting the fabric of spacetime and the light from the stars was being bent. Einstein turned into an overnight celebrity and became the most prominent scientist of the twentieth century, even though many people outside the world of science continued to have an understanding of gravity based upon Newton's theory. General Relativity has remained competitive by accounting for all scenarios the universe has thrown at it ever since. Of course, that is not to suggest that current theories of gravity cannot, and will not, be revised in the centuries to come.

THE SPACE AGE

On 4 October 1957, the Soviet Union successfully launched Earth's first artificial satellite, Sputnik 1, ushering in the Space Age and a space race between the Soviet Union and its Cold War rival, the United States of America.

The origins of the Space Age lie in impressive, if objectionable, developments German scientists made in rocket technology during the Second World War, during which German V-2 rockets could be launched in north-western Europe to rain down on London. After the war, former allies the Soviet Union and the United States tried to poach as many of these German scientists and disused V-2 rockets as possible for their own space and arms programs. The United States managed successfully to capture the V-2 project's chief engineer, Werner von Braun, who went on to become the "father" of the US space program.

In light of the fast emerging Cold War, the Russians and the Americans set these scientists, as well as their own,

to developing German V-2 technology into intercontinental ballistic missiles for their own arsenals. Both sides had successes in sending their own V-2 missiles to the edge of space. In 1957, the Soviet Union's top rocket engineer, Sergei Korolev, and his team were able to convince their government in Moscow that an artificial satellite sent into Earth orbit would provide the Soviet Union with a considerable triumph over the United States, where the idea of sending probes to space had been criticized for being too costly. In the months before its revolutionary launch in October, Korolev oversaw the building of Sputnik 1 and the testing of the rockets that would carry it.

The United States was taken aback; it had long seemed axiomatic that it was the leading technological power in the world, but the successful launch of Sputnik 1 called this belief into question. The United States rose to the challenge presented by the Soviet Union and restructured its space program. In October 1958, the National Aeronautics and Space Administration (NASA) was established. A large amount of funding was made available, and schoolchildren were encouraged to take an interest in the development of the space program, in order to create a new generation of engineers to help America get ahead in the emerging space race.

In the meantime, the USSR was pushing onward. On 3 November 1957, just one month after the launch of Sputnik 1, to celebrate the fortieth anniversary of the Russian Revolution, Sputnik 2 was sent into Earth's orbit, carrying the first animal to reach space, a dog named Laika. After several failures, the United States was able to narrow the gap and launched its first ever space probe, Explorer 1, on 31 January 1958. Although these missions had some scientific successes, and Explorer 1's data led to the discovery of the Van Allen Radiation Belt, they were mainly a matter of prestige.

The race to the moon
Both sides continued to send probes into space. The Soviet's Luna 1 became the first man-made object to orbit the sun in January 1959, only for the US to achieve the same feat two months later.

After placing a number of objects in space, the next obvious target was the moon. On 15 September 1959, the Soviet craft, Luna 2, crashlanded on the moon. This was a high point for the Soviet space program. The first man-made object to touch the surface of the moon carried pennants proudly inscribed with the Soviet emblem – the hammer and sickle. Smugly, the Soviet Premier, Nikita Khrushchev, presented the American president Eisenhower with replicas of the pennants on a visit to the USA, demonstrating that the space race was, by then, at the forefront of Cold War politics. The Soviets scored another important first, when Luna 3 sent back the first ever pictures of the far side of the moon. From the dawn of mankind until 7 October 1959, humans had only ever seen one face of Earth's satellite.

The United States was being quickly outpaced, but its probe, Ranger 7, took some of the first close-up pictures of the lunar surface as it crashlanded in 1964. But the Soviets were in the ascendancy when Luna 9 made a soft landing and took the first photographs from the surface of another world. In the latter half of the decade, one superpower tried to outdo the other, sending craft to the surface of the moon or into orbit. By 1967, many of the significant firsts had been achieved during the decade since Sputnik 1, and mostly by the Soviet Union. However, one task still eluded both: putting a man on the moon.

NASA began to fear that the USSR was on the verge of a manned landing, following the successful retrieval of a probe, Zond 5, and its crew of turtles, from a lunar orbit. Consequently NASA stepped up their lunar landing program. The Apollo 8 astronauts became the first men to leave Earth's gravity and orbit the moon. The success of this mission paved the way for the first moon landing by the crew of Apollo 11, Neil Armstrong and Buzz Aldrin, while the third crewman, Michael Collins, remained in the command module. America returned men to the moon on five further occasions, while the Soviet Union never achieved that goal, a result of the escalating costs of the space race being felt on both sides.

Manned missions

On 12 April 1961, the Soviet Union successfully put a man in space. Cosmonaut Yuri Gagarin spent 108 minutes orbiting the Earth once in the Vostok 1 probe, before he ejected himself from the module and parachuted to the ground. Less than a month after Gagarin's successful mission, on 5 May, Alan Shepard became the first American in space. He was put into a sub-orbital trajectory using a rocket that the Americans had developed with the help of German V-2 technology and scientists. It was not until February 1962 that an American successfully orbited the

Above: Soviet space poster, produced for the World Exhibition in Brussels, Belgium, 1958. This poster was made after the USSR launched the first artificial satellite, Sputnik 1. Launched in October 1957, Sputnik 1 weighed just over 83 kilograms and orbited the earth 1400 times, transmitting a pulsed radio signal. Its orbit decayed and it lost contact after 21 days.

Opposite: Laika, the dog who became the first animal in space, inside a mock-up of the cabin of the Soviet Sputnik 2 spacecraft. Sputnik 2 was launched on 3 November 1957. Laika was contained within a sealed cabin with a food store and an air conditioner. Instruments transmitted data to Earth about Laika's pulse, respiration, blood pressure and heartbeat for seven days until she died when her oxygen supply ran out. The spacecraft was not designed to be recovered and it burnt up as it re-entered the atmosphere on 14 April 1958, 162 days after its launch.

Previous page: Zarya and Unity. A view of the first two modules of the International Space Station. At center is the Russian-built Zarya control module which is joined to the United States-built connecting module Unity (lower center). The image was taken during the Endeavor Space Shuttle mission in 1998.

Earth; John Glenn, aboard Friendship 7, circled the Earth three times. However, in June the following year, the Soviet Union scored another first when cosmonaut Valentina Tereshkova became the first woman in space – a feat not matched for almost twenty years. The first American woman in Space was Sally Ride, as a crew member of the space shuttle Challenger.

Since the advent of manned space flights 34 countries have sent astronauts into space. The first non-Soviet, non-American person to be sent into space was a Czechoslovakian, Vladimir Remek in 1978. Initially most of these other nationalities came from the communist bloc of Eastern Europe, but, during the 1980s, astronauts from as far and wide as Vietnam, Syria, France, India and Canada were taken into space. Even Afghanistan sent a representative into space, alongside Soviet cosmonauts in 1988, a symbolic gesture at a time when the Soviets were beginning to exit from a protracted struggle in the country. The first British person in space was Helen Sharman after she entered a competition to become an astronaut. She was the first non-Soviet, non-American woman in space when she took off on 18 May 1991 to spend time on the Soviet space station, Mir. In 2003, the ill-fated mission of the space shuttle Colombia was carrying the first Israeli astronaut, Ilan Roman, who poignantly carried with him a drawing of the Earth as seen from the moon, by Petr Ginz, a fourteen-year-old boy. It was drawn during his incarceration in Theresienstadt concentration camp in Czechoslovakia, before being sent to his death at Auschwitz. In 1983 Guion Bluford became the first African-American astronaut, followed almost ten years later by Mae Jemison, the first African-American female in space. Franklin Chang-Diaz is often credited as the first Hispanic American in space, but also as the first Costa Rican because he moved to America when he was still in school.

A new space race

While these many people have added to the mix of nationalities participating in the the American, Soviet and Russian space programs, one of the most exciting recent developments took place in 2003 when China successfully sent a taikonaut (a Chinese astronaut), Yang Li-wei, into space. As the first country besides the USA or the Soviet Union and its successor state, Russia, to send a human being into space, this is an important step in the future of space travel. It is likely that China will become a major player in space exploration in the twenty-first century. Beijing has already planned its own lunar exploration missions resembling those of the USA and the Soviet Union during the 1960s.

Above: Yuri Gagarin's descent module, known as Charik or "little ball", on 12 April, 1961, at the end of the first manned spaceflight. Gagarin made one complete revolution round the Earth in the Vostok 1 spacecraft. The flight lasted 108 minutes, and Gagarin landed only six miles from the calculated point. Charik weighed 2400 kilograms and measured 2. 3 meters in diameter. Gagarin was killed while testing an aircraft on 27 March 1968.

Opposite: Apollo 11 astronaut Edwin "Buzz" Aldrin walks on the surface of the moon. Neil Armstrong and the Apollo 11 lunar module can be seen reflected in his helmet visor.

Echoing the twentieth-century space race, China has a likely rival: its neighbor, India, which has launched a number of satellites and is already planning its own trip to the moon by 2008.

Space tourism

On 28 October 2001, Dennis Tito, an American businessman, became the first space tourist, paying around $20 million to spend seven days aboard the International Space Station. A year later, in April 2002, he was followed by a South African businessman, Mark Shuttleworth, who paid a similar sum for a "space holiday" on the same facility. In October 2005, the third space tourist, Gregory Olsen, visited the space station, like his two predecessors, by buying a place aboard a Russian Soyuz mission. All three men had to undergo an intensive training regime to make themselves fit for the trip, as well as conduct scientific tests

aboard the space station. For the moment, space tourism is only open to those who can pay vast sums of money. However, if the cost of the trip can be reduced, it is a step towards making space travel accessible to ordinary people, not just states.

Space shuttle

The space shuttle is the common name given to NASA's Space Transportation System. The program began on 5 January 1972, when President Nixon announced its inauguration, as a low-cost, reusable alternative to the costly manned missions of the 1960s, such as Apollo. In September 1976 a proto-type named Enterprise was completed, and used for a series of flying and landing tests within Earth's atmosphere during 1977. Before Enterprise had even been tested, work had begun on what was to be the first shuttle in space, Columbia. After two years of tests at the Kennedy Space Center, during which two men lost their lives, the shuttle was finally launched on 12 April 1981, ushering in a new era of space travel.

Missions in space

Over the next four years NASA successfully launched a further three shuttles – Challenger in April 1983, Discovery in August 1984, and Atlantis in October 1985. The fleet of four shuttles undertook a variety of tasks, including deploying satellites, making repairs, launching probes from Earth-orbit and carrying out experiments. Atlantis deployed the planetary probes Magellan and Galileo on their paths to Venus and Jupiter respectively. Discovery launched the Hubble Telescope in 1990, and several shuttles have been involved in subsequent service missions to the giant instrument.

In 1995, the space shuttle began transporting men and supplies to the Russian space station, Mir. This was an important step in post-Cold War collaboration in space exploration between the two former rivals, Russia and the United States. Space shuttles made numerous journeys to the aging space station, until it was decommissioned in 2001. This helped prepare the shuttle crews for the assembly and service of the International Space Station, for which the shuttle is vitally important. Building this station has become the primary goal of the three shuttles remaining in the fleet.

Disasters in space

Seventy-three seconds after its launch on 28 January 1986, the Challenger space shuttle exploded, killing all seven astronauts on board. It was discovered that the cold January weather had meant that an O-ring, designed to seal one of the solid rocket boosters, had lost flexibility. Consequently, a gap was left unsealed, resulting in a leakage from the booster. Among the seven crew members was Christa McAuliffe, who had generated interest in this particular mission, as she had won a competition to be the first teacher in space. President Reagan postponed his State of the Union address, and instead opted for a heartfelt tribute from the Oval Office, which is often cited as one of the greatest, most poignant speeches of his presidency. It was two and a half years before a shuttle returned to space, when Discovery was launched on 29 September 1988. NASA began construction of a replacement shuttle the year after the loss of Challenger, but it was not until 7 May 1992 that Endeavor was launched.

Tragedy struck once again, seventeen years and four days after the Challenger disaster when, on 1 February 2003, the space shuttle Columbia exploded as it re-entered Earth's atmosphere. After launch on 16 January 2003, a piece of insulation foam broke away from the external fuel tank and struck the shuttle 82 seconds into the flight. The foam caused a breach of the hull, exposing the wing to super-heated gases when the shuttle re-entered the Earth's

atmosphere. This caused Columbia to disintegrate less than 20 minutes before its scheduled landing, killing all seven astronauts on board. Debris from the shuttle littered a vast area across the state of Texas.

The future of the shuttle

Again, it was over two years until the space shuttle was re-launched. Discovery blasted off from Florida on 26 July 2005. However, foam once again broke off the external fuel tank, but fortunately did not strike the shuttle this time. The craft successfully returned to Earth, but the reduced fleet of three has once again been grounded until 2007, pending further investigations into how this once-fatal error could occur twice. Delays to the shuttle program mark a setback to the completion of the International Space Station, initially set for 2010. After the completion of the space station the shuttle is to be retired in favor of a Crew Exploration Vehicle, capable of carrying humans to the International Space Station, the moon, Mars and possibly beyond.

The Soviet shuttle program

In response to the US Space Transportation System, the USSR developed its own, rival, reusable spacecraft program, commonly named Buran, after its first and only successful shuttle. Buran was successfully launched, unmanned, in November 1988 from Baikonur cosmodrome in Kazakhstan. The shuttle completed two Earth orbits before bringing itself back into land. This was

to be Russia's only brush with space shuttle glory; turmoil and financial crisis in the USSR meant that two more shuttles that were at advanced stages of construction, Ptichka and Baikal, went unfinished. Two more unnamed shuttles, in very early stages of construction, were completely dismantled. When the USSR collapsed, Kazakhstan inherited the shuttle program, making it one of only two countries to possess shuttle technology. But it is extremely unlikely that the Buran program will be restarted – Buran was destroyed in 2002, leaving only the unfinished Ptichka in Kazakh hands.

Opposite: Launch of the Saturn V rocket that carried the Apollo 11 spacecraft to the moon. Apollo 11 was the first manned mission to land on the moon. Apollo 11 had three parts: its command module is the cone at the tip of the rocket, its service module is the grey cylinder center, and the Lunar Module (LM) is in the white flared fairing at lower center. Astronauts Neil Armstrong, Michael Collins and Edwin Aldrin were launched in Apollo 11 on 16 July 1969. Armstrong and Aldrin used the LM to land in the Sea of Tranquillity on the moon on 20 July 1969. Collins orbited in the Command and Service Modules.

Above: International Space Station space walk, 21 May 2000. Astronaut James S. Voss holding a camera while he orbits above Earth. He is anchored to the remote manipulator system (RMS, robotic arm) of the Space Shuttle Atlantis. Together with astronaut Jeffrey N. Williams, he carried out several installations and repairs on the ISS exterior. Photographed during mission STS-101.

Above: Explosion of the space shuttle Challenger seventy-three seconds after lift-off from Kennedy Space Center, Florida, on 28 January 1986. All seven crew members were killed. It is thought that O-rings in a seal on the right-hand solid rocket booster failed, due to the extremely cold weather conditions experienced just prior to the launch. The subsequent leak of fuel resulted in the explosion.

Left: Launch of the space shuttle Discovery on 26 July 2005, from Launch Pad 39B, Kennedy Space Center, Florida, USA. Space shuttle mission STS-114, was the first launch of a space shuttle since the Columbia broke up on re-entry in February 2003.

Opposite: Mir space station seen above the Earth, with the moon at upper right. Heavy thunderclouds are seen on Earth (across bottom). Mir was launched by the USSR in 1986, and spent 15 years in orbit. It carried out a wide variety of scientific experiments. On 23 March 2001, it was allowed to fall back to Earth, breaking up in the atmosphere over the Pacific Ocean.

THE SOLAR SYSTEM

The solar system is the name given to the planetary system of which the Earth is a part. It comprises planets, moons, comets, meteors and asteroids which are all held together by the gravitational pull of a star, named either the Sun or Sol. The solar system is believed to have formed from one nebula, the solar nebula.

As gravity forced the nebula to condense it became more dense and pressure inside it increased, resulting in the creation of a proto-star, which began heating up to form the sun we see today.

The proto-star was surrounded by interstellar dust and gases which began clumping together as a result of gravity. This process, named accretion, continued for a long period of time, until, about 4.6 billion years ago, the clumps of rock and gas became much larger, and eventually gravity forced these irregular-shaped objects into the globular-shaped planets we see today. Many of the rocks did not become large enough to form planets and either remain today as asteroids, or they collided with the planets earlier in their history causing the large impact craters still visible throughout the solar system.

The planets

The known planets in the solar system can be divided into two groups. The four planets closest to the sun, Mercury, Venus, Earth and Mars, are called the "terrestrial planets" after the Latin word for "land" because they all share similar surfaces comprising solid rock surrounding dense, metallic cores. The four outer planets are known as the "Jovian planets", implying their similarities to the planet Jupiter – they are all much larger than the terrestrial planets, and do not share their rocky surfaces and metallic core. Instead they are giant balls of atmosphere, mainly comprising gases surrounding relatively small rocky cores.

The terrestrial and the Jovian planets are helpfully divided by a belt of asteroids, orbiting the sun between Mars and Jupiter. More recently Uranus and Neptune have been called Uranian rather than Jovian planets to highlight their differences to Jupiter and Saturn; mainly that they are appreciably smaller, are both bluish-greenish in color, comprise a significant amount of methane and have a thick coating of ice around their cores.

Pluto stands out as somewhat anomalous in the solar system. As a tiny ball of rock and ice usually far beyond the orbit of Neptune, it does not fit easily into either terrestrial or Jovian category. Moreover, Pluto's orbit is highly eccentric, resembling that of a comet rather than a planet. It is also very small and, had it been discovered today, would probably not have been classified as a planet at all. Instead it is better seen as being one of a number of trans-Neptunian objects, planetoids, asteroids and centaurs which make up the Kuiper Belt.

The Kuiper Belt is a vast field of icy asteroids of varying sizes, centaurs and periodic comet nucleii orbiting

the sun beyond Neptune. In July 2005, the discovery of a tenth planet orbiting the sun, twice as far away as Pluto, was announced. The anonymously named 2003 UB313 is larger than Pluto, and should be given planetary status if Pluto remains classified as a planet. However, improvements in telescopic technology have meant that more and more objects from the Kuiper Belt have been discovered, such as Sedna and Quaoar. They are similar in size to Pluto, although much farther out, but there are advocates who believe these two objects should be given planetary status.

Where does the solar system end?

It is difficult to calculate exactly where our solar system ends. It ends at the point at which objects are no longer affected by the sun's gravitational pull. This is also the area beyond the reach of solar winds and outside the sun's vast magnetosphere. The farthest reaches of the solar system are thought to be surrounded by a great halo, named the Oort Cloud, home to millions of comet nuclei and small icy rocks, which, it is speculated, lies a thousand times further from the sun than Pluto. However, more recent figures have suggested that Sedna might be the a part of the Oort Cloud and not the Kuiper Belt, indicating that the cloud might be much closer to the sun than initially thought. If this is the case, estimates of the size of the solar system might need to be reduced.

Above: An illustration showing the relative sizes of the major bodies in the solar system. The sun (orange) is in lower frame. Superimposed upon it are the four inner (terrestrial) planets. These are, from left to right: Mercury, Venus, Earth (with the moon to its left) and Mars. In the upper frame are the four major outer (gas giant) planets: Jupiter, Saturn (its rings are not seen), Uranus and Neptune. The furthest planet from the sun, Pluto, is seen upper right, along with its relatively large moon Charon. Pluto is a small rocky body that orbits at a distance of around 6 billion kilometers from the sun.

Opposite: An amateur astronomer, silhouetted against the horizon, uses a refractor telescope to view Venus (left of center) and a crescent moon. Photographed in the Grand Canyon National Park, Arizona, USA.

Previous page: Computer composite image of the four planets of the inner solar system, shown in their relative sizes and (at a different scale) their relative mean orbital distances. The planets are, left to right: Mercury, Venus, Earth and Mars. A representation of the sun is at far left. These inner planets all have rocky surfaces, unlike the outer "gas giants" such as Jupiter. Earth is the only planet where water is liquid at the surface, and thus suitable for organic life, although some features on Mars suggest the presence of surface water in earlier times. The planetary images come from data gathered by NASA space missions.

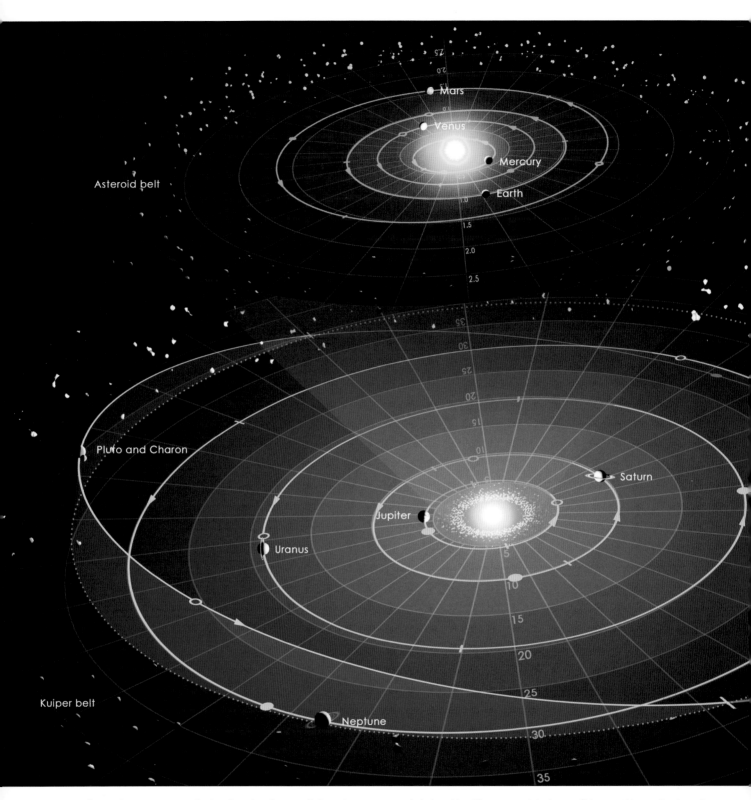

Mars

Venus

Mercury

Asteroid belt

Earth

2.5

2.0

1.0

1.5

2.0

2.5

35

30

25

20

15

10

Pluto and Charon

Saturn

Jupiter

Uranus

5

10

15

Kuiper belt

20

25

Neptune

30

35

Above: Computer artwork showing the planets of the solar system and their orbits. The terrestrial planets (Mercury, Venus, Earth and Mars) are separated from the gas planets (Jupiter, Saturn, Uranus, Neptune and Pluto). The asteroid belt (between Mars and Jupiter) and the Kuiper Belt (between and beyond Neptune and Pluto) are also shown. The open lines represent the points of orbit where the planets pass closest to the sun (perihelia), while the closed lines represent the points of orbit where the planets pass furthest from the sun (aphelia).

Timeline of the discovery of the planets and some of their moons

Date	
Before 16th Century	**The sun, moon, Mercury, Venus, Mars, Jupiter and Saturn**
1610	Moons of Jupiter - Callisto, Io, Ganymede and Europa
1656	Moon of Saturn - Titan
1671 - 1684	Moons of Saturn - Iapetus, Rhea, Tethys and Dione
1781	**Uranus**
1787	Moons of Uranus – Titania and Oberon
1789	Moons of Saturn – Enceladus and Mimas
1846	**Neptune**
1846	Moon of Neptune - Triton
1848	Moon of Saturn - Hyperion
1851	Moons of Uranus - Ariel and Umbriel
1877	Moons of Mars – Phobos and Deimos
1892	Moon of Jupiter - Amalthea
1898/1899	Moon of Saturn - Phoebe
1904/1905	Moons of Jupiter – Himalia and Elara
1908	Moon of Jupiter - Pasiphaë
1914	Moon of Jupiter - Sinope
1930	**Pluto**
1938	Moons of Jupiter – Lysithea and Carme
1948	Moon of Uranus - Miranda
1949	Moon of Neptune - Nereid
1951	Moon of Jupiter - Ananke
1966	Moons of Saturn – Janus and Epimetheus
1974/1975	Moons of Jupiter – Leda and Themisto (Themisto was soon lost and rediscovered in 2000)
1978	Moon of Pluto - Charon
1979	Moon of Jupiter - Adrastea
1979/1980	Moons of Jupiter – Thebe and Metis
1980	Moons of Saturn – Helene, Calypso, Telesto, Atlas, Prometheus and Pandora
1985/1986	Moons of Uranus – Puck, Juliet, Portia, Cressida, Desdemona, Rosalind, Belinda, Cordelia, Bianca and Ophelia
1989	Moons of Neptune - Proteus, Despina, Larissa, Thalassa, Naiad and Galatea
1990	Moon of Saturn - Pan
1997	Moons of Uranus – Caliban and Sycorax
1999	Moons of Uranus – Setebos, Stephano and Prospero
2000	Moon of Jupiter - Callirrhoe
2000	Moons of Saturn – Ymir, Paaliaq, Kiviuq, Siarnaq, Tarvos, Ijiraq, Thrymr, Skathi, Mundilfari, Erriapo, Suttungr and Albiorix
2000	Moon of Jupiter - Themisto*
2001	Moons of Jupiter – Kalyke, Iocaste, Erinome, Harpalyke, Isonoe, Praxidike, Megaclite, Taygete and Chaldene
2001	Moon of Uranus - Trinculo
2002	Moons of Jupiter – Hermippe, Eurydome, Sponde, Kale, Autonoe, Thyone, Pasithee, Euanthe, Orthosie, Euporie, Aitne and Arche
2003	Moon of Saturn - Narvi
2003	Moons of Jupiter – Eukelade, Helike, Aoede, Hegemone, Kallichore, Carpo, Cyllene and Mneme,
2004	Moons of Saturn – Methone, Pallene and Polydeuces
2005	Moons of Pluto - S/2005 P1 and S/2005 P2 (provisional names)

Missions to the edge

Voyagers 1 and 2 are the farthest reaching man-made objects in the solar system. After completing successful missions to the outer planets during the 1980s, the two spacecraft continued towards the edge of the solar system with the intention of reaching its outer boundary and entering interstellar space. In 2004, NASA announced that Voyager 1 had cleared the termination shock, the area of space where the solar winds begin to slow down and increase in temperature as they come up against interstellar winds.

It is hoped that the Voyager probes will continue transmitting data for several more decades, with luck, long enough to pass out of the solar system, where the solar winds have stopped altogether. But, despite the marvelous work of these missions to date, it would unfortunately take thousands of years for them to reach the nearest star, Alpha Centauri.

Other planetary systems

In the early 1990s, Aleksander Wolszczan discovered the first four extra-solar planets orbiting the star PSR 1257+12. Extra-solar planets can be detected using two methods. The most popular is to look for "wobbles" – small movements of a star resulting from the gravitational influence of a planet. Movements of a star caused by even the largest of planets are so minor they are difficult to detect using telescopes. As such, only extra-solar planetary systems with Jupiter-sized planets in orbits very close to their suns have been easily detected using this method.

Another method that is used is planetary transits. When Venus passes in front of the sun, its silhouette can be seen from Earth; likewise, when planets pass in front of a star, Earth-based telescopes note the dimming in the light of the star, which provides evidence of a planet around that star and can even show the planet's size. Again this process is only helpful for detecting Jupiter-sized planets, which cause sufficient dimming of the star to be detected on Earth, many light years away.

In the twenty-first century extra-solar planetary systems will become an area of keen astronomical study. NASA and the European Space Agency have plans to launch a Terrestrial Planet Finder in the coming decades, which will look for smaller, Earth-sized planets, and assess their chances of harboring life.

Left: Transit of Venus, 8 June 2004. View of the sun with Venus on lower right side.

Opposite: The optical telescopes of Keck I and II each have a 10-meter diameter mirror, which can be used together to provide more detailed images. Mauna Kea, an extinct volcano 4200 meters high, has several telescopes on its summit. Comet Hale-Bopp, seen in early 1997, was one of the brightest comets of the 20th century. Here, its two tails are seen. The gas or "ion" tail (blue) consists of ionized glowing gas blown away by the solar wind. The dust tail (white) consists of dust grains pushed away from the comet head by the radiation of sunlight.

THE SUN

Once thought to be exceptional, our sun is now known to be an ordinary and rather nondescript star situated on the outskirts of an average galaxy. It is easy to understand how successive generations held the sun in particular esteem – it is the source of life on Earth; it warms up our world and gives light during our daytime.

Nevertheless, in the grand scheme of the universe, the sun is just another middle-aged, Main Sequence star. Its stellar classification, G2, denoting its yellowish coloring and its surface temperatures of 5000⁰–6000⁰ Kelvin, is not extraordinary either; there are countless G2-type stars. Perhaps the sun's only distinction might prove to be that one of its planets harbors intelligent life.

Fusion

Scientists tried to understand just how the sun is able to emit so much energy. Initially it was thought that the sun was just one giant ball of fire, burning much like a candle. This theory is not tenable, because if the sun were burning like a candle, it would have been exhausted years ago. Another theory suggested that the sun's huge gravitational

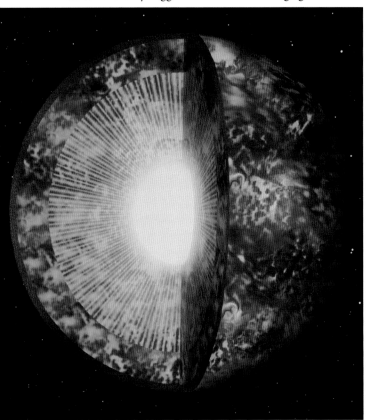

pull, the result of its large mass, was being converted into energy. Again, this does not account for the age of the sun, which must be more than 4.6 billion years old, the age of the oldest known rocks on the Earth.

At the beginning of the twentieth century, the German-born Jewish physicist Albert Einstein finally provided the answer when he stated that mass and energy were interchangeable, $E = mc^2$, where E is energy, m is mass and c is the speed of light. In the sun hydrogen nuclei collide with one another to create helium atoms. In this process, named fusion, mass is transferred into energy. Four hydrogen nuclei are required to produce one helium nucleus, which is slightly less massive; the excess mass is transferred into energy. This tiny process occurs millions of times simultaneously meaning that the energy we receive from the sun is enough to sustain life here on Earth. Fortunately for our descendants, this process will continue for some millions of years to come, until the last of the hydrogen in the sun is used up.

At the moment, the sun comprises 75% hydrogen, 23% helium and the remaining 2% consists of trace amounts of other elements. The period during which the sun generates energy through the process of fusion is called its Main Sequence. Our sun is estimated to be five billion years old; it is projected that its Main Sequence will last another five billion years.

Solar layers

The bright white disc that appears in the sky is the layer of the sun called the photosphere. The photosphere is essentially the surface of the sun – it emits the visible light that we see here on Earth. Temperatures in the photosphere of our sun are in excess of 5500⁰ Celsius. The surface of the sun has a granulated appearance, as hot gases rise to the surface and cooler ones fall back down to the convection zone below. Although these may appear as granules, relative to surface features on the Earth, they are vast in size. Although the photosphere is the outermost visible layer, there are others above it, often referred to as the solar atmosphere.

The solar atmosphere is divided into three layers, the chromosphere, the transitional zone, and the corona. All three are outshone by the photosphere so can only be observed as visible light during a solar eclipse. The chromosphere is a pinkish layer where much of the stormy weather on the sun is detected. Spicules, shortlived jets of gas, protrude outward from the interior of the sun through the chromosphere. The transition zone is where the temperature rises sharply from the 5500⁰ temperatures in the photosphere and chromosphere to levels in excess of one million degrees in the corona. The word corona comes from the Latin for crown, and during an eclipse it becomes obvious where this analogy comes from. The corona looks like a great crown, extending in all directions millions of kilometers away from the disc. It is caused by sunlight scattering onto, and projecting off, electrons and interstellar dust.

Above: Sunrise over the moon. Sunlight on the moon is much brighter than that on Earth, due to the moon's lack of an atmosphere. The seven Apollo landings all occurred during the early lunar morning. This allowed the astronauts to spot craters and boulders more easily, without the harsh sunlight during the day. Photographed during the Apollo 12 mission of 1969 (14-24 November).

Opposite: Computer graphic of the sun, showing its internal layered structure. The sun is a massive nuclear fusion reactor. The core (white) has a temperature of at least 14 million degrees Celsius where hydrogen atoms fuse into helium to release heat and light energy. This energy radiates out (lined layer) to form a turbulent layer. At the surface (red) is the photosphere, about 300 kilometers thick. The photosphere is affected by magnetic fields, producing phenomena like sunspots (cool areas, black); solar prominences (eruptions of charged particles); and solar wind. Its constant output of energy means that the sun loses about 4 million tons of mass each second.

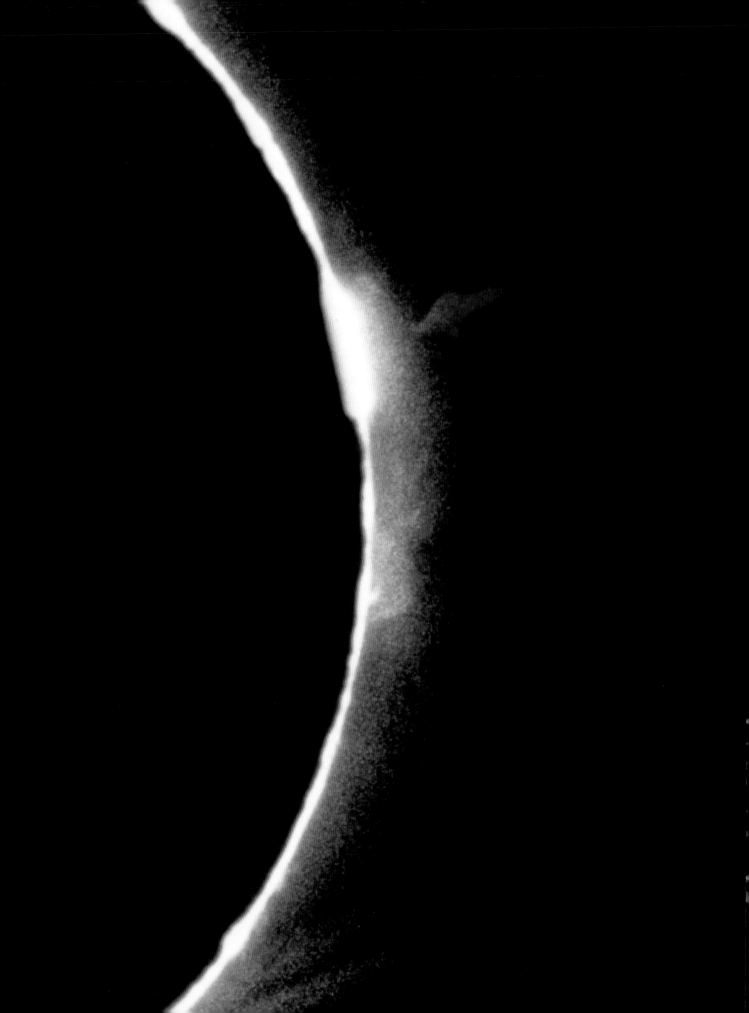

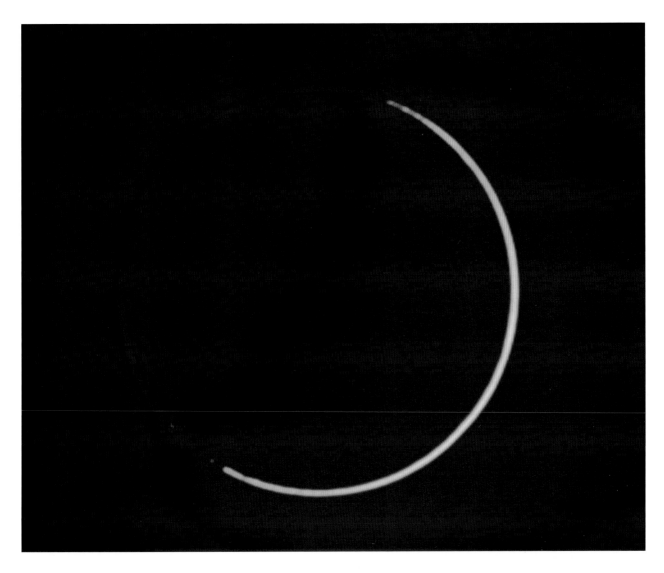

Beneath the photosphere is the sun's interior. The sun's core undergoes such intense heat and pressure that the process of fusion is unremittingly generated. Surrounding the core is the radiation zone. Photons emitted from the core in the process of fusion collide with ions in this layer and transfer small amounts of energy. The radiation zone eventually gives way to the convection zone, where the temperature is lower – particles are heated by convection. Less dense hotter gases rise to the surface of the sun, where they cool and sink back down to the depths of the convection zone where they are heated and rise to the surface once again.

Sunspots

In 1611 Galileo first reported seeing sunspots on the surface of the sun. These are minor regions, or spots, where the temperature of a small area of the photosphere is markedly cooler than its surroundings. This is a result of a

Opposite: A total eclipse of the sun showing Bailey's Beads, prominences, and the solar chromosphere. The dark moon is just covering the face of the sun. A narrow sickle of the brilliant light of the sun is seen through valleys and irregularities on the moon's surface, forming what are known as Bailey's Beads. The sun's lower atmosphere, the chromosphere, is seen as a red arc. Flame-like prominences protrude from the chromosphere into the surrounding upper atmosphere. These red prominences are made up of incandescent gas and may exceed 500,000 kilometers in length.

Above: Annular eclipse of the sun. An annular eclipse of the sun is when the moon in the middle of the eclipse conceals the central part of the sun's disk, leaving a complete ring of light around the border, 30 May 1994.

strong, localized magnetic field that prohibits heated particles from rising up to the surface of the sun. When sunspots are looked at in more detail, it can be seen that

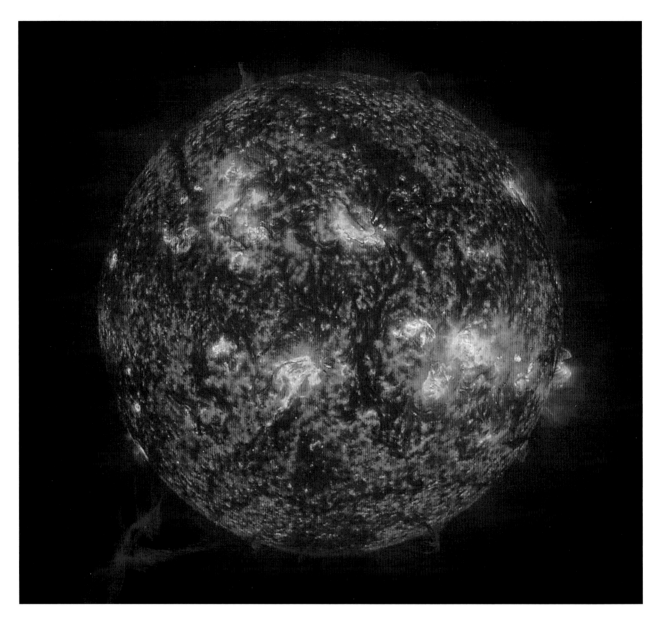

while the center, the umbra, is a blackish color, the surrounding spot, the penumbra, is gray. A solar cycle occurs every eleven years, when the sun is at its most active. At this time, known as the solar maximum, more than one hundred sunspots can be seen. However, during the solar minimum, there can often be no sunspots at all.

Solar flares

Solar flares were first detected by a British astronomer, Richard Carrington, during a particularly large flare in 1859. A solar flare occurs when energy that has built up in the sun's interior is suddenly released. The abrupt discharge of such an incredible amount of energy manifests itself in all forms across the electromagnetic spectrum as radio waves, gamma rays and X-rays, although it is difficult to see

Above: Solar prominence. SOHO (Solar and Heliospheric Observatory) image of a huge twisted prominence (lower left) in the corona of the sun. The prominence is a massive cloud of plasma confined by powerful magnetic fields. If it breaks free of the sun's atmosphere, such an event can cause electrical blackouts and auroral storms if directed towards Earth. This image was taken in the light of ionized helium (30.4 nanometers), which corresponds to a temperature of around $60,000^0$ Kelvin. It was taken on 18 January 2000 by the Extreme Ultraviolet Imaging Telescope (EIT) on board the SOHO spacecraft.

a flare on the visible part of the spectrum because the glare from the photosphere is too great. If particles from a solar flare come into contact with the Earth's magnetic field they

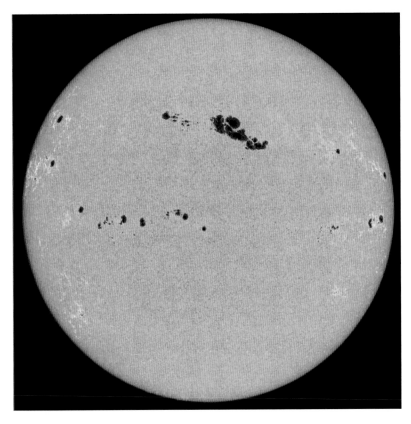

Left: An enormous sunspot group (dark, upper center) on the surface of the sun. Sunspots are relatively cool areas on the sun's surface associated with strong magnetic fields. At the end of March 2001, the area of this sunspot group was over 13 times that of the surface area of the Earth, making it the largest sunspot group seen during that solar cycle. Image taken by the Michelson Doppler Imager on board the SOHO (Solar and Heliospheric Observatory) spacecraft.

Below: Computer illustration of several large, dark sunspots. Sunspots are areas on the sun's surface which are around 2000° Celsius cooler than their surroundings, causing them to appear darker. The spots here have a dark region, the umbra, surrounded by a less-dark region, the penumbra. Sunspots are a sign of an active sun. The sun goes through a period of increased activity every 11 years or so. This is thought to be caused by the interactions between different layers of the sun, as they rotate at different rates.

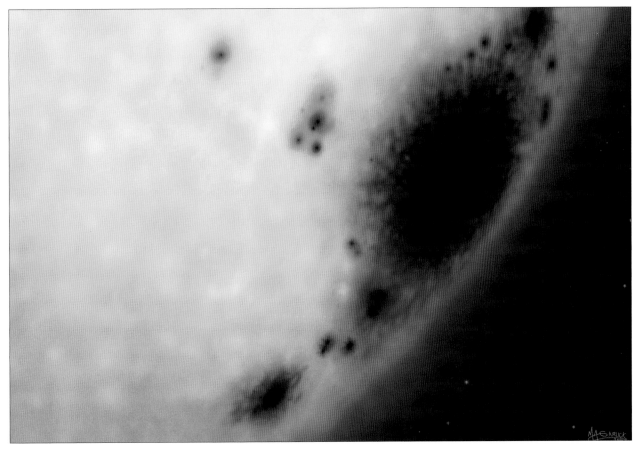

can disrupt communications such as radio and satellite links. Additionally, these particles are potentially lethal to astronauts working outside the Earth's atmosphere

Solar wind

Some particles are heated to such high temperatures that they are able to escape the sun's gravity. These move at rapid speeds of around 300 miles per second as a stream of particles called solar wind. Many of the planets in the solar system generate a magnetic field, which protects them from the solar wind, preventing it reaching the planet. Sometimes, solar particles are caught in a planet's magnetic field and drawn to the planet's poles, where they interact

Above: Solar flare, Skylab 1 image. This flare, or prominence, is erupting from the chromosphere (orange), which lies above the sun's visible surface. Prominences are dense clouds of plasma, or ionized gas, in the sun's outer layer, the corona. Upon erupting, the flares become part of the solar wind. They may be associated with strong magnetic activity inside the sun, and some flares are powerful enough that, on reaching Earth, they can disrupt telecommunications and satellite systems. Solar flares can extend hundreds of thousands of kilometers into space.

Opposite: Colored image of a solar flare (upper center). The flare is erupting from the chromosphere, or photosphere. Solar flares are explosive eruptions associated with active regions of the sun. The temperature within a flare, which normally lasts for a few minutes, can reach hundreds of millions of degrees Celsius.

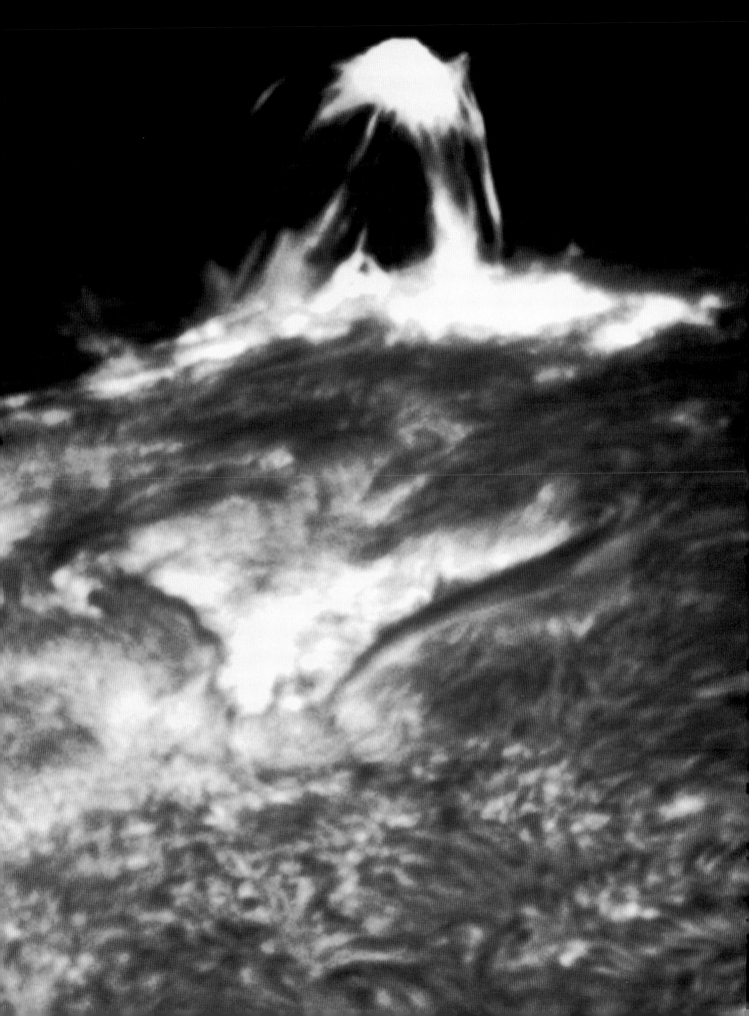

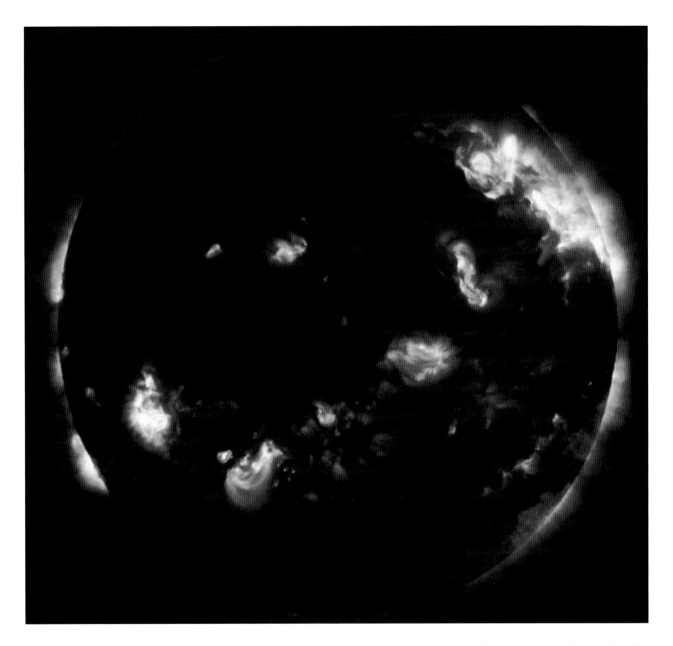

with atmospheric gases causing fantastic light displays named auroras, like Earth's Aurorae Borealis and Australis. Auroras increase in frequency when the sun is at its period of maximum activity, which occurs every eleven years.

Observing the sun

Never look directly at the sun, even when it seems that the sun's brightness has been reduced by cloud, sunglasses or some other method. Certainly do not look at the sun through binoculars, telescopes or cameras. Galileo went blind in the later years of his life, possibly as a result of his solar observations. The best way of observing the sun is by projecting its image onto a screen through the lens of binoculars or a telescope.

Above: Solar corona. X-ray image of the activity of the solar corona obtained by the Normal Incidence X-ray Telescope (NIXT). The image was taken before the onset of a solar eclipse and the round feature at right shows the shadow of the lunar disc. The corona is formed by gas at very low density but an extremely high temperature (1 to 5 million degrees Kelvin) which causes the intense emission in the X-ray band. The brightest areas are solar active regions where sunspots would be seen in visible light; the darkest regions are coronal holes where the gas density is extremely low and from which the solar wind, a stream of charged particles, is ejected into the interplanetary space.

Opposite: View of the sun setting behind a cloud. The sun appears redder and dimmer at sunset and sunrise as its light passes through more of the atmosphere and becomes scattered.

Sun/Earth Comparison

	The sun	Earth
Discovered by	Known by the Ancients	-
Age	About 5 billion years	About 4.6 billion years; the oldest rocks have been dated at around this age
Distance from the Earth to The sun (minimum)	149,597,000 km Light from the sun (travelling at 299,792 km/sec) takes about 8 minutes and 20 seconds to reach the Earth	
Diameter	1.390,400 km 109 Earths would be needed to fit across the sun's disc	12,756 km
Circumference	4,379,000 km	40,075 km
Surface area	6,087,799,000,000 km^2 11,990 times the area of the Earth	510,065,700 km^2
Orbital period (length of year)	The sun takes about 225 million years to make one revolution around the center of the Milky Way. During this period, the sun travels about 10 billion times as far as the distance between it and the Earth	365.25 Days
Rotational period (length of day)	25 days 9 hours 7 mins	23 hours 56 minutes
Surface gravity	274 m/s^2 28 times the gravity on Earth	9.8 m/s^2 If you weigh 100 kg on Earth you would weigh about 2822 kg on the sun
Temperature range	10 – 20 million° C (core) - 5,504° C (surface)	-89.6° to 59° C
Atmosphere	The sun is, at present, about 75% hydrogen and 23% helium by mass. This changes slowly over time as the sun converts hydrogen to helium in its core	Nitrogen, oxygen, carbon dioxide, argon, water vapor
Mass	1.99 x 1030 kg Approx. 333,400 more massive than the Earth and contains 99.86 of the mass of our entire Solar System	5.97 x 1024 kg
Volume	1.14 x 10^{18}km^3 Equivalent to 1,300,000 Earths	1.1 x 10^{12} km^3
Density	1.4 g/cm^3 (average) About one quarter the density of The Earth	5.5 g/cm^3
Surface	The surface of the sun (the photosphere) is about 500 km thick. Its temperature is about 6,000°C. The outer layers of the sun's atmosphere are chromosphere and the corona	The surface of the Earth is divided into dry land and oceans - the dry land occupying c.149,000,000 million km^2, and the oceans c.361,000,000 km^2

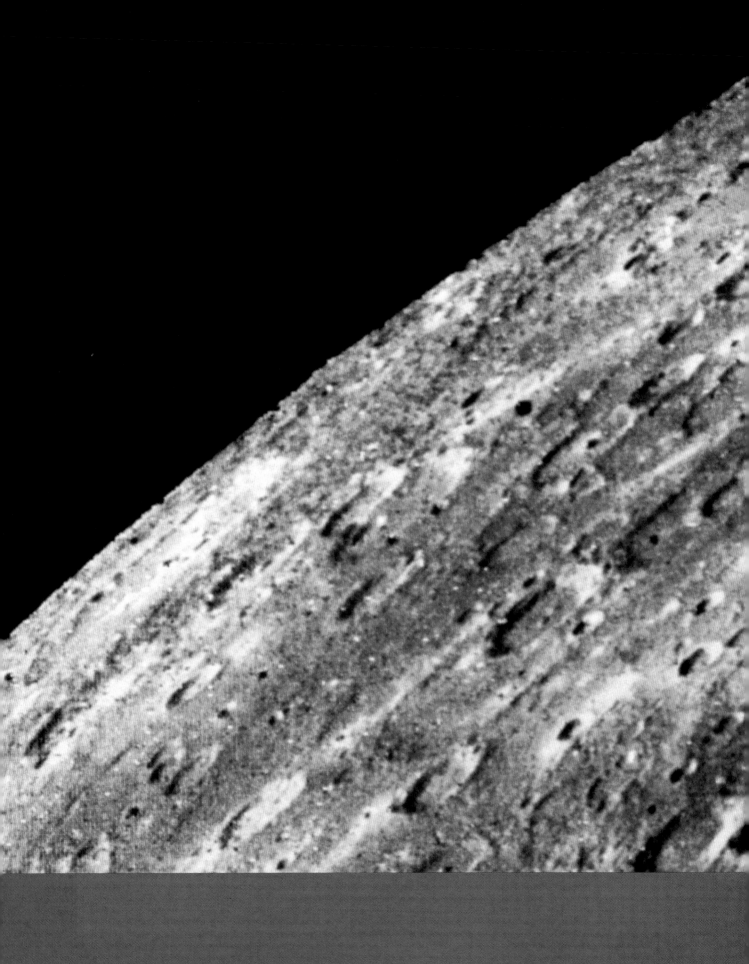

MERCURY

Very little was known about Mercury, the nearest planet to the sun, until Mariner 10 visited in 1974. Beforehand, it had been very difficult to observe through a telescope due to its small size and proximity to the sun, so difficult in fact that it is said Copernicus never managed to see Mercury for himself.

Mercury's closeness to the sun means that it is best observed during the hours of dawn and dusk, because during such twilight hours it is not overpowered by the luminosity of the sun. To view Mercury, it is best to wait until it is at maximum elongation – the greatest angular distance between an inferior planet and the sun, as seen from Earth. Mercury's maximum elongation is a mere 27°, meaning even when it appears to be at its furthest distance from the sun, a would-be observer must always seek to find the planet in the direction of the sun.

Orbital data

The planet was named by the Romans after Mercury, the messenger to the gods, because they likened its quick movement across the sky to the speed at which the messenger was believed to move. As the closest planet to the sun it completes one orbit in a mere 88 days, at breakneck speeds of 50km per second, making it the fastest planet in the solar system. Mercury can be seen moving from elongation on one side of the sun, to elongation at the other side in just a matter of months. In the late nineteenth century, Giovanni Schiaparelli asserted that the period of time it took Mercury to rotate on its axis was equal to the time it took Mercury to orbit the sun, 88 days. This would mean that Mercury would only ever present one face to the sun, just as the moon only ever presents one face to the Earth. His theory was proved wrong in the 1960s because the far side of Mercury was deemed too warm to have

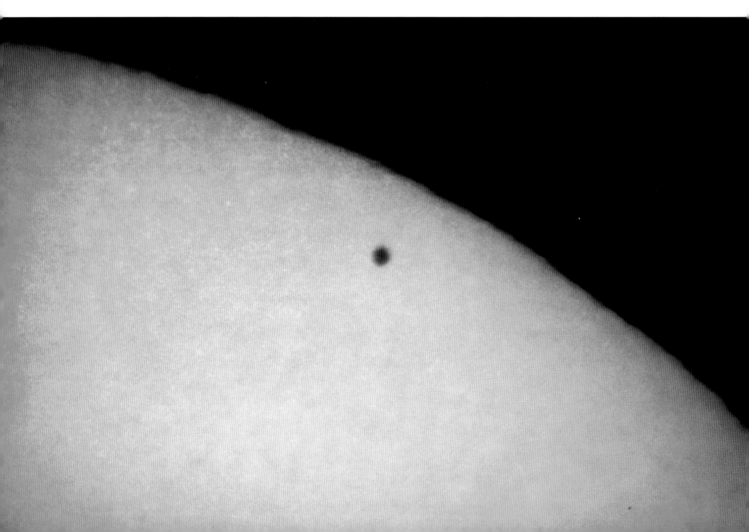

endured perpetual darkness; instead it was calculated that it takes Mercury 59 days to rotate on its axis, which would still leave part of the planet in long periods of night.

The first probe

Mariner 10 was launched in November 1973. Previously, it had been considered too costly to build rockets powerful enough to break Earth's orbit and lock into Mercury's even faster orbit, but a new method was used: the gravitational pull of Venus was employed to assist Mariner 10 on its mission to Mercury, the so-called gravity-assist or "slingshot" maneuver. Mariner 10 flew past Mercury twice in March and September 1974, and then once again in March 1975. Together the three flybys managed to cover just under half of the surface of the planet. Mariner 10 unexpectedly identified a magnetic field. It was thought that the planet's core would have solidified long ago, but the existence of a magnetic field suggests that Mercury has a metallic core that remains partially molten. This core is thought to be very large indeed, perhaps larger than the

Above: Mariner 10 photograph of Mercury, the innermost planet, showing its heavily cratered surface. Mariner 10 was the first spaceprobe to visit the planet, with three separate encounters during 1974-5. This image is a mosaic constructed from photographs taken as the spacecraft approached the planet for its first flyby on 29 March 1974.

Opposite: Optical photo of the planet Mercury transiting the sun. Mercury appears as a small black dot silhouetted against the brillant disc of the sun. Thirteen times a century the planet Mercury passes directly between the Earth and the sun.

Previous page: Mariner 10 photograph of the surface of Mercury. The dark, ridge-like structure visible near, and roughly parallel to, the right-hand edge of the image is known as Antoniadi Dorsum.

Earth's moon as, despite the fact that Mercury is much smaller than Earth, it has a similar average density; a high density points to a large iron core.

First impressions

When Mariner 10 arrived, it quickly became apparent that Mercury was a cratered world, much like the Earth's moon. During the probe's first approach to the planet a massive crater was discerned, subsequently named Kuiper, after Gerard Kuiper, a famous planetary scientist who died shortly before Mariner 10's arrival at Mercury. The planet's craters are most likely the result of meteorites colliding with the surface; one particularly large instance of a collision is the Caloris Basin. The basin is estimated to be 1300km across and the impact was so severe that mountains were thrown up on the opposite side of the planet.

The existence of smooth plains indicated that molten lava was once present, but the abundance of craters suggested that the planet was no longer geologically active, otherwise Mercury's pockmarked face would have been smoothed over. Massive cliffs, as high as three kilometers in places, are further indication that Mercury has cooled down. These cliffs are the likely result of the crust contracting as the planet cooled.

Mariner 10 mapped less than 50% of Mercury's surface. Although the rest of the surface is expected to be similar, a different terrain cannot be ruled out; one need only look at the example of Mars to see that a planet once written off as cratered and dead proved an erroneous judgement and that there exists an altogether more dynamic world.

Temperatures

Mercury has a very weak atmosphere, with the resulting effect that the planet retains very little light; therefore, the skies would be dark in spite of daytime temperatures reaching as high as 350⁰ Celsius. During the long night, temperatures can drop as low as minus 170⁰C. As Mercury spins on an axis with almost no tilt whatsoever, seasons do not exist, as the sun remains strongest at the equator all year long. Corresponding lines of latitude are at similar temperatures because neither hemisphere is notably closer to the sun. With such high daytime temperatures the existence of water in any form is highly unlikely. Nevertheless, in 1991, scientists bounced radio waves off

the surface of Mercury, in an experiment which produced an anomalous reading around the north pole, perhaps indicating that frozen water might be present, hidden deep inside craters, safe from the sun's rays because Mercury's perpendicular axis means that the sun cannot penetrate inside.

Atmosphere

Mercury's atmosphere is so tenuous that scientists often term it an exosphere instead of an atmosphere. The exosphere is the outermost layer of the Earth's atmosphere where molecules have enough velocity to escape the planet's gravitational pull. As the whole of Mercury's atmosphere is like the outermost layer of Earth's atmosphere, most of its atoms and molecules are lost into space. The sun plays an important part in the loss of these particles. Potassium and sodium molecules have an approximate life-span on Mercury of just three hours, which is reduced to merely an hour and a half when Mercury is at perihelion (its closest point to the sun). When Mariner 10 visited Mercury, helium, hydrogen and oxygen were discovered in the atmosphere. The following decade, in the 1980s, potassium and sodium were also discovered; between them these two elements alone are now thought to

Right: Mercury temperature map. Colored radio image of the surface of the planet Mercury, showing the range of temperatures across its surface. This image was obtained by the VLA (Very Large Array) radio observatory at a two centimeter wavelength. The hotter regions are represented by the yellow color. Mercury has two hot poles on its equator, produced by the intense heat of the nearby sun. The far pole is hidden, but may be deduced by the heating at the edge of the disc at lower right.

Opposite: Composite of images of Mercury seen from the Mariner 10 spacecraft. Numerous meteorite impact craters are seen. Mercury is the closest planet to the sun, orbiting at an average distance of 58 million km, less than half the sun-Earth distance. Mercury is 4880 km across, less than half the size of Earth. It is a rocky planet that orbits the sun in 88 Earth days. With a rotational period of 59 Earth days, it rotates three times in two Mercury years, with one sunrise in those two Mercury years. Its temperatures range from 420 to -170 degrees Celsius.

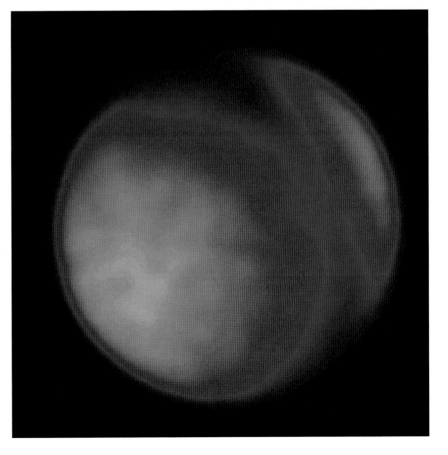

comprise more than 50% of the atmosphere. Mercury's magnetosphere is able to capture ions from solar winds, ensuring the atmosphere is constantly replenished, in spite of the rapid loss of molecules into space. Mercury is also restocked with sodium and potassium particles by meteorites that impact the surface.

The future

Given that it performed only three fleeting flybys, Mariner 10's mission has perhaps raised more questions than it has solved. For example, how can there be a magnetosphere on Mercury if the surface features indicate a core that has cooled and solidified, when, to the best of our current knowledge, we understand that a magnetosphere is generated by a molten core. Such questions have led to a new mission to Mercury, just over thirty years after Mariner 10's flybys. The aptly named MESSENGER mission was launched on 3 August 2004. Although MESSENGER reflects the profession of Mercury's namesake, the messenger to the gods, it actually stands for MErcury Surface, Space ENvironment, GEochemistry, and Ranging. It is destined to rendezvous with Mercury in March 2011, after one flyby of the Earth and two flybys of Venus. MESSENGER will complete the map of Mercury's surface, as well as establish an understanding of the internal structure of the planet, and attempt to discern its geological history. Furthermore, the mission will try to establish the exact composition of the thin atmosphere and discover more about the surprising magnetosphere. It will also investigate the north pole of Mercury to try to understand the odd reading from the 1991 radio waves emissions, to see whether frozen water might be found deep inside a crater. The European Space Agency also intends to send a probe, BepiColombo, to Mercury early in the next decade. The mission will have three parts: a planetary orbiter, a magnetospheric orbiter and, most excitingly, a lander, fitted with a camera, which will beam back the first photographs from the planet's surface.

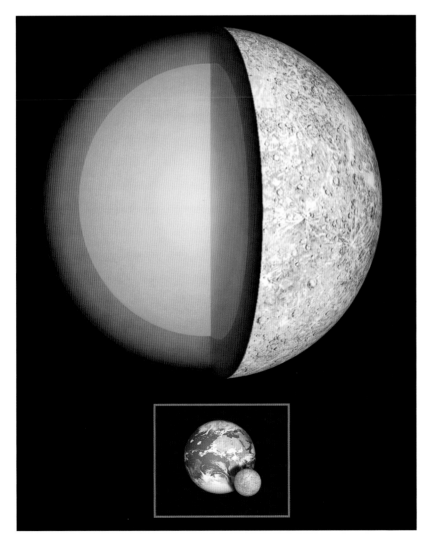

Left: Internal structure of Mercury, cutaway artwork. The inset box shows Earth and Mercury at the same scale. Mercury is a rocky planet. Its interior comprises a large iron core (yellow). This underlies a thick silicate crust (orange). Mercury has a very thin atmosphere, which does not trap much heat. Because of this, and its proximity to the sun, it undergoes drastic surface temperature changes, from around -200° Celsius at night to over 400° Celsius in the day.

Opposite: Mariner 10 spacecraft mosaic image of Mercury. Areas for which data is missing are blank. The surface of Mercury is heavily cratered due to impacts from meteorites. It also has lines of cliffs which are up to 3km high and 500km long. These escarpments may have been formed by the planet's crust wrinkling as the core cooled and contracted billions of years ago. The surface rocks are generally dark and a poor reflector of sunlight. Mercury has about the same density as Earth, though it has only about 5% of the volume and mass of our planet. The Mariner 10 spacecraft imaged Mercury on three flybys during 1974-75.

Above: Artwork of the nine planets of the solar system arrayed from bottom to top in order of their distance from the sun. Mercury is the nearest planet to the sun at 57 million kilometers. The size of each planet is to scale. The four small, rocky planets of the inner solar system are Mercury, Venus, Earth and Mars. The four large, gas giant planets of the outer solar system are Jupiter, Saturn, Uranus and Neptune. Finally, Pluto is a small planet of rock and ice.

Opposite: Mosaic photograph showing the heavily cratered surface of Mercury, the innermost planet. This photo is a mosaic of more than 200 photos taken by the spaceprobe Mariner 10 in 1975.

Mercury/Earth Comparison

	Mercury	Earth
Discovered by	Known by the Ancients	-
Date of Discovery	Unknown	-
Distance from the Earth (minimum)	77,269,900 km	-
Average Distance from sun	57,909,175 km	150,000,000 km
Average Speed in Orbiting sun	48 km/sec The fastest of the planets	30 km/sec
Diameter	4,878 km Approximately 40% diameter of Earth	12,756 km
Circumference	15,329 km	40,075 km
Surface area	74,800,000 km²	510,072,000 km²
Number of known satellites	0	1
Tilt of Axis	0°	23.5°
Orbital period (length of year)	88 Earth Days	365.25 Days
Rotational period (length of day)	59 Earth days Mercury completes three rotations for every two orbits around the sun. If you wanted to stay up for a Mercury day (sunrise to sunrise), you would have to stay up for 176 Earth days	23 hours 56 minutes
Surface gravity	3.7 m/s² (39% of Earth) Mercury's smaller mass makes its force of gravity only about a third as strong as that of the Earth. An object that weighs 100 kilograms on the Earth would weigh about 38 kilograms on Mercury	2.6 times that of Mercury
Temperature range	-173° to 427° C	-89.6° to 59° C
Atmosphere	Potassium, sodium, oxygen, argon, helium, nitrogen, hydrogen Dry, extremely hot and almost airless	Nitrogen, oxygen, carbon dioxide, argon, water vapor
Atmospheric pressure	Trace	1.03 kg/cm²
Mass	3.30×10^{23} kg Mercury is the second smallest planet	5.97×10^{24} kg If Earth was the size of a baseball, Mercury would be the size of a golf ball
Volume	6.1×10^{10} km³ Approx 5% the volume of the Earth	1.1×10^{12} km³
Density	5.4 g/cm³ Mercury is the second densest body in the solar system	5.5 g/cm³ Earth is the densest
Surface	Covered by a dusty layer of minerals (silicates), the surface is made up of plains, cliffs, and craters	Water (70%), air, and solid ground. It appears to be the only planet with water

Only one spacecraft has ever visited Mercury: **Mariner 10** in 1974-75. NASA has launched a new mission to Mercury called MErcury Surface, Space ENvironment, GEochemistry, and Ranging (MESSENGER) which will orbit Mercury toward the end of this decade

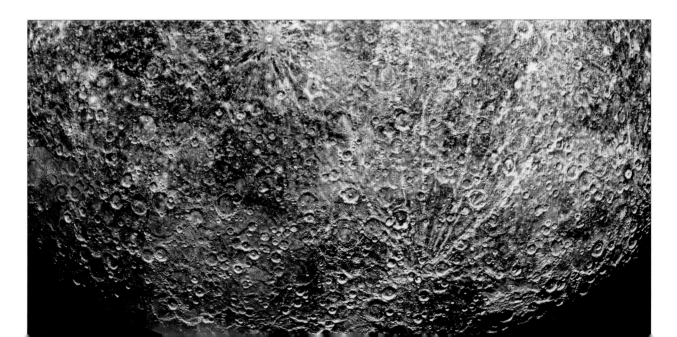

VENUS

The Romans named the second planet in the solar system Venus, after their goddess of love and beauty, perhaps because it shines gloriously in the evening or morning sky. Its dense cloud cover is a great reflector of light, which makes Venus the brightest planet in the solar system.

So bright in fact that Venus can sometimes be seen during Earth's daylight hours, making it the only celestial body, aside from the moon and the sun, to be visible during an Earth day. Venus is closer to the sun than Earth and, as such, when searching for it in the sky, it must be looked for in the direction of the sun. Venus's greatest elongation is almost 50 degrees and, therefore, it is not as easily outshone by the sun as Mercury, the other inferior planet. Although it is best seen around the hours of dawn and dusk, it has a much greater window of visibility than its partner inner planet. Venus lasts longer into the night sky, or rises earlier in the morning, and thus can be seen against a darker background, making it more visible to a stargazer than Mercury, and earning it the historic titles of both Morning Star and Evening Star.

Below: False- projection of the surface of the western hemisphere of Venus. This image was constructed largely from data gathered by the Magellan radar-mapping spacecraft during its first cycle of observations in 1991. The north pole is at the top of the image. The bright band across the disc shows the extent of Aphrodite Terra, a "continent" about the size of Africa. At the left edge of the disc is the largest upland region. Just below this is a circular valley-like feature called Artemis Chasma. The Magellan data has been supplemented by data from the earlier Pioneer Venus, with a general color hue based on Russian Venera surface photographs.

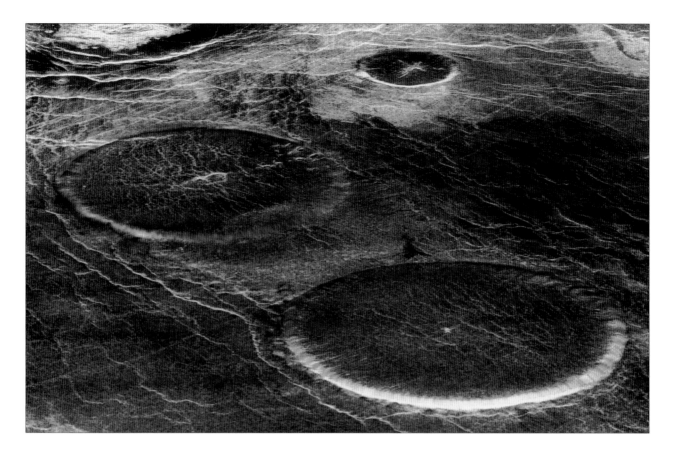

Orbit

The orbit of Venus has long been watched and recorded. A 21-year record of the appearance of Venus was found in an ancient Babylonian library, thought to date as far back as 1600 BC. The Mayan civilization of central America also noted the movement of Venus, which they revered as their "Great Star", over one synodic period – the time it takes a planet to reappear in the same spot in the sky. The orbits of both inferior planets, Mercury and Venus, cross the sun, as viewed from Earth, and they both exhibit certain phases. In 1610 Galileo Galilei first noted these phases, which seemed to vindicate Copernicus's theory that the sun and not the Earth was at the center of the solar system. When Venus was a smaller crescent, Galileo observed that it appeared much larger in the sky than when it was full. This happens because when Venus is at inferior conjunction to the Earth, although it is full, it is in line with the sun, and thus outshone by it. As such, from Earth a full Venus can only be observed at superior conjunction, i.e. the far side of the sun; that is why it appears much smaller in the sky.

The transit of Venus

When Venus is at inferior conjunction it usually passes above or below the sun. However, rarely, when both Earth's and Venus's orbital planes cross, a rare sight, the transit of

Above: Artwork of volcanic domes on Venus. Venus has the hottest planetary surface in the solar system, with temperatures of nearly 500⁰ Celsius. This is due to its carbon dioxide atmosphere that traps the sun's heat. Layers of sulfuric acid clouds cover the planet. The surface was mapped with radar by the Magellan space probes. The gravity is only slightly less than that on Earth.

Previous pages: Computer-generated false-color 3D view of a Venusian landscape, looking towards Sapas Mons.

Venus across the sun, can be observed. The same occurs as with a solar eclipse of the Earth by the moon, but Venus is much farther away than the moon and the effect is far less pronounced. Instead, the small outline of Venus can be seen crossing the sun. A transit of Venus is a rare sight indeed. Transits occur in pairs, with over a hundred years difference between each couplet. The most recent transit was in 2004; before that, the last transit pair was in 1874 and 1882. The partner to the 2004 transit, is expected on the evening of 5 June 2012; it will be best observed from the Pacific Ocean. In Europe, the last stages of the transit can be seen on the morning of 6 June. It is important to remember not to look directly at the sun – use a pinhole projecting system instead.

Above: Computer-generated perspective view, looking east toward the Maxwell Montes range on Venus. Maxwell Montes (just above center) is the tallest mountain range on Venus, reaching 11km above the mean planetary radius, and lies on the eastern edge of the northern hemisphere "continent" Ishtar Terra. The data for this image were gathered by the Magellan radar-mapping spacecraft. This view has been colored to reflect the basaltic rocks of the surface. The clouds, mist and atmospheric haze are computer generated.

Left: Transit of Venus. Venus is the black dot seen on the sun at lower left. This image was taken at 05:41 U.K. time on 8 June 2004 from Waldenburg, Germany. A transit occurs when Venus passes in front of the sun as seen from Earth. This was the first transit since 1882. Venus does not appear to cross the sun's disc during every orbit as the orbital paths of the Earth and Venus are not in exactly the same plane. Venus transits occur in pairs separated by eight years, with alternating intervals of 121.5 and 104.5 years in between pairs. As viewed from Earth, only Mercury and Venus can transit the sun.

Rotation

Venus is unique in that a Venusian day lasts longer than a Venusian year. It takes Venus 243 Earth-days to rotate on its axis, while it takes just 225 Earth-days for Venus to orbit the sun. Further irregularities are noted in that Venus rotates on its axis from east to west, instead of the conventional direction from west to east. Therefore, on Venus the sun rises in the west and sets in the east, the reverse of what we are used to on Earth. It would appear that Venus is rotating in a retrograde fashion at an axial inclination of just two degrees. However, many astronomers believe that Venus is upside down, with its north pole 178° from the perpendicular, which would mean that Venus is rotating in a direct, conventional fashion, but upside down. Either way, it is likely that this odd rotation was caused by a massive impact with a celestial body sometime in Venus's past. The fact that the planet has only a very weak magnetic field might be caused by its slow rotation.

In spite of these peculiarities, Venus is exceptionally conformist in other ways; for example, its polar diameter and its equatorial diameter are almost identical, making Venus nearly a perfect sphere, indeed the most spherical planet in the solar system. Venus also has the most circular orbit of all the planets in the solar system, with its eccentricity measured at just 0.0070.

Atmosphere

Venus is often referred to as Earth's sister planet, not only because they are one another's nearest neighbors in the solar system, but also because they are very similar in size – Venus and Earth have similar diameters, surface areas, volumes and masses. Without being able to see beneath Venus's cloud cover, and given the similarities to the Earth, observers throughout the centuries believed that Venus perhaps had Earth-like qualities, such as oceans, forests, vegetation and even life.

However, in 1962 this fancy was corrected with the arrival of the first successful probe, NASA's Mariner 2, which proved that the average surface temperature was between 400 and 500° Celsius. Such temperatures, which could melt lead, could almost certainly not sustain plant or animal life. Further Soviet and NASA probes charted the Venusian atmosphere, indicating more bad news: more than 90% was made up of carbon dioxide. Today that figure has been refined to an estimated 96% of Venus's atmosphere comprising the gas.

Venus's high temperatures cannot be explained by being closer to the sun than the Earth because Mercury's highest recorded temperatures fall almost 100 degrees Celsius short of the average Venusian temperature. The explanation is that Venus is being heated like a greenhouse.

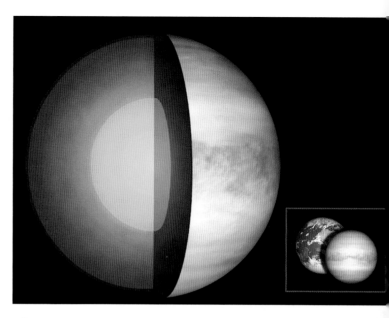

Above: Cutaway artwork shows the internal structure of Venus. The inset at lower right illustrates Earth and Venus on the same scale, showing that they are around the same size. At the center of Venus is a primarily solid iron core (yellow), which underlies a thick mantle (orange) made mainly of silicate minerals. On top of this is a very thin crust, which is only around 30km thick (compared to a maximum of around 70km for Earth's crust). Venus also has a thick, acidic atmosphere, which traps the heat of the sun (a runaway greenhouse effect). This makes Venus the hottest planet in the solar system.

All planets with atmospheres have a naturally occurring greenhouse effect. Energy from the sun is able to penetrate through the gases in the atmosphere on its way in to the planet because such solar energy has very short wavelengths. Waves that reach the surface are either absorbed or reflected. Those reflected are emitted as infra-red, which has a longer wavelength than the incoming rays, meaning their escape from the planet's atmosphere is not as easy as was their entrance. While some infra-red rays manage to escape into space, many are absorbed by atmospheric gases which reflect the infra-red back towards the surface, thus heating up that planet. It is the sheer abundance of carbon dioxide in Venus's atmosphere, and not its thick cloud cover, that traps the heat, leading to a greenhouse effect that is more exaggerated than on any other planet in the solar system. In fact rather than contributing to the planet's warmth, the cloud cover actually keeps Venus cooler, because it refuses entry to some of the sun's rays before they are able to reach the surface. The energy absorbed by the carbon dioxide is reflected back onto the surface of the planet, resulting in Venus possessing the hottest surface temperatures in the solar system.

Cloud cover

With such high surface temperatures, the layer of clouds which obscure the Venusian surface form much higher up in the atmosphere than clouds do on Earth. Most clouds on Venus form in a belt between 45km and 65km above the surface, while clouds on Earth seldom reach much higher than 10km. The clouds comprise mainly sulfuric compounds which are moved rapidly round the planet by fast winds of up to 300 km/h. Such rapid winds are only to be found at the cloud tops; at the surface, winds travel at relatively modest speeds, just a few kilometers per hour. Venus also experiences rain, but unlike Earth's water-based rain, Venusian rain consists of sulfuric acid. Such rain would be highly corrosive on the landscape, but it most likely evaporates under the intense heat before it reaches the surface.

The first probes to Venus

Prohibited by dense cloud cover from conducting clear observation of the Venusian surface, both the United States and the Soviet Union made it their desire to understand more what lay beneath. America began successfully charting the surface of the planet in the 1950s, before Mariner 2's arrival, by projecting radio waves from Earth. However, this only gave insight into part of Venus's surface, because it only ever presents one face to the Earth. This may be a result of chance, but it is speculated that, in a similar fashion to the relationship between the Earth and the moon, the Earth and Venus might be tidally locked when Venus makes its closest approach. Thus, like the moon, the far side of Venus remained unknown for centuries

In 1970, the Soviet probe Venera 7 landed on Venus and became the first successful landing of a spacecraft on a planet. Venera 7 relayed less than half-an-hour of data, under the strenuously demanding conditions – temperatures of over 470^0 Celsius, and an atmospheric pressure assessed at ninety times that experienced on the Earth's surface, bearing more resemblance to the depths of Earth's oceans than to the surface of the Earth itself. Humans would be crushed under the pressure immediately; this has ruled out a manned mission to Venus for the forseeable future. Instead, the emphasis has been placed on Earth's other neighbor, Mars, where the atmosphere would be much more hospitable to a human landing.

In October 1975 our perception of Venus changed forever as two Soviet probes, Venera 9 and Venera 10 landed on Venus within one week of one another – both probes photographed the Venusian surface for the first time. The black and white pictures revealed rocky remnants

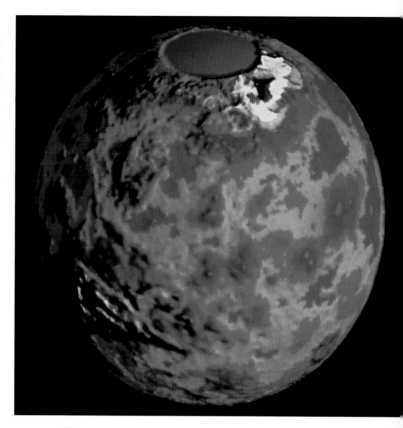

Above: Color-coded topographic map of the surface of Venus, compiled from radar data recorded by the Pioneer Venus spacecraft. The smooth circle at top marks the north pole, an area not mapped by the spacecraft. Most of the planet's surface is covered by relatively smooth plains, colored blue in this image. Two large highland regions are visible (yellow), Ishtar Terra (upper left) and Aphrodite Terra (lower right). Ishtar Terra is a "continent" about the size of Australia, containing the Maxwell Montes (red), the highest mountains on Venus.

Opposite: Colored radar map of the eastern hemisphere of Venus. The map was created using data gathered by the Magellan radar-mapping spacecraft in 1990-94. The colors indicate the elevation of the surface relative to the mean planetary radius (6041km). Blue colors denote land below the mean radius; land above the mean radius is colored green, brown, pink and white (highest). The equatorial zone is dominated by the upland "continent" called Aphrodite Terra. To the north are the lowlands of Niobe Planitia, to the south is Aino Planitia.

of lava from volcanoes, suggesting that Venus might be the only inner planet, aside from Earth, that had active vulcanism. In order to answer that question a series of mapping missions followed during the 1980s, with NASA's Pioneer Venus program and more Soviet Venera landings. These visits crudely mapped out most of the surface, identifying two massive areas of highlands, Aphrodite Terra and Ishtar Terra. The highest point on Venus, Maxwell

Montes, was discovered in Ishtar Terra, by Pioneer Venus. It is difficult to calculate its exact height, given that there is no sea level, but when measured from the average surface elevation, it is thought to be around 11.5km tall, over 2km higher than Mount Everest. Maxwell Montes is the only landform on Venus to have a male name; all the others are named after women, in keeping with the astrological tradition that Venus is a feminine planet. Maxwell Montes was named after James Clerk Maxwell, a nineteenth-century Scottish physicist who first identified light as an electromagnetic wave.

Mapping the surface

In 1990, the data from the Venera and Pioneer Venus missions were given further clarity by NASA's new spacecraft, Magellan. It was able to reveal, in detail, approximately 98% of Venus's surface. A total of 167 volcanoes with diameters greater than 100km were discovered, and many thousands of smaller volcanoes were observed. Venus was also shown to have a much smoother exterior than the Earth, as much of its surface was created by lava flows. However, the question of whether Venus continues to be geologically active remains.

The Venusian surface is thought to comprise mainly relatively young, basaltic rock, perhaps between 200 million and 800 million years old, indicating recent volcanic activity. On Earth, the surface rocks are all of different ages, while on Venus, the whole planet seems relatively young, and this has led scientists to believe that the volcanoes were not created by plate tectonics, as on Earth. Instead, one theory holds that molten rock had difficulty reaching the surface as lava and, consequently, magma, heating up in the mantle, built up to such great pressure that a cataclysmic eruption occurred across vast swathes of the planet. This would explain why we see very little variation in the ages of the rocks on Venus and would also mean that we are unlikely to see isolated volcanic eruptions. It also suggests that we will remain unsure whether Venus is geologically dormant until the cataclysm comes again.

Future missions to Venus

Venus is set to be visited again, this time by European explorers. The European Space Agency plans to launch its Venus Express by the end of 2005, for an arrival in early 2006. Once it reaches its destination, the Venus Express will

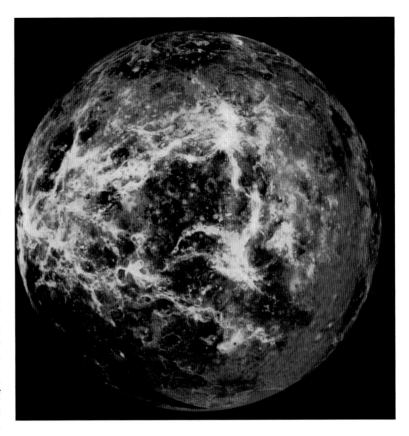

Above: False-color radar map of the west hemisphere of Venus. The image is centered on the equator at 270 degrees east (90 degrees west) longitude, with the north pole at top. Four major radar-bright upland features are seen. Running down the image just right of center are Beta Regio (top), Phoebe Regio and the less-distinct Themis Regio (bottom). The bright area at center left is the eastern extent of the continent Aphrodite Terra. The data for this image were gathered by the Magellan radar-mapping spacecraft. Areas of missing Magellan data have been filled in with lower-resolution Pioneer Venus data. The color was suggested by Soviet photographic data.

Opposite: Clouds over Venus. A false-color image made at ultraviolet wavelengths of the upper cloud layers over Venus, from data gathered by the Pioneer Venus orbiter. The general structure of these clouds has remained the same over many years. There are two dense bands of cloud near each pole, and the cloud banks at lower latitudes form bow-shaped waves. These high clouds are mainly sulfuric acid droplets. At the top of the clouds (about 80km altitude), wind speeds may reach 360km/h.

measure surface temperatures from orbit, as well as try to give greater clarity to our understanding of the Venusian atmosphere and clouds. Japan also has plans to launch an orbiter, Planet-C, in 2007, to search for volcanic activity and lightning, as well as to continue analysis of the Venusian atmosphere.

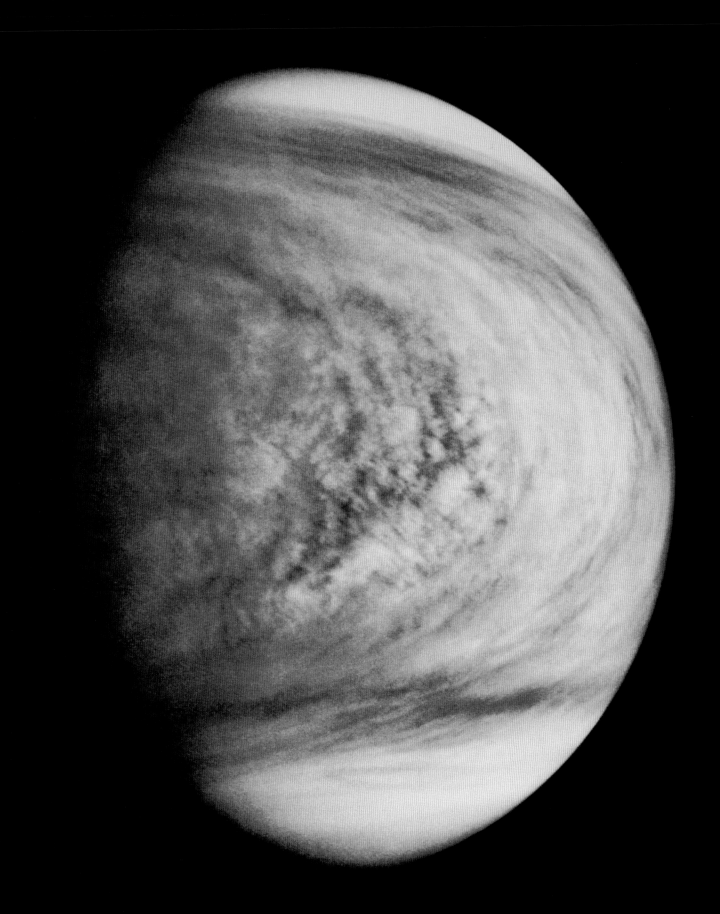

In the mid-1960s the gravity-assisted technique was developed. This enabled a spacecraft to gain a transfer of energy from a planet if it approached close enough, using the planet as a slingshot to catapult the craft to its destination in a much shorter time, with the use of less fuel. This gravitational slingshot idea has meant that Venus has been the indirect destination of many crafts, acting as an vital slingshot to propel them to the depths of the solar system. In a bid to make the probes less costly and more time-effective, most are given mini-missions to assess the planet that is catapulting them. Venus, as Earth's nearest neighbor, and the obvious contender to play slingshot, is a great beneficiary of this technique. For example, the Cassini probe orbited Venus twice in 1998 and 1999 to gain the necessary speed to reach Saturn, probing Venus's surface with radio waves and searching for lightning. Similarly, the probe Galileo photographed Venus when it used the planet as a slingshot in 1990 in order to get to Jupiter. It is not just missions to the superior planets which employ Venus as an accelerator, NASA's MESSENGER probe will require two Venusian flybys in 2006 and 2007 in order to reach Mercury, as will Europe's planned mission to Mercury, BepiColombo. The gravity-assist technique has ensured that Venus will never go long without a visit from Earth, as we try to understand more about our "sister planet".

Above: Maat Mons, Venus. Computer-generated false-color 3D view of a Venusian landscape, looking toward Maat Mons. This 5km high volcano appears in the center of the horizon. Radar-bright lava flows dominate the surrounding scene. In the foreground (towards bottom right) is an impact crater. This view was made by combining radar imaging and altimetry data from the Magellan radar-mapping spacecraft, extending the vertical scale by a factor of 10. The colors were suggested by previous photographic data. The viewpoint is 634km north of Maat Mons, at an elevation of 3km above the local terrain.

Opposite: Computer-generated topographical view of Sif Mons, a volcanic feature on the surface of Venus. This image was derived from radar and altimeter data gathered by the Magellan radar-mapping spacecraft whilst in orbit around the planet. The view is from the northeast towards the southwest. Sif Mons is 2km high and 300km in diameter, located within the 2300km by 2000km rise in the western Eistla Regio region. A series of bright lava flows is seen spreading 120km from the peak. The lava is relatively rough, and was formed during recent volcanic activity from highly fluid material. It is thought that the Eistla Regio itself was formed by an upswelling of hot material within the planet.

Venus/Earth Comparison

	Venus	Earth
Discovered by	Known by the Ancients	-
Date of Discovery	Unknown	-
Distance from the Earth (minimum)	38,150,900 km	-
Average Distance from sun	108,208,930 km	150,000,000 km
Average Speed in Orbiting sun	35 km/sec	30 km/sec
Diameter	12,104 km	12,756 km
Circumference	38,025 km	40,075 km
Surface area	460,200,000 km^2	510,072,000 km^2
Number of known satellites	0	1
Tilt of Axis	3°	23.5°
Orbital period (length of year)	225 Earth Days	365.25 Days
Rotational period (length of day)	243 Earth days A day on Venus is longer than its year. It rotates retrograde, or "backwards," spinning in the opposite direction of its orbit around the sun and is the only planet where the sun rises in the west and sets in the east	23 hours 56 minutes
Surface gravity	8.9 m/s^2 (89% of Earth)	If you weigh 100 kg on Earth you would weigh 91 kg on Venus
Temperature range	462° C The thick atmosphere allows the sun's heat in but does not allow it to escape, resulting in surface temperatures over 450 °C; hotter than the surface of Mercury, which is closest to the sun	-89.6° to 59° C
Atmosphere	Carbon dioxide, nitrogen, argon, carbon monoxide, neon, sulfur dioxide	Nitrogen, oxygen, carbon dioxide, argon, water vapor
Atmospheric pressure	93 kg/cm^2 The pressure is so intense on Venus that standing would feel like the pressure felt 900 meters deep in Earth's oceans	1.03 kg/cm^2
Mass	4.87 x 10^{24} kg About 80% of mass of Earth	5.97 x 10^{24} kg
Volume	9.3 x 10^{11} km^3	1.1 x 10^{12} km^3
Density	5.2 g/ cm^2 A "portion" of Venus would weigh a little less than an equal-sized "portion" of Earth	5.5 g/ cm^2
Surface	A rocky, dusty, waterless expanse of mountains, canyons, and plains, with a 200-mile river of hardened lava. Covered by more than 1,000 volcanoes or volcanic craters larger than 20km in diameter	Water (70%), air, and solid ground. It appears to be the only planet with water

The two planets are similar in size, mass, composition, and distance from the sun

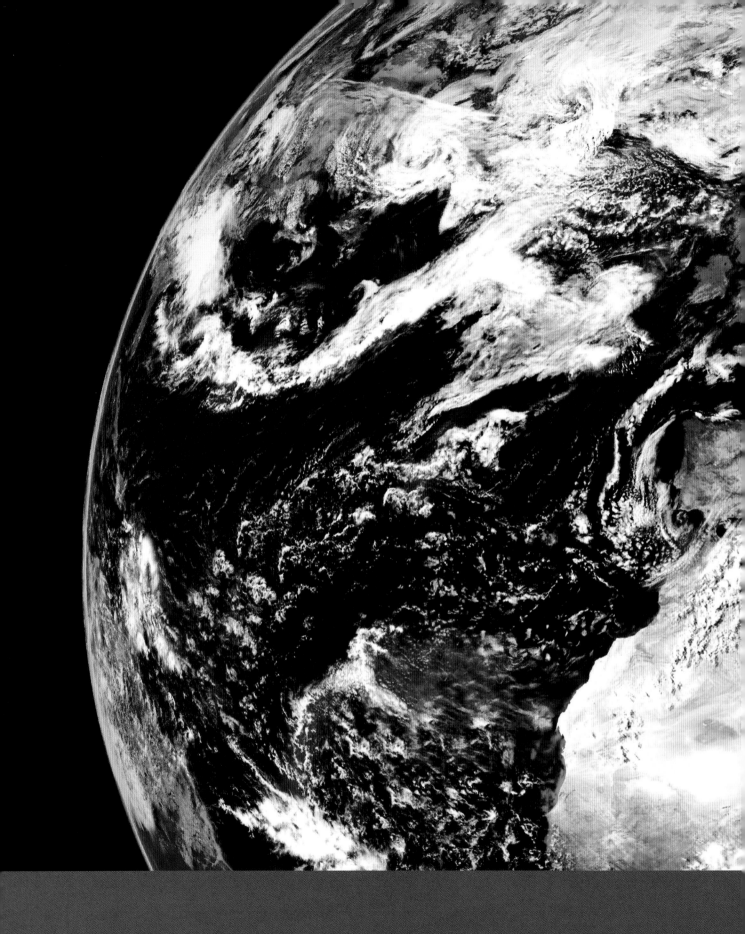

EARTH

The third "rock" from the sun is called Earth; it is also sometimes referred to as Terra, after the Roman goddess of the Earth, in keeping with a solar system named after characters from classical mythology. The Earth is unique in the solar system as the only planet with a nitrogen-oxygen atmosphere with liquid water oceans that cover more than 70% of the surface, and it is the only planet known to harbor life.

The Earth remains geologically active; the surface is under constant, gradual change. It has a relatively large satellite, the moon, which is more than one quarter the size of the Earth. As a consequence of this size ratio the two objects are often called a double planet.

Seasons

The Earth takes 365.26 days to orbit the sun at an average distance of 150 million kilometers. It takes the planet 23.93 hours to revolve once on its axis. Earth's axis is not perpendicular to the planet's orbital plane, but is tilted 23.5 degrees. This tilt means that a particular line of latitude will receive a different quantity of solar heat as the Earth proceeds on its orbit. If the north pole is pointed towards the sun, the sun will be overhead at the tropic of Cancer, the line of latitude 23.5 degrees north of the equator, with the result that the northern hemisphere will be undergoing summer. Meanwhile, the southern hemisphere will be experiencing a three-month winter. Half a year later, the Earth will have moved to the far side of its orbital path and consequently the south pole will be angled towards the sun. Halfway between winter and summer, for both hemispheres, the sun will be at its zenith above the equator meaning that in one hemisphere it will be spring and in the other it will be the fall. The seasons proceed from spring to summer to the fall to winter but climatic changes are more noticeable in the temperate and polar regions of the Earth. While most places experience longer hours of sunshine

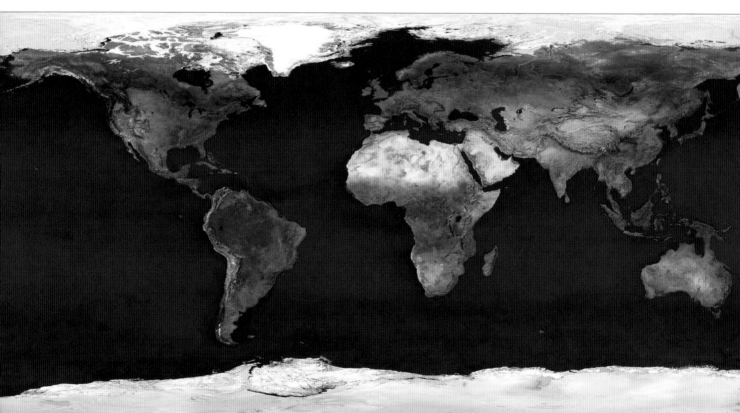

during summer and more hours of darkness in winter, the closeness of the polar regions to the poles means this seasonal change is exaggerated. During summer, when the pole is tilted towards the sun, the surrounding polar regions experience long hours of daylight often called "White Nights" or "Midnight Sun". Conversely, during the winter, polar regions suffer much of the day in darkness.

Biosphere

The Earth is the only planet we know to support life. Life appears to be resilient; every part of the planet plays host to some form. Life has been discovered at depths of 10,000 meters below sea-level and at heights in excess of 20,000 meters above sea-level. Life can be found in the ocean, in the skies, in the desert and in the polar regions but it is found in greatest abundance in the tropical regions. The fact that life proves so resilient on Earth indicates that it might be able to exist, in some form, elsewhere in the solar system, which is why many scientists have not abandoned hope of finding life there.

Living organisms function in small units within their environment called eco-systems. Within each eco-system is an established food chain, where all the members are locked into a circle of life, allowing one another to exist and survive. When an eco-system is upset, species within it might become endangered and eventually might cease to exist. The dodo became extinct in the seventeenth century when non-indigenous humans entered their habitat and disrupted their eco-system on the island of Mauritius. Among the many flora and fauna facing extinction is the dromedary camel, which is now extinct in the wild and the cheetah which is also vulnerable.

A floating crust

In its youth, the Earth was a ball of molten rock. As the planet cooled over time, the surface layer crusted over leaving molten rock beneath. The process of cooling has left the Earth in the state it is today. A solid iron inner core, more than 5000km below the surface, is enveloped by a molten iron-nickel outer core. Surrounding the outercore is the mantle. A layer of semi-molten rock of a viscous consistency ranging from 30km to almost 3000 kilometers in depth, the uppermost part of the mantle is termed the

Above: Crescent Earth. View of the Earth taken from the Apollo 4 spacecraft, in orbit 17,960km above the surface. The large amount of cloud cover makes it difficult to identify any surface features in the sunlit side. Apollo 4 was an unmanned test of the Apollo/Saturn V launcher combination. It was launched on 9 November 1967 into a low orbit. The third stage was then used to climb to over 18,000km before heading back to Earth. The speed at re-entry was similar to that expected for Apollo flights returning from the moon. This test validated the design of the crew capsule.

Opposite: Whole Earth map based on satellite data. The land is dominated by vegetation (green) or arid land (brown), such as the deserts of North Africa. The polar regions are covered by snow and ice (white) on sea and on land. The map is based on year-long observations by American NOAA weather satellites for cloud-free coverage. Ocean coastal color (due to chlorophyll content) is provided by the Nimbus 7 weather satellite. The polar regions were imaged with the DMSP weather satellites which are in polar orbits. This map is a latitude-longitude cylindrical projection that distorts and magnifies polar regions relative to equatorial regions.

wave is refracted, it indicates that it is entering different media or thicknesses of rock. Secondary shockwaves from earthquakes cannot penetrate liquids, and seem to halt abruptly at depths of almost 3000km, which first suggested to scientists that the outer core might be a molten liquid.

However, a decisive understanding of our planet's internal structure will be best achieved by going there. The deepest drills have barely scratched the surface of the crust but that will all change if a new Japanese mission to the upper mantle is successful. The mission, intended to be completed by 2007, aims to bring back rocks directly from the mantle for analysis.

Plate tectonics

The surface of the Earth undergoes constant change because the crust is fractured into a number of plates. All the plates glide slowly over the asthenosphere but not all move in the same direction. This means that plates are bound to collide, diverge or rub against one another as they move about, with the result that plate boundaries are rather precarious areas, which give rise to volcanoes, earthquakes or often both. If two plates are moving away from one another, chasms open up to the mantle below allowing hot magma to well up to the surface and form new land. This process usually occurs in the depths of the ocean and so is often termed "sea-floor spreading". As new land is created the old land is pushed further apart. This is occurring in the depths of the Atlantic Ocean, where a mid-Atlantic ridge of mountains has formed. This means that Europe and the Americas are gradually moving apart. This process of sea-floor spreading has changed the face of the Earth over the years. Initially there was one great continental land mass, named Pangaea, and the continents have since drifted away from one another. A careful look at a map reveals that the continents fit together like a jigsaw puzzle.

There is only a finite amount of room on the surface of the Earth, meaning that when land is constructed at some plate margins, it must either be destroyed or elevated at another. If two continents collide, the result is that the land is pushed upward to form great mountain ranges. This is how the Himalayas were formed, when India crashed into the south of Asia. However, when a continental plate collides with an ocean-based plate, the result is destructive. Oceanic plates comprise basaltic rock, which is heavier than the mostly granite continental plates and so when they collide, the heavier oceanic plates are forced beneath the lighter continental plates into the mantle below, a process called subduction which results in the destruction of part of the crust. The process is slow; there may be no activity for many years while the plate builds up pressure. Eventually an almighty surge occurs as the oceanic plate

Above: The sun setting behind the limb of the Earth. Photographed by the Apollo 12 mission of 1969 (14-24 November), returning from the second manned landing on the moon.

Opposite: Satellite image of the Earth, centered on the Arabian Peninsula. The Arabian Peninsula is separated from Africa (lower left) by the Red Sea. It is also surrounded by Europe (upper left), the rest of Asia (upper center to upper right) and the Indian Ocean (lower right).

asthenosphere. Above the mantle is the Earth's crust, which averages 30km in thickness. The top of the crust is the surface layer of the land but much of it is sea-bed and therefore cannot be seen. However, the parts of the surface above sea-level carve out the familiar shapes of continents we recognize today.

The internal make-up of the Earth has been discovered through the science of seismology. When earthquakes strike, some of the shockwaves penetrate through the Earth. Seismologists can look to see how these waves behave once in the interior; for example, when a

charges into the mantle causing earthquakes and tidal waves. A tsunami in December 2004 killed an estimated quarter of a million people when the oceanic Indo-Australian plate was forced beneath the Burmese plate causing the displacement of water in the Indian Ocean. Water and other volatile materials, which accompany the plate into the mantle, cause a great deal of pressure, eventually resulting in a great explosion back through the crust in the form of a volcano. The Andes and the Rocky Mountain ranges were formed in such a fashion. If two converging plates are both oceanic in origin, one is still forced beneath the other and the resulting pressure causes the creation of a volcanic island along the plate margin. This sort of tectonic activity resulted in the creation of a new island at Krakatoa in 1883; the eruption was so violent it was heard in Australia and Africa. As this process of island building continues over many years, volcanic island arcs, called archipelagos, result. Japan, the Philippines and New Zealand are all such island arcs.

Faults and hotspots

Not all earthquake and volcanic activity need occur at plate margins. Plates are fractured by smaller fault lines. When the rocks surrounding a fault line slip in opposing directions, the result is earthquake activity. Faults explain how earthquakes, such as the Dudley earthquake in Britain in 2002, can strike areas that are far removed from plate boundaries.

Volcanoes can also occur away from plate boundaries, on hotspots. In some parts of the world, the core heats the mantle to a greater extent than usual, with the result that the material rapidly rises through the mantle as a plume of molten rock. If sufficient pressure is built up, the material will punch its way through the core to the surface, forming a volcano. The volcanic islands of Hawaii, far from a plate boundary, are formed and volcanically sustained by a hotspot. Hotspot vulcanism is thought to have been responsible for the super-volcanoes found on Mars. Although on Mars, the volcanoes never moved off the hotspot, on Earth they do; meaning that hotspot volcanoes eventually become extinct. Yellowstone National Park in the United States is now known to sit on a large hotspot. Remnants of its last eruption, thousands of years ago, lie across the entire country, indicating that another explosion would be catastrophic, resulting in millions of deaths, and perhaps even global climate change.

Above: Popocatepetl. This volcano (5452 meters elevation) is the second-highest peak in Mexico. It had been dormant for around 60 years when it became active again in 1994. Moderate eruptions and earthquakes have occurred every few months, as of early 2001. As here, these can be accompanied by a column of ash and gas rising for several kilometers into the sky, posing a hazard to aviation. The largest eruption for 1000 years occurred in December 2000. Monitoring of the volcano and evacuation alerts help to protect the surrounding population. Photographed in December 1998.

Opposite: Sun setting behind the Earth as seen from the Space Shuttle Columbia. The tops of thunderclouds (center right) are seen towering high into the atmosphere. The glow of the sun is also seen reflecting off the upper layers of the atmosphere, providing a sharp dividing line between the Earth and space. Photographed during mission STS-109 (1-12 March 2002), while Columbia was orbiting over the Java Sea near Indonesia.

Evolution of the atmosphere

The Earth's atmosphere comprises approximately 78% nitrogen, 21% oxygen, and 1% argon, with trace amounts of other noble gases, hydrogen and carbon dioxide. The evolutionary process of the atmosphere remains uncertain, but the current composition is thought to be the third arrangement of the atmosphere since the creation of the Earth. The first would have consisted primarily of hydrogen gas together with some helium. This first atmosphere would have evaporated into space relatively early in Earth's existence, when the planet was still molten. When the surface cooled sufficiently to crust over, volcanoes formed, spewing carbon dioxide and steam into space. Earth's gravity would have held the volcanic gases close by, forming a second atmosphere. This would be composed primarily of carbon dioxide and water vapor, and some hydrogen probably also remained present. Over a long period of time, the water vapor in the atmosphere would have rained down to form oceans, into which much of the carbon dioxide would have been absorbed. Carbon compounds in liquid water oceans provided the breeding ground for bacterial life and later plants, both of which would have converted carbon dioxide into oxygen over time. The conditions then became ripe for the nitrogen cycle to begin; decomposing flora led to the presence of ammonium in the soil, which reacted with nitrifying bacteria, eventually resulting in atmospheric nitrogen.

Troposphere

The Earth's atmosphere is divided into a number of layers. Ascending from the surface to a height of 8km at the poles and 18km at the equator is the troposphere, named after the Greek word for mixing, because in this layer the atmosphere is circulated by winds. Conditions in the troposphere vary from region to region and from time to time; the state of the atmosphere in any given place at any given time is called weather. Weather is caused by differences in the amount of energy an area receives from the sun, which leads to variations in atmospheric pressure, temperature, humidity, wind and cloud cover.

The greenhouse effect, responsible for insulating the Earth with vital thermal radiation, occurs mostly in the troposphere, where there is an abundance of greenhouse gases, particularly water vapor and carbon dioxide.

The troposphere becomes less dense with height, meaning that there are fewer particles to absorb the heat, with the result that temperatures in the troposphere decrease with height. Clouds, comprising tiny droplets of condensed water vapor form mostly in the troposphere. There is a wide variety of cloud. Wispy cirrus clouds form high in the troposphere, where temperatures are cooler, and therefore comprise suspended ice crystals; at lower levels, stratus (layered) and cumulus (mounded) clouds form at middle and lower levels of the troposphere. Cumulo-nimbus clouds, large vertical clouds that can ascend high into the troposphere, are associated with perilous weather such as thunderstorms and hail.

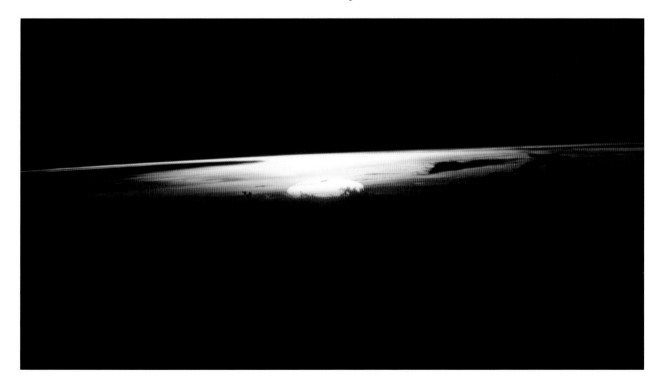

Left: Cutaway computer artwork showing the internal structure of the Earth. From the center outwards, the five layers shown are: inner and outer core, inner and outer mantle, and crust. The core is around 15% of the volume of the Earth, and the mantle is around 80%. The crust is a thin (5-70km thick) rock layer over the 12,756km diameter Earth. The core is heavy iron and nickel metal that sank to Earth's center. The inner core is solid, but the liquid outer core generates the Earth's magnetic field. The mantle is molten rock, and the inner mantle is more fluid than the outer mantle due to higher temperatures, which exceed 6000° Celsius in the core.

Opposite: Hurricane Katrina over the Louisiana coast on 29 August 2005. Katrina first made landfall near Miami, Florida on 24 August as a category 1 hurricane. It then moved south into the Gulf of Mexico where it intensified to a category 5 storm. It made landfall in Louisiana on 29 August as a category 4 storm with sustained winds of 240km per hour. Katrina caused immense damage and flooding and killed nearly 1000 people. Early estimates put the cost of the hurricane at $25 billion, making it the most expensive ever. Hurricanes are enormous rotating storm systems that form over tropical seas. They can be hundreds of kilometers wide. Image taken by the MODIS instrument on board NASA's Terra satellite.

Stratosphere

The layer immediately above the troposphere is the stratosphere, ascending to heights of 50km above the Earth's surface. Commercial airliners tend to fly very low in the stratosphere to avoid the turbulence they face in the troposphere.

Infrequently, nacreous clouds can be seen in the stratosphere in polar regions. As they are so high, they reflect sunlight several hours before dawn and dusk, beautifully brightening the night sky.

Air in the stratosphere is not heated by convection as air is in the troposphere, it is heated instead by ultraviolet radiation, which is absorbed by ozone particles found in the stratosphere. Many of the ozone particles are located higher up in the stratosphere, where they form the Ozone Layer. A greater abundance of ozone higher up in the stratosphere means that temperatures become hotter with increasing distance from the surface. In the 1970s it was discovered that levels of ozone in the atmosphere were decreasing and many scientists made a link between harmful substances, such as chlorofluorocarbons, and ozone depletion. The discovery of a hole in the Ozone Layer over Antartica in the mid-1980s led to a world-wide ban on chlorofluorocarbons by 1996. Tentative research shows that the ban has had a positive effect, as the rate of ozone depletion seems to have slowed.

Above the stratosphere

Above the stratosphere is the mesosphere, from the Greek for middle. The mesosphere ascends from 50km above the surface to approximately 85km. Temperature once again decreases with distance from the surface of the Earth, and temperatures in the upper mesosphere are lower than -70°C. Shooting stars or meteors can be found in the mesosphere because meteoroids that strike the Earth are usually burned up in this layer.

Noctilucent clouds, Earth's highest cloud type, can be found in polar regions in the mesosphere. The name noctilucent means "luminous at night"; because they are so high in the atmosphere they are lit up by the sun for the

found in the exosphere, particularly lighter gases – hydrogen and helium – can escape into outer space. Many of the satellites orbiting the Earth are located within the exosphere.

Magnetic field

The movement of iron and nickel alloys around the liquid outer core is thought to be the primary reason that the Earth has a magnetic field, the strongest of all the terrestrial planets. The Coriolis effect – the fact that the Earth has different speeds of rotation at different lines of latitude – is also held partly responsible. Earth has two magnetic poles, both of which are located near the poles of Earth's axis; the magnetic north pole is currently located in the far north of Canada and magnetic south pole in Antarctica. These positions are not static as the poles move over time. Clues in the shifting magnetic orientation of rocks over thousands of years have led scientists to believe that the poles interchange sometimes, so that the north pole becomes the south pole and vice versa.

The magnetic field provides the Earth with vital protection from solar wind; without the magnetic field solar wind could scorch the Earth, by eroding the atmosphere and causing the oceans to evaporate, making it uninhabitable for any life forms. The solar wind fans the Earth's magnetic field into a three-dimensional teardrop-shaped object called a magnetosphere; the strength of the magnetic field trails off with distance, leading to a long tail extending 50,000km from the planet in the direction away from the sun. Not all the solar wind is deflected by the magnetosphere; the Earth is vulnerable at the magnetic poles, where charged particles from the solar wind can race down inside the magnetosphere either to be stored in the Van Allen Belts or react with atmospheric gases to cause a fantastic light displays called aurorae. The Van Allen Belts are two doughnut-shaped radiation zones. They were discovered in 1958 by the United States' first successful space probe, Explorer 1. The belts were named after James Van Allen, who was instrumental in building the probe. Aurorae, meaning "dawn" in Latin, are a spectacular sight; unfortunately they are usually confined to polar and sub-polar regions which means that most people will never get the chance to see them first hand. In the northern hemisphere the aurora is called the "Northern Lights" or Aurora Borealis and in the southern hemisphere it is termed Aurora Australis.

Changing climates

Earth's climate can be divided into a number of different categories because there is sharp variation in global climate. Surrounding the equator are tropical regions, like

most part of the night. They seem to be a relatively recent phenomenon, having only been noted since the end of the nineteenth century and scientists are still unsure exactly what causes them; suggestions range from meteor trails and volcanic eruptions to space shuttles and climate change.

Above the mesosphere is a large layer called the thermosphere, extending from 85km to as far as 450km away from the surface of the Earth. Ionization occurs in the thermosphere because solar radiation is able to strip atoms of their electrons.

Beyond the thermosphere is the exosphere, a very rarefied layer extending from 450km above the surface to distances of perhaps 10,000km. The atmospheric gases

the Amazon basin which are hot, wet and humid areas covered in rainforests. Some parts of the Earth are barren, arid deserts, caused by a lack of rain, low sea-surface temperatures, or atmospheric circulation. At the poles there are ice caps; while the south pole is covered in a permanent ice sheet, named Antarctica, the north pole is surrounded by pack ice, floating in the Arctic ocean.

The Earth's climate has always been undergoing change. During its history the Earth has undergone many ice ages; the most recent, the Pleistocene, ended just 10,000 years ago. Climate change occurs naturally on the Earth over the years as a result of volcanic activity, or as plate tectonics have caused the movements of continents into different climatic zones. The Earth's orbit is not static and undergoes a cycle of change, meaning that the amount of solar energy reaching the Earth has varied over time. The sun has also become hotter as it has grown older, which has direct implications for the Earth's climate.

However, the process of climate change has accelerated over the past century as a result of human agency, in a process called global warming. There is controversy surrounding the exact causes of recent global warming, but it seems likely that it is the result of vastly increased greenhouse gas emissions, especially carbon dioxide, caused by burning fossil fuels, coupled with a deforestation of the flora that absorbs much of the carbon dioxide. The increase in greenhouse gases in the atmosphere has exaggerated the greenhouse effect and consequently the Earth has heated up. Human exploitation of the Earth shows few signs of relenting and, in the forseeable future, global warming will continue. A feared result of climate change is that the increased temperatures will melt the polar ice caps causing the world to become wetter, as well as hotter. This climate change is predicted to happen so fast that animal and plant life will not have sufficient time to adapt, posing great threats to their eco-systems and thus their survival.

Left: Crescent Earth, photographed in July 1969 from the Apollo 11 spacecraft, during its historic flight to the moon for the first manned lunar landing.

Opposite: Composite image of astronaut David R. Scott walking on the moon during the Apollo 15 mission, with Earth in the background. The Lunar Roving Vehicle (LRV), used for the first time on this mission, is right of Scott. Apollo 15 landed in the Hadley-Apennine region on 30 July 1971. During their 67-hour stay on the moon, Scott and James B. Irwin (who took the photograph of Scott) made three excursions totalling 18 hours 35 minutes. The LRV enabled them to travel a total of 28km. They took numerous samples of lunar soil on this journey. Apollo 15 returned to Earth on 7 August 1971. Alfred M. Worden piloted the Command Module.

MOON

To call the moon Earth's only natural satellite might be misleading, given that the diameter of the moon is more than a quarter of the diameter of the Earth. Perhaps it might be more accurate to refer to the Earth and the moon as a double planet.

The moon is tidally locked into a synchronous orbit of the Earth – it takes the same amount of time to rotate on its axis as it takes to orbit its parent planet. Therefore, during its 27 day, 7 hour and 43 minute rotation and orbit, the moon only ever presents one face to the Earth. The far side of the moon remained a mystery until 7 October 1959 when the Soviet probe Luna 3 first photographed it. The moon and the Earth are only 384 thousand kilometers apart, meaning both bodies exact a strong gravitational pull upon one another, causing both bodies to bulge toward one another. This bulge is scarcely noticeable; however, the gravitational attraction causing it results in the tides we see on Earth's oceans.

Early observations of the moon

The moon, as the largest object visible in the night sky, has understandably captivated audiences on Earth since the dawn of humanity. In ancient Chinese culture, the moon was identified as Yin, the feminine, while Yang, the sun, represents the masculine. It is thought that the association

of the moon with femininity arose because the lunar cycle is similar in length to a female's menstruation cycle. This association persisted in to ancient Greece and Rome where the sun gods were male, while gods associated with the moon were female, for example Selene, Phoebe and Artemis in ancient Greece or Luna and Diana in ancient Rome. In the Middle Ages, the link between the moon and femininity resurfaced, when links were made between the pagan ritual of worshipping the moon and witchcraft. The lunar-feminine link has remained to this day through the practice of astrology, in which the moon represents the irrational, spontaneous side of a person's character – traits which were traditionally associated with femininity. But, equally, there were civilizations with male lunar deities such as the Eygptian god, Thoth, or the Shinto god, Tsukuyomi, as well as gods of Mesopotamia and the Aztecs. Whether male or female, the moon featured heavily in the religious practices of ancient civilizations.

Given the moon's important religious connotations, scientific understanding of the moon made slow progress over the centuries, In ancient Greece, Anaxagoras was imprisoned for suggesting that the moon, as well as other

Above: Apollo 11 astronaut Edwin "Buzz" Aldrin is photographed on the surface of the Moon, next to the United States flag. Part of the lunar module is seen on the left of the photograph. Apollo 11 was the first manned lunar landing mission and was launched on 16 July 1969. It landed on the moon on 20 July 1969.

Opposite: Apollo 11 Lunar Module returning from the surface of the moon to dock with the orbiting Command Service Module, while in the background the Earth rises above the horizon of the moon. The dark area on the surface of the moon is Smith's Sea.

Previous pages: Astronaut Edgar Mitchell using seismic equipment on the surface of the moon, during the Apollo 14 mission of 1971 (31 January to 9 February). The device, known as the thumper, detonated mini explosive charges to create small localized moonquakes. These quakes were recorded so that a profile of the lunar interior could be made.

celestial bodies, was spherical. Since ancient times it had been thought that the dark patches on the moon might be large seas of water and that the moon harbored life. However, with the arrival of the telescope in the

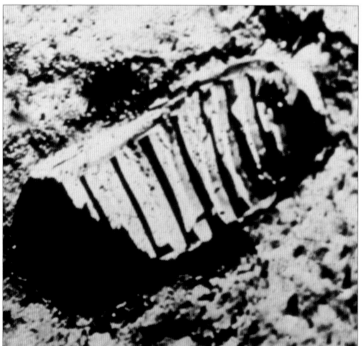

Above: Earthrise. This photograph of a blue and white Earth rising over the horizon of the moon was taken from the Apollo 11 spacecraft in July 1969. The lunar terrain in the field of view is in the area of Smith's Sea.

Left: The footprint of Neil A. Armstrong's first step on the moon on 20 July 1969. Apollo 11 was launched on 16 July 1969 and was the first manned lunar mission.

Opposite: Crater Tsiolkovsky on the far side of the moon, photographed from the Apollo 8 spacecraft in 1968. The moon's orbit of Earth is locked so that only one hemisphere faces Earth at all times. The far side was seen for the first time when Russian probes photographed it in the late 1950s, and many of the named features on that side are named after Russians. Apollo 8 lasted from 21-27 December 1968, and carried James Lovell, William Anders and Frank Borman to the moon. They orbited it ten times but did not land on its surface.

seventeenth century, the moon was shown to be a dry, cratered world, seemingly incapable of supporting life, or holding liquid water.

This did not stop the belief in extra-terrestrial life on the moon; in 1835, the New York Sun wrote a hoax report that John Herschel had discovered life on the moon. It caused widespread excitement as many believed the report, demonstrating that popular belief in lunar life had not been widely extinguished with the development of the telescope. The idea of intelligent life dwindled, but the prospect of microscopic life remained into the 1960s – NASA placed the three Apollo 11 astronauts into quarantine in case they returned with a lunar pathogen, which could have contaminated the atmosphere. Given that these quarantine procedures were breached when the command module was opened in the ocean, it is perhaps fortunate that it seems there is no life on the moon.

Formation

It is speculated that the moon might originally have come from the Earth, the resulting debris broken off when Earth was impacted by a massive object early in our planet's history. Such an impact might have been responsible for the tilt of Earth's axis. The Earth and the moon also seem to be moving apart at a rate of an inch each year; if this process has continued throughout history, the Earth and the moon would have been much closer together in their past. Whether these two bodies were once one or not, analysis of rock from the moon suggests that the moon and the earth are very similar in age, and that they might even have been formed from the same nebula at the same time. However, this would not account for similarities in the composition of the moon and the Earth's mantle. Another theory is that the moon is a large asteroid caught in the Earth's gravitational pull; this is unlikely because the moon is spherical and orbits its parent in a direct fashion, unlike captured moons which are rarely spheroid and frequently have retrograde rotations.

Surface

It is not difficult for an observer from Earth to distinguish darker and lighter patches on the moon. The darker patches are named maria, the Latin for seas, because for generations it was believed that the darker patches were likely to be oceans. These "seas" are smooth, lowland areas comprising basalt, which are the result of lava flows. Over three billion years ago, large meteor impacts would have exposed molten rock beneath the crust, which would have

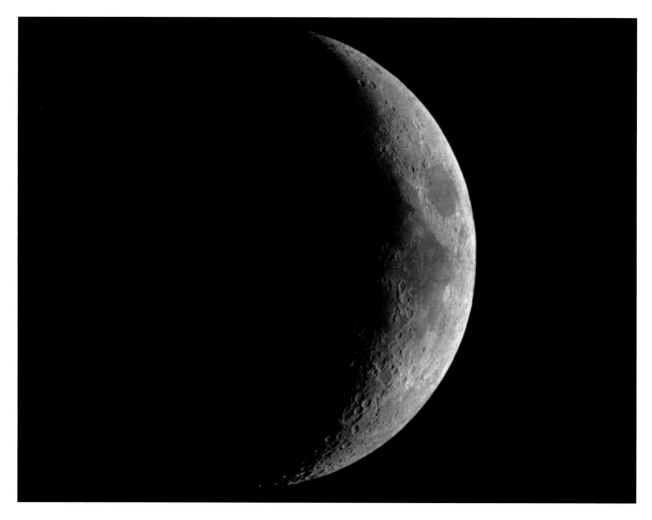

flowed out, forming the lava plains we see today. The moon is too small to have retained its heat for a long period and is now cool, but the number of meteor impacts has significantly declined and the maria remain relatively smooth. Perhaps the most famous of all the maria is the Sea of Tranquillity, famed for playing host to the first moon landing.

Surrounding the maria are the highland areas which are far from smooth, rather they are pockmarked by craters, the scars of a long history of impacts with comets and meteors. The ray-shaped crater Tycho, named after the famous Danish astronomer Tycho Brahe, is particularly noticeable from Earth as, from its position in the south central section of the moon, it reflects light from the sun. Another prominent crater is Copernicus, located just to the west of the moon's center and, although it is not as impressive as Tycho, it can be observed clearly with binoculars.

The highland areas are covered in regolith, a fine rock and dust coating, which are the result of consecutive meteors breaking up upon impact and spreading their

Above: Image of a waxing (increasing in apparent size) crescent moon 5 days into its 28-day cycle. The lunar phases arise as the moon's orbit of the Earth shows the Earth-facing side moving into and out of the light of the sun. This Earth-facing side of the moon is locked in place by the gravitational influence of the Earth. This results in a lunar day that equals the length of the lunar Earth orbit. On a waxing moon the day-night line (terminator) marks the lunar dawn.

Opposite: Crescent moon with Earthshine. The moon does not produce its own light, but can be seen because it reflects light. The bright crescent is lit by the sun whilst the darker part is lit by "Earthshine" or sunlight reflected from the Earth. Earthshine is most readily observable shortly before and after a new moon. When the moon is new, the Earth appears fully lit as viewed from the moon. Sunlight is reflected from the Earth to the night side of the moon, and then back to observers on the Earth. The dark patches on the moon are maria, areas of ancient lava flows. A prominent starburst impact crater is at lower left on the moon's surface.

debris across the surface. This regolith is more reflective than the basalt, which has the effect that the seas appear darker than the surrounding highlands. The far side of the moon has far fewer maria than the near-side, instead it appears pockmarked by years of meteor impacts, which did not cause bleeding of molten rock from the mantle onto the surface; this indicates that the crust is thicker on the far side of the moon than it is on the nearside of the moon, which has considerably more maria.

In 1989, the Galileo probe, en route to Jupiter, flew by the moon. It discovered a vast impact crater at the moon's south pole, the Aitken Crater. In 1994, NASA sent the probe, Clementine, to investigate, but the probe raised more questions than it answered. Radar signal from the bottom of the crater, which is permanently covered in shadow, indicated that there might be frozen water at the bottom of the crater. Ice would have arrived on the moon with comets that impacted the surface during its history. If the ice has remained in permanent shadow for many years, it may not have melted and evaporated into space. In 1998, NASA sent another probe, Lunar Prospector, to investigate. Lunar Prospector was crashed onto the surface of the moon, near the south pole; it has confirmed the evidence of water, but scientists have remained conservative in their

assessment of quite how much water. When man returns to the moon, these ice deposits will provide an obvious target for a closer look.

Lunar phases

The moon, as it appears in the night sky, undergoes phases, changing from a full moon to a crescent, half or gibbous moon, or even no moon at all – a new moon. These phases are caused by the changing angle at which the illuminated face of the moon can be observed from Earth. Such changing angles occur because the moon is moving around the Earth, but not rotating on its own axis. Therefore, whenever a full moon cannot be seen, it means that a portion of the far side of the moon is illuminated, but we cannot see the far side from Earth.

After 27.3 days the moon, having completed one revolution of the Earth, returns to its original position and the cycle begins again. The cycle begins with a new moon when the moon lies between the Earth and the sun, and therefore the far side is lit up, consequently, no moon can be seen from Earth. Between the new moon and the full moon, the moon is said to be waxing because the portion of near side of the moon being lit up by the sun is growing. Half way between the full moon and the half moon, when

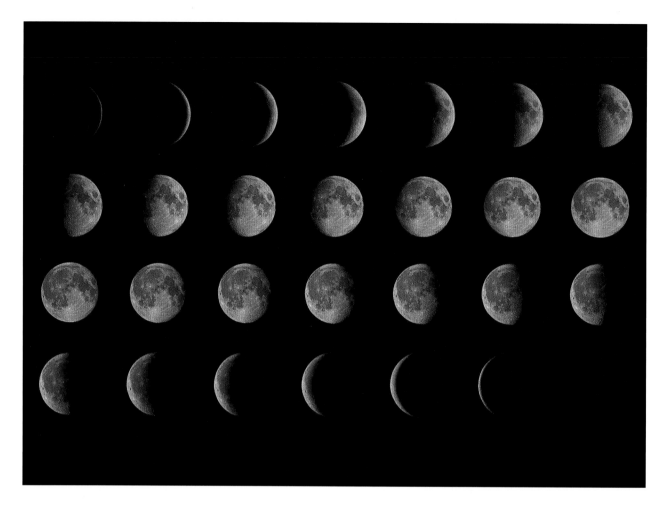

Above: Composite image showing the moon at each stage of its 28-day cycle (a lunar month). Along the top row, the moon is a waxing (growing in apparent size) crescent, reaching a half moon after 7 days. For the next seven days it is a waxing gibbous (between half and full), reaching a full moon (far right of second row) after 14 days. The moon is then a waning (decreasing in apparent size) gibbous, reaching another half moon 21 days into the cycle. On the bottom row it is a waning crescent, reaching the new moon stage at bottom right. The phases of the moon are due to it revealing differing amounts of its sunlit face as it orbits the Earth.

Opposite: Photograph of the south-east portion of the moon taken through a 30cm telescope from Orange, California. The four dark patches on the moon's surface are lava-filled basins called maria: Mare Tranquillitatis at top left, Mare Crisium at top right, Mare Nectaris at bottom left and Mare Fecunditatis at bottom right. On the edge of the Mare Fecunditatis is the bright, rayed Langrenus crater. The prominent crater on the day-night boundary to the north west of the Mare Nectaris is Theophilus.

the moon intercepts the orbital path of the Earth we see a half moon, because half of the nearside is illuminated. Between the new moon and the half moon we see a crescent moon, as only a sliver of the moon is revealed to us. Between a half moon and full moon, we see a gibbous moon. Half way through the moon's orbit, we see a full moon, as the moon moves behind the Earth, so that the whole of the near side of the moon is illuminated. After a full moon the phases repeat the first half of the moon's orbit as a mirror image because the moon is on the other side of the Earth. The moon is now said to be waning, as it appears to be declining in size from the full moon to the new moon.

Solar eclipse

When there is a new moon, the moon lies between the sun and the Earth, but cannot be seen because only the far side, unseen from Earth, is lit up. New moons occur once every 27.3 days, and usually the moon passes above or below the elliptic plane, the plane upon which the Earth and the sun lie. However, sometimes the new moon enters the ecliptic plane and obscures the sun; this is called a solar eclipse. The

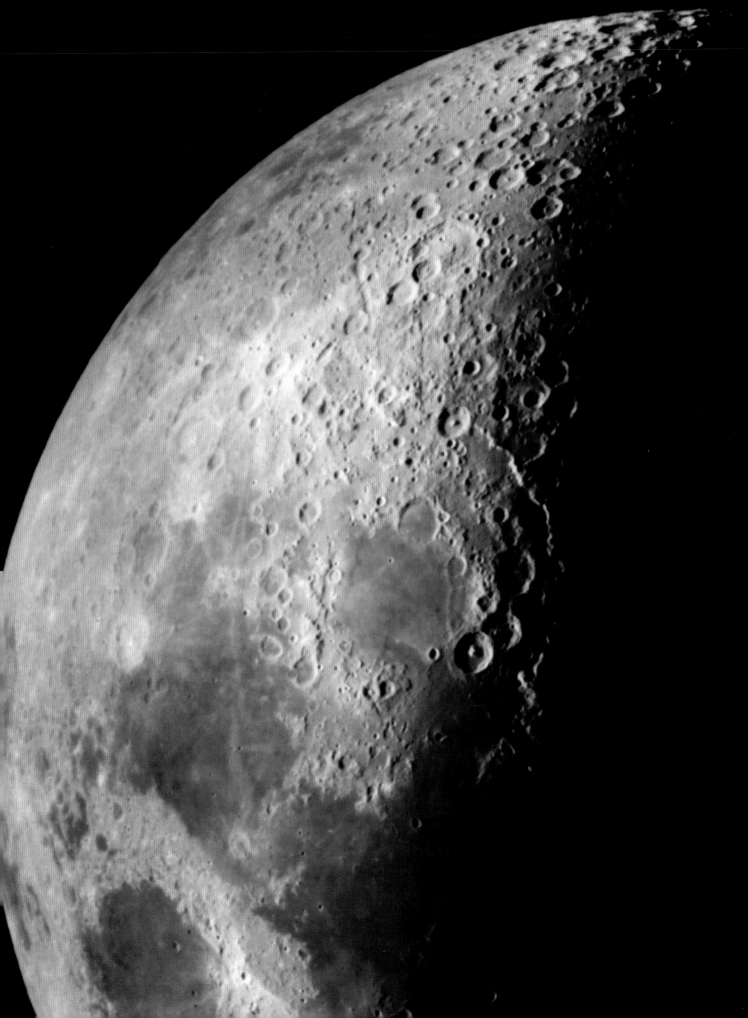

term eclipse can be misleading; an eclipse is when an object passes into the shadow of another object, instead, what we see is an occultation, which is when one body passes in front of another body, as they are seen from Earth. The moon's orbit of the Earth is not a perfect sphere, meaning that when it moves into the ecliptic plane, the moon is not always in the same position. When it is closest to the Earth, the moon appears larger in the sky, and therefore blocks out the entire disc of the sun, causing a total solar eclipse. When the moon is farthest away from the Earth it is not large enough to block the disc of the sun entirely; here we get an annular eclipse, and a ring of the sun can be seen encircling the dark disc of the moon. During a total eclipse, the area completely shadowed by the moon is named the umbra; the part of the Earth's surface within the umbra is the area from which a total eclipse can be seen. Meanwhile, the moon also casts a partial shadow, named the penumbra, over some parts of the Earth; a total eclipse can not be seen from these areas; instead, observers get treated to a partial eclipse when the disc of the moon will not block

Opposite: Optical image of a full moon 14 days into its 28-day cycle. The moon is full when the Earth-facing side is fully lit by the sun. The continuing motion of the moon in its orbit around the Earth will begin to move this Earth-facing side out of the sunlight. Darkness will encroach (here, from the right-hand side) as the lunar night falls on a waning moon. The Earth-facing side of the moon is locked in place by the gravitational influence of the Earth. This results in a lunar day that equals the length of the lunar Earth orbit. Taken in October 2001.

Left: Waning (decreasing in apparent size) gibbous moon 19 days into its 28-day cycle. The lunar phases arise as the moon's orbit of the Earth shows the Earth-facing side moving into and out of the light of the sun. This Earth-facing side of the moon is locked in place by the gravitational influence of the Earth. This results in a lunar day that equals the length of the lunar Earth orbit. On a waning moon the day-night line (terminator) marks the lunar sunset. The moon is gibbous when it is more than half full.

out the entire disc of the sun. Total solar eclipses are not actually that rare, they occur somewhere on Earth every one to two years, but it is rare for a recurrence in the same spot on the Earth's surface for several decades.

If the moon enters the ecliptic plane on the far side of the Earth, the Earth casts a shadow onto the moon, this is a lunar eclipse. When the moon enters the umbra of the Earth's shadow, it does not usually disappear from sight, because sunlight is refracted by Earth's atmosphere onto the moon, and the moon shines with a reddish hue. Lunar eclipses are not uncommon, at least two occur every year; however, they are not always so spectacularly colored, sometimes the refraction of sunlight might be obstructed by cloud or dust and the moon will appear much darker.

Missions to the moon

The moon was one of the greatest benefactors of the Cold War. As mankind entered the age of space travel, the moon, as the largest and brightest body in the night sky, became the obvious target for both superpowers, the United States and the Soviet Union. On 15 September 1959, the Soviet probe, Luna 2, crashed onto to the surface of the moon.

Although no further developments were made for science, Luna 2 became the first man-made structure to land on the surface of another world. A month later, another Soviet probe, Luna 3, sent back the first ever pictures of the far side of the moon. The fact that the Soviet emblem, the hammer and sickle, was sitting on the surface of the moon amidst the wreckage of the Luna 2 probe, did not sit well with the United States. In 1962, President Kennedy, desperate for the USA to gain ascendancy in the space race, announced that the United States would send a man to the moon by the end of the decade. America's lunar program did not get off to a successful start, its three Able space probes had failed to reach the moon in 1958. But by 1964, the United States had begun to redress the balance by crashing its first probe on to the moon. Ranger 7, took the first close-up pictures of the moon's surface as it crashed in July 1964.

As the decade progressed, consecutive American and Soviet missions to the moon, deepened our understanding of Earth's satellite. In 1966, the Soviet Probe, Luna 10, became the moon's first artificial satellite. Its greatest achievements were identifying and measuring

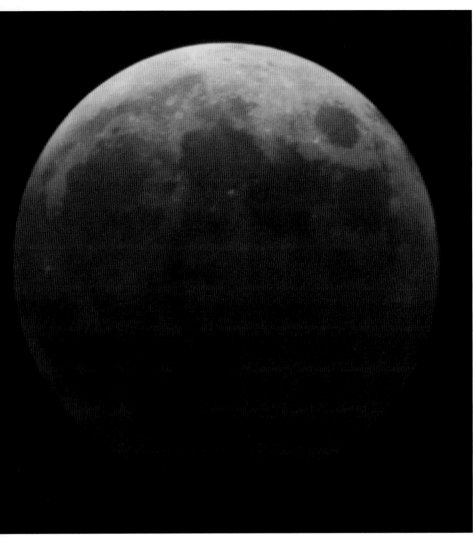

Michael Collins, accompanied the craft on one and a half orbits of the Earth and then its journey to the moon. On 20 July, the lunar module, Eagle, separated from the command module, Colombia. Michael Collins remained on Colombia, while Aldrin and Armstrong descended to the moon's surface in the Eagle module. As an estimated 500 million people around the world watched in amazement, the module landed successfully on the moon as Neil Armstrong uttered the first of his two iconic quotes of the day, "The Eagle has landed". Just before 9pm – the time in mission control, Houston, Texas – Neil Armstrong stepped out of the probe onto the powdery surface of the moon and uttered perhaps the most famous quote of the twentieth century, "That is one small step for man, one giant leap for mankind". Indeed it was, the moon had been the center of popular imagination for millenia, and finally, humanity had reached it. Twenty minutes after Armstrong, Buzz Aldrin stepped on to the moon, to become the second man on the moon. Both Aldrin and Armstrong spent over two hours outside the module on the moon's surface. In this time they took rock samples, photographed the lander so that engineers could later see

the moon's weak magnetosphere as well as detailing lunar radiation. The same year, American probe, Lunar Orbiter 1, took the first pictures of the Earth as seen from the moon and the following year, in 1967, successfully landed a probe, Surveyor 3, on the moon's surface; it was equipped with a mechanical scoop to analyze the lunar soil. When the Apollo 12 crew picked up the Surveyor 3 probe, three years later, it was discovered that bacteria, which had got into the probe before its launch, had been able to survive on the moon for three years. As a result subsequent probes are fully sterilized to avoid contaminating their destination.

how the exterior had responded to the landing and perfected techniques for moving about in the moon's weaker gravity – which is just one sixth of the strength of the gravity on Earth – meaning that the astronauts could make some impressive jumps. Before re-embarking the lunar module, the astronauts planted an American flag and received a phone call from US President Nixon, the first phone call to the surface of the moon. The lunar module successfully rejoined the command module and the three men made their descent to Earth with moon rock for geologists to study.

Apollo 11

In December 1968, the United States successfully sent a manned mission into lunar orbit. Apollo 8's orbit of the moon gave people a taste for what was to come the following year. On 16 July 1969, Apollo 11 blasted off from the Kennedy Space Center in Florida. Aboard the three astronauts, Edwin "Buzz" Aldrin, Neil Armstrong and

The Apollo Program

Before the decade ended, America returned to the moon; Apollo 12's lunar module landed on the moon on 18 November 1969. Apollo 12 landed in a different sea to Apollo 11. It landed in the Ocean of Storms, while the first moon landing had been in the Sea of Tranquillity. Rocks returned to Earth by both missions revealed that the maria

Above: Lunar landscape. Basalt rocks littering the south rim of the Camelot crater, in the valley of Taurus-Littrow, on the surface of the moon. The rocks were ejected from underlying lava flows by the impact that formed Camelot about 70 million years ago. Photographed during the Apollo 17 mission of 1972.

Opposite: Eclipsed lunar disc. Image of a partial phase of a lunar eclipse at totality. Lunar eclipses are caused by the entry of the moon into the cone of the shadow cast by the Earth. During a lunar eclipse the moon does not generally disappear. It is still visible thanks to the sunlight refracted onto its surface by the Earth's atmosphere. Since red light is refracted less than blue light the moon has a red-coppery color. The lunar disc appears to be darker and redder when eclipses occur after strong volcanic eruptions. This is caused by the large amount of ash thrown into the atmosphere which scatters blue light more strongly than red light.

had formed at different periods. This gave scientists the first indications that the maria had been formed by lava bleeding on to the surface after severe meteor impacts.

Over the next three years NASA sent a further five Apollo missions to the moon, the most memorable being the mission of Apollo 13. In April 1970, an oxygen tank exploded while Apollo 13 was making its way towards the moon. The moon landing was of course cancelled and, remarkably, all three astronauts returned to Earth safely. Apollo 14, in January 1971 resumed the successful moon landing program and one of the crew, Alan Shepard, famously practiced his golf swing on the moon; given the low gravity, it might have been one of the longest golf swings in history.

Apollo 14 was followed by three further successful missions, Apollos 15, 16 and 17. These last three missions all included a lunar rover, also known as a "moon buggy". This vastly increased the area the astronauts could cover; astronauts from the Apollo 17 mission covered over 30km of ground in their lunar rover and astronauts from Apollo 16 hold the record for the fastest speed for a wheeled vehicle on the moon: 11 miles per hour. Three further Apollo missions were planned but Apollos 18, 19 and 20 never got off the ground, and Apollo 17 became the last manned mission to the moon to date.

The United States government did not believe they could justify further funding when so much data had been gathered already and the country was fighting a costly war in Vietnam. Moreover, the Apollo program had not resulted in any fatalities, even Apollo 13 had got back to the Earth safely. By quitting while it was ahead, NASA ensured it maintained a clean sheet in terms of returning its astronauts to Earth.

In 2004, US President, George W. Bush, announced that America would return to the moon by 2020. The last time a President had set a date on a manned lunar mission, the US met the challenge and successfully landed the first man on the moon before the time expired. Even if President Bush's timeframe is not met, it is a reliable bet that humans will once again walk upon the surface of the moon.

Below: Lunar landing module. The lander (lower center), Challenger, in the Taurus-Littrow valley on the surface of the moon during the Apollo 17 mission of 1972 (7-19 December). The rocky craters at left are known as Camelot and Horatio and the hill in the background is the South Massif.

Opposite: A close-up image from Earth of the crescent moon in daylight.

Moon/Earth Comparison

	Moon	Earth
Discovered by	Known by the Ancients	-
Age	Scientists believe that the moon was formed approximately 4.5 billion years ago (the age of the oldest collected lunar rocks)	-
Distance from the Earth (minimum)	384,000 km Because of the gravitational pull of the sun, the extreme ranges of the moon from the Earth are from 356,400 km to 406,700 km	-
Average Speed in Orbiting Earth	1 km/sec	Orbits sun at 30 km/sec
Diameter	3,474 km	12,756 km
Circumference	10,916 km	40,075 km
Surface area	37,932,330 km^2	510,065,700 km^2
Tilt of Axis	1.5°	23.5°
Orbital period (length of year)	27 days 7 hours 43 mins	365.25 Days
Rotational period (length of day)	27 days 7 hours 43 mins From Earth, we see the same face of the moon all the time because the moon rotates just once on its own axis in the same time that it travels once around Earth. This is known as "synchronous rotation"	23 hours 56 minutes
Surface gravity	1.6 m/s^2 The gravitational forces between the Earth and the moon affect the level of the ocean tides, causing the Earth to have two high tides per day	9.8 m/s^2 If you weigh 100 kg on Earth you would weigh 16 kg on The moon
Temperature range	-233 to 123° C	-89.6° to 59° C
Atmosphere	None	Nitrogen, oxygen, carbon dioxide, argon, water vapor
Mass	7.35 x 10^{22} kg The ratio of the mass of the moon to Earth is far larger than the similar ratios of other natural satellites to the planets they orbit, with the exception of Charon and Pluto	5.97 x 10^{24} kg
Volume	2.2 x 107 km^3 If the moon were seen next to the Earth, it would look like a tennis ball next to a football	1.1 x 1012 km^3
Density	3.3 g/cm^3	5.5 g/cm^3
Surface	The light areas are lunar highlands. The dark features, called maria, are impact craters that were filled with dark lava between 4 and 2.5 billion years ago	The surface of the Earth is divided into dry land and oceans - the dry land occupying c.149,000,000 million km^2, and the oceans c.361,000,000 km^2

MARS

M ars was, perhaps hastily, referred to as the "dead planet" following Mariner 9's 1971 flying visit, from which the first pictures of the Martian surface revealed a dusty, moon-like, cratered world, devoid of other discernible features.

This all changed in the later 1970s, when the Viking missions reached Mars and revealed super-volcanoes, gigantic valleys and areas that appeared to be ancient, giant flood plains. The question of whether Mars is dead does however remain pertinent. Scientists remain unclear about the possibilities of life, water and volcanic activity on Mars, and, consequently, the jury is still out on the vitality of the planet.

Owing to its small size and mass, the Martian atmosphere is exceptionally thin, approximately one hundredth the density of Earth's atmosphere. The chief component of the Martian air is carbon dioxide, which comprises around 95% of the atmosphere, while on Earth it is only found in trace amounts. The remaining 5% mainly consists of argon and nitrogen, with traces of oxygen. Although the composition and concentration of the atmosphere might render manned missions difficult, it has enabled Mars to be the recipient of a rich space program, for Venus, the closer of Earth's two neighbors, has a much thicker atmosphere than the Earth and probes would burn up very easily upon entering the Venusian atmosphere. This is not the case on Mars, which several successful unmanned landing probes have visited.

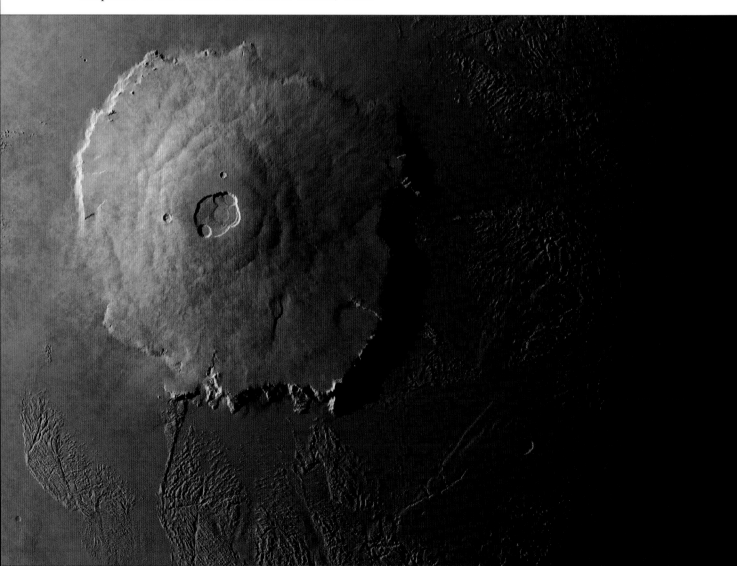

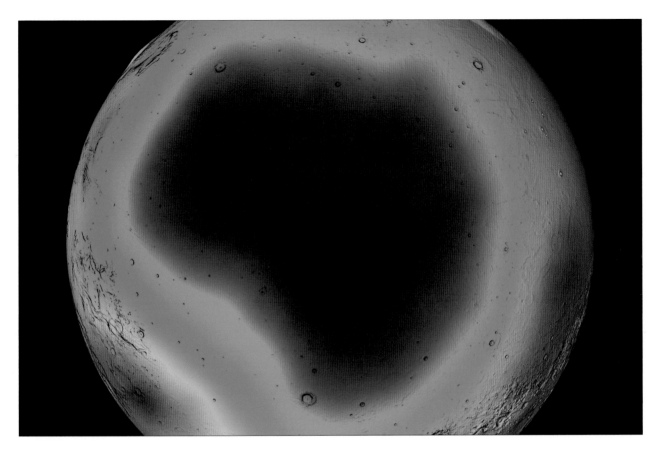

Weather systems

Mars is a cold planet. The average surface temperature is minus 60° Celsius. In the summer months, the equator can reach temperatures of around 20°C. Such temperatures cause low pressure, and cold air rushes in from the poles to fill the gap left behind as this relatively hot air rises. This creates winds on Mars which can reach speeds of several hundred miles per hour. These fast Martian winds pick up dust particles and engulf Mars in massive, planet-wide dust-storms. When probes have taken color photographs of Mars, the sky appears a pinkish-tan color. This is the result of the iron-rich dust particles, which are whipped up from the surface by Martian winds, and are almost always present in the atmosphere. However, when the dust subsides the Martian sky changes to a dark blue.

The search for water

Water exists on Mars, in both frozen and vapor form, but it has not yet been found as liquid. This is because the surface of Mars is far too cold. Therefore, surface water is only to be found in frozen form and this is largely confined to the northern polar ice cap. Both poles have a residual cap that exists all year round, and both exhibit seasonal ice caps which can be found during the winter months.

Mars experiences similar seasons to Earth, although

Above: Water ice on Mars. During the Martian summer, a large expanse of frozen water (blue) is seen on the surface of Mars. During winter, much of the ice is obscured by layers of carbon dioxide frost or snow (dry ice, green). This image shows the northern hemisphere of Mars. The water-rich soil layer is the Martian equivalent of permafrost. This image, showing the composition of elements in the top meter of the surface of Mars, is based on data from the gamma-ray spectrometer on board NASA's Mars Odyssey spacecraft.

Opposite: Artwork of Olympus Mons, the largest known volcano in the solar system. Its summit rises 27km above the surrounding plains (Mount Everest is 8.8km high), while the base measures 600km across, resulting in a gentle surface slope. Also visible is the cliff that marks the base of the slope. The rough, crinkly patches around the volcano form the Olympus Mons Aureole. Both the Aureole and the basal cliff are poorly understood, although it is thought that their origins may be related.

Previous page: Martian canyons. This image was taken in 2004 by the High Resolution Stereo Camera (HRSC) on board Mars Express and shows a perspective looking north for 600km over the central part of the Valles Marineris region. The Valles Marineris canyon system is over 4000km long. This area is about 300km wide. The canyons are Ophir Chasma (across top, pale color), Candor Chasma (across upper center, dark) and Melas Chasma (also dark, across lower center). Each canyon is about 200km wide and between 5 and 7km deep.

Above: Artwork of Mars as it is today: a dry, barren planet. It is thought that liquid water existed on Mars early in its history, but was lost to space over time. This may have been due to Mars's weak gravity, thin atmosphere and weakening magnetic field. If liquid water did exist on Mars, there is a chance that life may have begun there. Numerous probes have so far failed to find any evidence for this. In the future, it may be possible to return Mars to a wet state artificially, and create an environment suitable for life once again. This process is called terraforming.

Opposite: Evidence for life on Mars. Colored scanning electron micrograph of a tube-like structure (colored turquoise) on a meteorite which originated from Mars. Structures such as this have been interpreted as possibly being microfossils of primitive, bacteria-like organisms which may have lived on Mars more than 3.6 billion years ago. The structures are less than 1/100th the diameter of a human hair. The meteorite, called ALH84001, was discovered in Antarctica in 1984, and has since been studied at NASA's Johnson Space Center and at Stanford University.

as a Martian year is almost twice as long as Earth's, the seasons last proportionally longer. As such, in winter, the seasonal ice cap in the northern hemisphere can reach as far south as a latitude of 45°, which is equivalent to southern France on Earth. It is only the residual, northern ice cap which is constructed of water-based ice, the southern ice cap and both seasonal caps are thought to comprise mainly frozen carbon dioxide. However, a more conclusive understanding of the southern pole will come with the arrival of NASA's Phoenix probe in 2008, and scientists are hopeful of finding evidence of water ice there too.

The concept of liquid water on Mars is age-old, perhaps because the ice caps could be observed through telescopes. Telescopes had also picked up dark lines across the surface, which popularized the nineteenth-century idea that canals existed on the planet. When Mariner 4 reached Mars in 1964 it revealed a dead, cratered surface, putting paid to the idea of liquid water. But since Mariner 4 the case in favor of liquid water has been mounting; NASA's Viking missions, a decade later, detected the existence of fluvial valleys and channels in the northern hemisphere, and such evidence was bolstered by NASA's Pathfinder mission in 1997 which suggested that the layout of rocks in a region called Ares Vallis indicated they had been formed by a flood.

When NASA's Rover, Opportunity, reached Mars in the early twenty-first century, it seemed to have stumbled upon Martian bedrock. The area Opportunity investigated was smooth and dark rock with indentations which could have been caused by salt-water crystals. NASA remains unwilling to unequivocally announce the existence of a liquid, watery past on Mars, but the evidence is becoming increasingly convincing.

Liquid water

With favorable evidence of a liquid-water past, scientists are faced with two questions. Firstly: how did the water flow? The volcanoes on Mars could have created a greenhouse effect by emitting carbon dioxide. As a result, the atmosphere could have warmed, melting frozen water which would then have flowed in liquid form across the surface of the planet. Alternatively, if Mars has always been as cold as it is today, oceans of water could have flowed under a vast covering of ice, melted by friction as the ice moved across the surface of the planet.

The second question is: where did all the liquid water go? More recent missions to Mars have hoped to make sense of this conundrum. Convincing explanations include evaporation into space or that liquid water subsequently froze to form the ice caps we see today. A

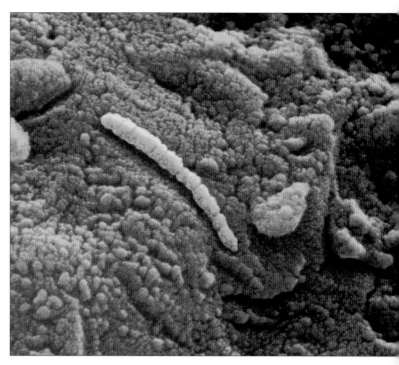

more recent theory is that a large amount of water might be locked in the sand dunes, cementing them together, explaining why they have been so durable over the years, and have resisted the fierce wind and dust. In 2002, NASA's Odyssey probe gave the most powerful indications yet of the presence of liquid water on Mars; it gathered evidence suggesting that vast amounts of water might be stored a few feet beneath the surface. If this proves accurate, it would not only re-ignite the possibility of manned settlements on Mars in the distant future, but it would also give scientists a clearer indication of where to search for fossilized evidence of Martian life forms.

The search for life

In 1877, when Mars passed closest to the Earth, Giovanni Schiaparelli developed a map of Mars, from observations through a telescope at his observatory near Milan. The map became the most influential document on Mars until the first space probes reached the Red Planet just under a century later. Schiaparelli's map displays lines criss-crossing Mars, which he termed "canali", the Italian for channels. However, his term was frequently mistranslated from the Italian "channels" to the English "canals" which not only indicated the existence of water at some point in the history of Mars, but also implied that someone or something had built such waterways.

The idea of intelligent life on Mars was not new. In the Middle Ages it was often taken as a given that all the planets were inhabited, even the sun. However, the possibility of "canali" focused attention on the idea of life

on Mars. This led to a flurry of popular interest in all things Martian. Particularly successful was H.G. Wells's classic, *The War of the Worlds*, in which Martians invade Surrey, England. Written in 1898, not long after Schiaparelli published his map in 1890, Wells's book has had enduring success. Famously, in 1938, Orson Welles broadcast a radio version of the novel, set in the United States, which sent Americans into a panic, believing the report to be true. *The*

War of the Worlds has also had two successful big-screen outings, in 1953, and more recently in 2005, showing that interest in the concept of intelligent life on Mars has not dwindled.

On many occasions, NASA has risen to the challenge of searching for life on Mars. Several of the Lander missions were dispatched with a mandate to see whether Mars was ever home to some form of life, and even

to uncover whether microscopic life forms have endured in the Martian soil. Viking 1's mission in the 1970s was fitted with a robotic arm to test the soil. The results were inconclusive as the soil was seen to have produced oxygen. Initially it was thought that this indicated the existence of microbes, but it was later believed that oxygen was simply being produced by non-biological chemical reactions in the soil. Most other Mars missions have included an additional mandate to search for life, and some missions, such as Britain's failed Beagle 2 mission in 2003, have this focus as the primary function of the expedition.

The debate as to whether there is life on Mars escalated in 1996 when NASA's analysis of a meteorite from the planet was released. The meteorite, ALH84001, was discovered in Antarctica in 1984, and it is estimated that the 4.5 billion-year-old rock fell to earth 13,000 years ago. The rock contained microscopic structures similar to bacteria on Earth. Such evidence points to the existence of life on Mars, but critics claim that the life forms are merely fossil

Above: The dry, rocky surface of Mars, taken by the panoramic camera on the Mars Exploration Rover Spirit before it left its lander on 18 January 2004. Spirit landed successfully in the Gusev crater on the planet on 4 January 2004. NASA scientists chose this location because the 145 kilometer-wide crater may once have contained a lake.

Opposite: An optical image of Mars taken when the planet was 68 million kilometers from Earth. The Martian summer in the northern hemisphere results in a large south polar ice cap (white, bottom). Two seasonal dust storms can be seen, one at top center and one over the Hellas impact basin at lower right. Photographed on 26 June 2001 by NASA's Hubble Space Telescope.

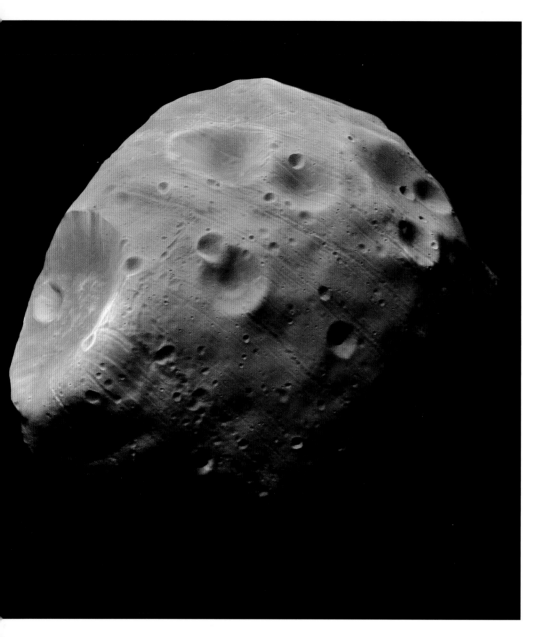

Left: A Mars Express image, taken by the High Resolution Stereo Camera (HRSC), showing Phobos, the larger of the two Martian moons. Phobos is irregular in shape, measuring 19x21x27km. The large Stickney Crater (center left) is 10km across. Phobos orbits 9400km above Mars, taking just over 7.6 hours to complete an orbit. This is the Mars-facing side of the moon, taken from a distance of less than 200km. Mars Express has been orbiting the planet since December 2003.

Opposite: The surface of Mars, showing the Ruell Vallis channel, which was created at a time in the the past when water flowed on the planet. The area is to the east of the Hellas Basin and measures 100km across. This image, with north at the top of the picture, was taken from a height of 273km on 15 January 2004 by the HRSC on board Mars Express.

microbes from Earth which infiltrated the rock after it landed. However, this is refuted by some scientists who point out that the life forms are only found at the center of the rock and not at its crust, as would be expected if they had permeated the rock after landing. Moreover, they argue that other, non-Martian, meteors found in Antarctica do not contain similar life forms. ALH84001 has put the pressure on both factions in the debate over life on Mars, but only rock samples collected on Mars will be able to prove or disprove the meteorite's reliability. NASA intends to move closer to a more conclusive answer as to whether there is life on Mars by sending Phoenix in 2007 followed by the Mars Science Laboratory in 2009, with more missions likely in the near future.

Martian moons

Mars has two moons, Phobos, meaning fear, and Deimos, meaning dread, after characters in Homer's *Iliad*. Both moons were discovered by the American astronomer Asaph Hall in August 1877. They were undiscovered before because they are both so small. It is most likely that they strayed into Mars's gravitational pull from the asteroid belt.

Phobos is the largest of the two. It orbits Mars more closely than any other moon orbits its parent planet, meaning that Phobos creeps ever closer to the Roche Limit – the area within which a moon will break up due to gravitational tidal forces exerted upon it by the planet. When this happens, several million years in the future, the debris from Phobos will turn into a planetary ring around

Mars. Meanwhile, Phobos orbits Mars faster than it rotates on its own axis, so it rises and sets twice during one Martian day, while it takes Deimos just over two Martian days. It becomes apparent how quickly both moons orbit Mars when they are contrasted with our moon's 28-day revolution period.

Tectonic activity

When Mariner 9 reached the planet in 1971, Mars was in the midst of a dust storm. As the dust subsided, the first image seen by scientists showed the tops of four massive volcanoes: Olympus Mons, Arsia Mons, Pavonis Mons and Ascraeus Mons. It was quickly realized that Olympus Mons was the biggest volcano in the solar system, towering over Earth's largest, Mauna Loa. It is seventeen miles high and 350 miles in diameter, eleven miles higher and 275 miles wider than Mauna Loa.

It is doubtful that there are plate tectonics on Mars; there are no significant mountain ranges or patterns in the locations of the volcanoes. The Martian crust is perhaps too cold for Earth-like plate tectonics, and instead, Martian volcanoes were produced by hotspots. A hotspot is formed when one area of magma in the mantle is hotter than the surrounding molten rock. The hotter lava rises to the surface and erupts in the form of a volcano. A similar process can be observed in Hawaii, where Mauna Loa is situated. Hawaii was formed by a hotspot, but owing to plate tectonics on Earth, the crust above moves, and so the volcanoes were shifted off the hotspot, stunting their growth in comparison to the Martian volcanoes which probably did not move off the hotspots which formed them. In which case, they grew to mammoth proportions.

The question remains as to whether these Martian super-volcanoes might still be active. Scientists monitoring Olympus Mons have suggested that it last erupted between 20 and 200 million years ago. This is not a long period, geologically speaking. However, the flows seem to have been very small, implying that volcanic activity on Mars might be running out of steam as the mantle cools. If this is the case, it would be a shame that the planet has begun to burn out, just as humanity begins traveling there.

Missions to Mars

The race to reach Mars coincided with the Cold War. The first probe, the Soviet Union's Mars 1, was launched on 1 November 1962, just days after the Cuban Missile Crisis – the most tense point in the hostilities – had ended. The USSR lost radio contact with the probe before it reached Mars. With the failure of the Soviet mission, it was the turn of the rival superpower, the USA. America launched its probe Mariner 3 to investigate Mars, but this mission also failed when its protective shroud failed to eject.

The first successful mission to Mars was launched in November 1964, just weeks after Mariner 3's failure. Mariner 4 reached its destination in mid-July 1965. Without rockets to slow it down, the probe traversed Mars at great speed, managing to snap twenty-one photographs of the Martian surface. The pictures Mariner 4 returned finally ruled against the existence of canals on Mars. Craters, and not canals, covered the Martian surface. As a result, Mars became known as the dead planet; it bore more similarity to the moon than to the Earth. Nevertheless, history had been made, and the Mariner 4 mission was to usher in an era of charting and analyzing Mars.

The US maintained the monopoly on successful visits to Mars. Soon after the moon landing, in summer 1969, the US probes Mariners 6 and 7 reached the Martian equatorial region and the southern polar region, respectively. They measured surface temperatures and atmospheric pressures, as well as taking more than one hundred photos, still showing Mars as a dead planet riddled with craters.

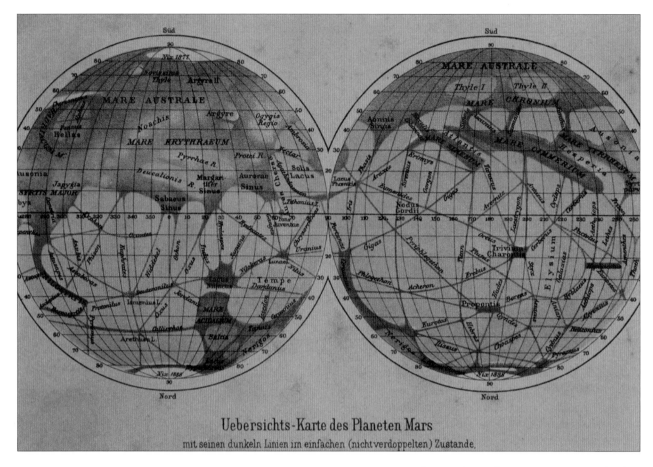

Uebersichts-Karte des Planeten Mars
mit seinen dunkeln Linien im einfachen (nichtverdoppelten) Zustande.

Above: Historical map of the surface of Mars. This drawing was made by the Italian astronomer Giovanni Schiaparelli (1835-1910) between 1877 and 1888. It was published in 1898 in Germany. Schiaparelli called the straight surface features "canali", and also noticed that the patterns on the surface changed with the Martian seasons. He wrongly assumed this to be due to seasonal changes in vegetation. It is now known that Mars is swept by powerful dust storms which alter the surface features. The idea that there was life on Mars was very popular around the end of the nineteenth century.

Opposite: Cutaway artwork which illustrates the internal structure of Mars. The inset at lower right shows Earth and Mars at the same scale. Mars is a rocky planet. It has a partially molten core of iron and iron sulphides (yellow). Overlying the core is a thick mantle (orange), which underlies the crust (brown). The crust of Mars is around 100km thick, compared to the 10-70km thick crust of Earth. The lack of a completely molten region around the core means that Mars does not generate a uniform strong magnetic field, which would have protected the planet's atmosphere from the solar wind. It is thought the Martian atmosphere was stripped away after the core cooled.

Not to be outdone, the USSR sent two further missions to Mars in 1971. Both Mars 2 and Mars 3 were intended not only to orbit Mars, but also to dispatch landing craft for the first time. On 27 November, Mars 2's lander touched down on the Martian surface but failed to transmit any data to Soviet mission control. Mars 3's lander followed suit a week later; it relayed blurred images and data for just a few minutes before shutting down. A planet-wide dust storm is thought to be the reason for the failure of both landing craft. The Orbiter components of both Mars 2 and 3 continued to relay data for four months until March 1972.

When it entered orbit in November 1971, the US's Mariner 9 became the most successful probe to reach Mars up to that point. Initially, Mariner 9 sent back featureless photographs as Mars was in the midst of a planet-wide dust storm, similar to that which ruined the Mars 2 and 3 lander missions. After the dust subsided, Mariner 9 managed to map most of the surface of Mars, sending back thousands of photographs, enabling the creation of a new atlas to replace Schiaparelli's, drawn up almost a century earlier. It was the first map to identify Mars's four large volcanoes and its vast valley, Valles Marineris, to which Mariner 9 gave its name.

This mission delighted those who had previously written off Mars as a featureless, dead planet. The limited scope of previous missions had distorted the impression Earth had gained of Mars. Mars was not nearly as cratered as had previously been thought, the northern hemisphere in particular showed signs of landslides, lava plateaus and channels, perhaps resulting from great floods. Mariner 9 was kept in operation until late October 1972, spending almost a year as the first artificial satellite of another planet.

Viking missions

During 1973, the USSR embarked on a series of ill-fated missions to Mars. Mars 4, 5, 6 and 7 were all launched within a few months of one another. Mars 4 missed its planned orbit of Mars and only managed a few photographs before falling into a heliocentric orbit. Mars 5 managed to enter orbit, but only transmitted data for three days. Mars 6 and 7 were flyby missions, which were to deploy landers as they hurtled past. The lander from Mars 6 gave only two minutes of data as it parachuted to the surface, while that from Mars 7 missed the planet altogether.

In 1975, the US stole the USSR's thunder in doing what its superpower rival could not, successfully landing not just one, but two probes on the Martian surface. On 20 August the US probe Viking 2 was launched followed on 9 September by the probe Viking 1. Viking 1 landed first, on 20 July 1976; Viking 2 landed in early September 1976. The two missions were mandated for a mere ninety days, but Viking 2 ended up charting Mars for nearly four years, and Viking 1 for over six. Although their search for life proved inconclusive and their seismographs failed to settle the debate over Martian earthquakes and plate tectonics, the two landers, together with their orbiters returned unprecedented insights into the Martian world.

Pathfinder missions

The missions to Mars dwindled as the Cold War drew to a close. NASA's Viking missions had been the most productive. In 1988, in the dying days of the USSR, the

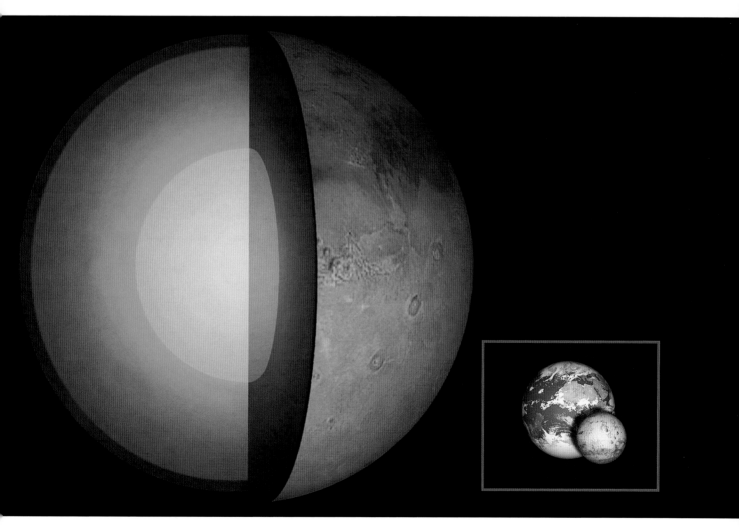

Soviet Union made one last attempt at sending a probe to Mars and her moons. The probe Phobos 2, while taking some useful photographs of the Martian moon, Phobos, as well as making the important discovery of water vapor in Mars's atmosphere, failed in its main function, namely to send a landing craft to Phobos. Just two months after it reached Mars, Phobos 2 stopped transmitting, and with its failure, the USSR's Martian exploration program passed into history. The USA was left the main superpower in the world, and NASA's Mars program ran largely unmatched.

The post-Cold War era of visits to Mars had shaky beginnings after the failure of NASA's Mars Observatory in 1993. This early setback was rectified on Independence Day in 1997 when the Mars Pathfinder mission touched down in the Ares Vallis. The arrangement of rocks in the valley seemed to confirm that water had once existed, as they appeared to have been laid down by a great flood. The Pathfinder mission brought about the democratization of interplanetary travel, as millions could now watch daily feeds of Pathfinder's activities over the internet. Pathfinder contained a rover, named Sojourner, which gave NASA flexibility to move around the Martian surface and analyze the Martian soil. Pathfinder also discovered an iron core and identified two colors of clouds, one white, comprising water vapor, the other blue, which probably contains carbon dioxide. Shortly after Pathfinder, an orbiter, Mars Global Surveyor, was launched to examine the atmosphere and begin an even more extensive mapping of the surface using its orbital camera to take extremely close-up images of the surface.

Mars Surveyor program

Russia, seemingly unperturbed by the collapse of the Soviet Union, attempted to send a probe called Mars 96, named after the year of its launch. It was equipped with two surface infiltrators, which were to have investigated the

Opposite: Mars Global Surveyor's (MGS) image of clouds (white) over the surface of Mars. These high, wispy clouds mainly comprise water ice. At lower left they are seen covering the peaks of the three large Tharsis Ridge volcanoes. At far left, clouds are also seen around the peak of Olympus Mons, the largest volcano in the solar system, while top center the ice cap covering the north pole can be seen. This image was taken by the Mars Orbiter Camera (MOC) on board the MGS spacecraft.

Right: A robotic Sojourner rover vehicle on the surface of Mars sampling the large rock known as "Yogi" which was the second rock to have its composition studied by Sojourner, using its Alpha-Proton X-Ray Spectrometer (APXS). Sojourner also carries a high-resolution camera. The rover, whose tracks can be seen in the fine soil, was controlled by an operator on Earth. The vehicle weighed 9kg, was 63cm long and 48cm wide, and was powered by a solar panel which allowed for a few hours movement per day.

interior structure of Mars. Unfortunately, the probe failed to escape Earth's orbit and plunged into the Pacific Ocean.

However, it has not always been plain sailing for the USA in its endeavors to understand more about the Red Planet. The Mars Surveyor program of 1998 resulted in disaster for NASA. Two sister probes, the Mars Climate Orbiter and the Mars Polar Lander, were launched separately in December 1998 and January 1999 respectively. The Mars Polar Lander was destined for the south polar cap, and outfitted with an additional probe, Deep Space 2, which was to test for water. While the Mars Polar Lander and Deep Space 2 never reported back to mission control, the Mars Climate Orbiter was lost in the most embarrassing of circumstances. It emerged that while one team at NASA had been working in imperial units, another had been operating a metric system. Consequently, it is thought that the Mars Climate Orbiter burnt up because it entered orbit at far too low an altitude. NASA ended the century which had seen a series of spectacular and unprecedented visits to Mars on a low. The huge financial cost of the failed missions led to a restructuring of NASA's Mars program, which included scrapping the lander mission of the 2001 Mars Odyssey probe, in favor of sending just an orbiter.

Above: Columbia Hills on Mars, photographed in June 2004. NASA's Mars Exploration Rover Spirit took the photographs for this composite, true-color image from a distance of 300 meters from the base of the hills, later traveling to them to analyze their composition.

Opposite: Martian caldera. A 3-dimensional oblique view of the surface of Mars showing the summit caldera of the Albor Tholus volcano. Dust from the surrounding plateau appears to be falling into the crater at left. Albor Tholus is in the Elysium region of Mars. The volcano has a diameter of 160km and is 4.5km high. The 30km-wide caldera is 3km deep, far deeper than calderas on Earth. This image was taken on 19 January 2004 by the HRSC on board Mars Express.

The twenty-first century

Investigation of Mars reached greater heights in the new millennium with the "Mars Rush" of winter 2003-2004. The Japanese probe, Nozomi, was destined to reach Mars during this period. It had initially been scheduled to enter orbit in 1999 but had encountered a run of bad luck. Initially a loss of fuel meant that Nozomi was put on a new trajectory around the sun which caused its arrival date to be set back four years until the winter of 2003. With a prolonged heliocentric orbit, Nozomi was damaged by a solar flare, which caused an electrical malfunction.

Japanese scientists spent much of 2003 trying to fix the problem, but it proved too difficult and at the last minute, in December 2003, mission control diverted the probe into space to avoid it crashing into Mars; Japan's first interplanetary mission was abandoned.

Following Japan's Martian foray, it was Europe's turn. The European Space Agency, ESA, sent an orbiter, the Mars Express, with a British-led lander mission, Beagle 2, which was to search for signs of life. While the Mars Express continued Odyssey's role of searching for underground water reservoirs, Beagle 2 was lost.

Meanwhile, NASA recovered from the failure of the Surveyor program by successfully sending two exploration rovers, Spirit and Opportunity, to Mars. The rovers were designed to cover up to one hundred meters a day, which meant that they could cover much more of the Martian surface than other landers. Opportunity gave further evidence of water, as its landing site, Terra Meridiani, appears to have been the shore of what is likely to have been a great body of water. Both rovers have far exceeded their allotted time of operations and continue to explore and analyze the surface.

On 12 August 2005 NASA launched the Mars Reconnaissance Orbiter. This probe will continue the search for water, past or present, and also act as a telecommunications base for future missions. In 2007 NASA intend to launch their next lander, Phoenix. Unlike Spirit and Opportunity, Phoenix is to be a stationary lander, designed to investigate the northern ice cap. Another NASA rover mission is scheduled for 2009, followed two years later, if all goes well, by a second chance for the European Space Agency to send a roving lander to Mars to search for life.

Men on Mars?

President George W. Bush announced in 2004 that man would return to the moon by 2020 to create a staging post for a manned mission to Mars. Humans are needed to make faster and more far-reaching discoveries than probes and, like the moon landing, a manned mission to Mars would proudly denote a key stage in humanity's evolution. However, a manned mission to Mars is a journey into the unknown. Scientists are not sure just how well man would fare on Mars; the atmosphere or the dust might be too challenging for even the best spacesuits. A manned mission would also be extremely costly and many would argue that such vast sums of national revenue might be better spent on healthcare and education on Earth. President Bush's plans have also to survive the contingencies of numerous other presidencies and events, which may well change priorities and postpone visits to Mars. But it is almost certain that at some point in our future, a human being will stand on Mars.

Above: Martian plain. A Mars Express perspective of part of the Elysium Planitia region of Mars. This area, just north of the Martian equator, is flat and covered in dust, with two impact craters at center right and upper right. It is thought that this area, a few tens of kilometers across, is a dust-covered frozen sea. Mars is a cold desert world, with an atmosphere of carbon dioxide and no liquid water. This image was obtained from the High Resolution Stereo Camera soon after Mars Express began operating in December 2003.

Opposite: Olympus Mons on Mars. Artwork of Olympus Mons (darker area, upper center), as seen from the north. It is the largest known volcano in the solar system. Its summit rises 27km above the surrounding plains (Mount Everest is 8.8km high), and the base measures 600km across. In front of the volcano is a region of ridges and hills known as the Lycus Sulci (rough area, center).

Mars/Earth Comparison

	Mars	Earth
Discovered by	Known by the Ancients	-
Date of Discovery	Unknown	-
Distance from the Earth (minimum)	56,000,000 km	-
Average Distance from Sun	227,936,640 km	150,000,000 km
Average Speed in Orbiting Sun	24 km per sec	30 km per sec
Diameter	6,796 km	12,756 km – almost twice as wide as Mars
Circumference	21,344 km	40,075 km
Surface area	144,100,100 km^2	510,072,000 km^2
Number of known satellites	2	1
Tilt of Axis	25°	23.5°
Orbital period (length of year)	687 Earth Days	365.25 Days
Rotational period (length of day)	24 hours 38 minutes	23 hours 56 minutes
Surface gravity	0.38 m/s^2 (38% of Earth) A 100kg object on Earth would weigh 38 kg on Mars	2.63 times that of Mars
Temperature range	-143° to 17° C	-89° to 59° C
Atmosphere	95 % carbon dioxide with traces of nitrogen, argon, oxygen, carbon monoxide, neon, krypton, xenon, and water vapor	Nitrogen, oxygen, carbon dioxide, argon, water vapor
Atmospheric pressure	0.007 kg per cm^2 This low pressure means a person would survive no more than a few seconds without a pressure suit	1.03 kg per cm^2
Mass	0.64^{21} x 10^{24} Mars weighs about 0.107 times the Earth's weight	5.97 x 10^{24} kg, nine times as massive as Mars
Density	3.94 grams cm^3	5.52 grams cm^3 - 40% more dense than Mars
Surface	Canyons, dunes, volcanoes, and polar caps of water ice and carbon dioxide ice	Water (70%), air, and solid ground. It appears to be the only planet with water
Seasons	**Mars (estimated days)**	**Earth (Northern hemisphere in Earth days)**
Spring	170	93
Summer	196	94
Autumn	176	89
Winter	145	89

JUPITER

Jupiter, the fifth planet in our solar system, is so massive that it contains more than twice the mass of all the other eight planets combined, and well over 1000 Earths could fit inside it. As the largest member of the solar system, Jupiter appears brighter than the brightest star when it comes into opposition, approximately every thirteen months.

With good binoculars a flattened disc can be observed; Jupiter is not a perfect sphere, its equatorial diameter is almost 10km more than its polar diameter. Such flattening of the poles is caused by Jupiter's rapid rotation on its axis – the planet spins at more than 45,000 kilometers per hour. Consequently, it takes the giant just under ten hours to complete one rotation of its axis. The result is that the planet appears to bulge at its equator.

Jovian gas giants

Jupiter is the first of the four gas giants, the collective name for which, the Jovian planets, is a direct reference to the fact that they are Jupiter-like. (Although Uranus and Neptune are now considered less so than originally thought). Over 80% of Jupiter's atmosphere is composed of hydrogen and much of the remainder is supplied by helium. Oxygen, sulfur and nitrogen are also found in the atmosphere where they mix with the predominating hydrogen to form water, hydrosulphides and ammonia.

Cloud decks

The presence of these three substances in the atmosphere leads to three cloud decks because each substance condenses at a different level in the troposphere. The top layer of clouds is made up of ammonia and is brightly colored. Beneath, in the middle deck, ammonia hydrosulfide crystals give Jupiter its dark red color. The bottom deck appears as bluish cloud, and comprises water which is likely to be frozen, as the temperature is well below 0^0 Celsius.

In 1995, when the Galileo atmospheric probe relayed data during its descent through the Jovian atmosphere, it revealed only a thin layer of ammonium hydrosulfide clouds. Scientists believe this was a rare

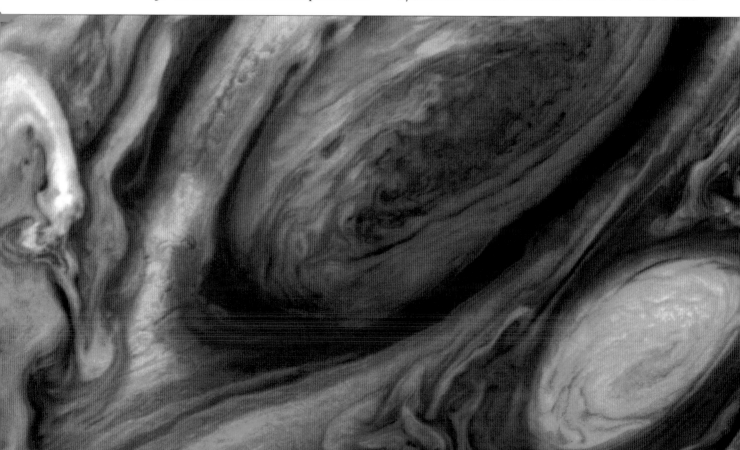

exception rather than the norm on Jupiter as the probe had unfortunately descended in a spot which was unusually barren of clouds.

Belts and zones

Jupiter's atmosphere is visibly divided into belts and zones, which can be seen from Earth with a telescope. These are caused by rapid winds traveling in opposing directions. In a zone the wind travels from east to west, and the clouds sink. In a belt, the opposite is occurring, the wind is traveling from west to east and the clouds are rising. The zones and belts appear well defined because of the sheer speeds of the winds propelling them. When the Galileo probe descended it measured wind speeds of 400km/hr which rose to incredible speeds of 600km/hr at 40km depth. The fact that the wind speed increases, in spite of the fact that the sun's intensity diminishes behind the cloud cover, indicates that the energy generating Jupiter's weather comes mainly from within the planet itself.

Great Red Spot

Jupiter's Great Red Spot is the most notable feature on the planet. It is a giant storm, which flows anti-clockwise across an area in excess of 24,000km in length and 12,000km in width. This giant anticyclone is greater than twice the diameter of the Earth. The storm is known to be almost three hundred and fifty years old, as it is believed that the astronomer Robert Hooke first observed the phenomenon in 1664.

The spot's red color probably comes from the reaction of phosphorus, dredged up from the depths by the storm, with the sun. It is not only its color which makes the Great Red Spot so pronounced; it is also because the cloud tops of the storm are elevated at least 8km above the surrounding cloud tops. Scientists are unsure if this is a permanent feature. On Earth, hurricanes dissipate when they move over solid land because of the resulting friction, but there is no solid landmass on Jupiter to cause the necessary friction to disperse the storm. Additionally, the storm seems to be being fuelled by heat from Jupiter, rather than the sun. All of this means that there appears to be no reason for the storm to die out. However, the Great Red Spot has been getting smaller during the last one hundred years in which it has been being recorded, perhaps indicating that one day it will disappear altogether.

In 1997, a planetary scientist observed a dark spot near Jupiter's north pole. In 2000 the Cassini-Huygens probe confirmed the presence of a Great Dark Spot, even larger than the Great Red Spot. This feature seems to be transitory; it disappears only to reappear at another stage, which is perhaps why it went undetected for so long.

The interior

Jupiter, like the other gas giants, does not contain the same layered rocky structure as Earth and the other terrestrial planets. Instead, the interior of Jupiter is mainly composed of hydrogen and helium. Beneath the cloud cover, the pressures on Jupiter are so great that the hydrogen and helium are found in liquid form. As the pressure and heat increase further, to incredible levels, it is thought that the liquid hydrogen might possess the characteristics of a metal, where electrons are able to move about, transferring electric charges between atomic nuclei. In this state the element is known as liquid metallic hydrogen. This substance does not exist on Earth, and it has also proved difficult to create it in the laboratory, therefore the

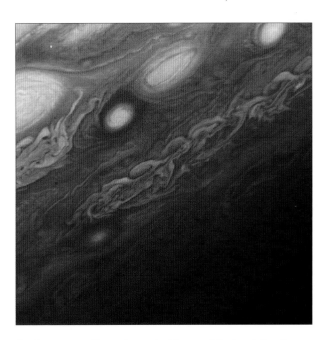

Previous pages: True color optical image of Jupiter, taken from a mosaic of shots by the Cassini spacecraft on 29 December 2000. Passing at a distance of 10 million kilometers, Cassini provided the most detailed images of the planet yet produced. Powerful jet streams create bands of colored clouds in the planet's atmosphere, dotted with spots marking atmospheric disturbances which can persist for many years. The largest such spot is the Great Red Spot (below center). The clouds are made of ammonia, hydrogen sulfide and water.

Opposite: Voyager 2 view of Jupiter's Great Red Spot, recorded on 6 July 1979 from a distance of 2.6 million kilometers. A long, narrow, white cloud is seen along the Great Red Spot's northern boundary; the presence of this cloud prevents small cloud vortices from circling the Spot in the manner seen by the Voyager 1 spacecraft three months earlier.

Above: Voyager 1 picture of Jupiter limb and white ovals.

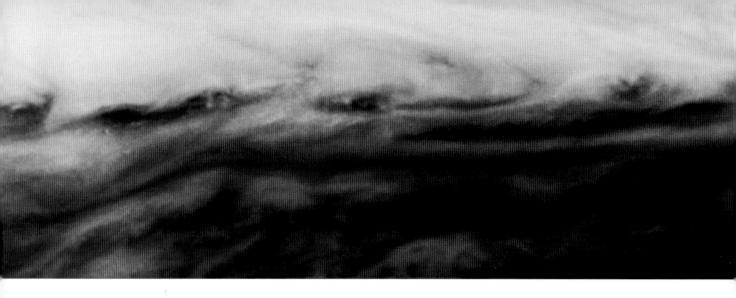

metallization of hydrogen under such extreme temperatures remains unconfirmed. However, if it does exist on Jupiter, the most helpful way of imagining it might be to think of the element mercury, a liquid metal at room temperature. Beneath the layer of liquid metallic hydrogen, there is thought to exist a relatively small core containing iron and rocks.

Jupiter undergoes a process of differential rotation; the rotational period of the poles is five minutes longer than the rotational period at the equator, because the fluid liquid and gases of the planet do not rotate together as a solid body as rock does on terrestrial planets.

Dark rings

In 1979, the Voyager 1 spacecraft discovered rings encircling Jupiter. Jupiter's rings are much darker than those of its neighbor, Saturn, and this explains why they were not detected from Earth. The inner ring has been named the Halo Ring because it is very faint and cloud-like. The next, called the Main Ring, is over 6000km wide but only 30km thick, giving it a squashed appearance. When the Galileo probe reached Jupiter it also discovered an outer ring, the Gossamer Ring, divided into two sections, surrounding the orbits of the Jovian satellites Thebe and Amalthea.

It is likely that Jupiter's rings are formed from material sheared off the moons surrounding them; the Main Ring is thought to comprise dust resulting from the impact of meteoroids with the moons Adrastea and Metis, while the Gossamer Ring consists of fine particles of debris from Thebe and Amalthea.

Magnetosphere

A magnetosphere is the area surrounding a planet in which the planet's magnetic field is stronger than the space around it. Jupiter's is generated by the layer of liquid metallic hydrogen in the planet's interior.

Jupiter's magnetosphere is not only the largest magnetosphere of any planet in the solar system, but it is also the largest entity in the solar system, even larger than the sun – although the sun's magnetosphere is as large as the solar system itself. If it could be seen by the naked eye on Earth, it would appear larger than the moon in the sky. Jupiter's magnetosphere is so large that its tail reaches beyond the orbit of Saturn, meaning that, for a short time, Saturn can be found inside Jupiter's magnetosphere.

Moons caught inside Jupiter's magnetosphere, most notably Io, sometimes leave a trail of debris as they interact with it, This trail is called a torus, so called because of the doughnut-shape the debris forms. These particles become trapped within Jupiter's magnetic field and undergo a process of ionization. The resulting ions and electrons remain in the magnetosphere. This means that huge areas within the magnetosphere carry such intense amounts of radiation that a manned mission to Jupiter or its satellites could potentially be lethal.

Above: Colored Galileo spacecraft image of bands of cloud in an equatorial region of Jupiter's atmosphere; the colors approximate to natural tones. In the center of the frame is a boundary between two zones of clouds (red and white). The colors of the clouds depend upon the exact mix of chemicals within them. The clouds are stretched into fine filaments and curls by violent, turbulent winds in the atmosphere. This image was made by combining near-infrared and violet light observed by Galileo's solid state imaging system on 5 November 1996 at a distance of 1.2 million kilometers. Observations at these frequencies provide information on the clouds' composition and altitude.

Opposite: Southern hemisphere of Jupiter, imaged by NASA's Cassini spacecraft. Jupiter's moon Io and its shadow are also seen. Jupiter's outer layer is composed of the gases hydrogen and helium, with some water, carbon dioxide, methane, and other simple molecules. High speed winds in the outer layer are confined to wide bands which encircle the planet: light bands are known as zones, whilst dark bands are known as belts. The Great Red Spot (bottom center) is a high pressure region which has been visible from Earth for over 300 years. This image was taken by Cassini as it passed Jupiter on its way to Saturn.

Moons

In 1610, Galileo discovered four moons orbiting Jupiter, which were later given the names Europa, Io, Callisto and Ganymede after four of the god Jupiter's many lovers and servants. It was not until 1892, 282 years later, that a fifth moon, Amalthea, was discovered. Today, following the Galileo probe's successful mission to the planet, we have knowledge of sixty-three moons. However, the four Galilean moons remain the most interesting. They are easily visible through a telescope and the observer is regularly treated to the fascinating sight of their transit across the planet.

The Galilean Moons

Io, the closest Galilean satellite to Jupiter, is the most volcanically active body in the solar system. In 2001, the largest eruption in the recorded history of the solar system occurred on Io where it is not uncommon for volcanic plumes to rise over 150km from the surface, some even exceeding 280km. Io's vigorous geological activity is caused by tidal heating by Jupiter, Europa and Ganymede. The orbits of these four bodies are locked. Europa orbits Jupiter twice for every one orbit of Io and Ganymede orbits Jupiter twice for every orbit of Europa. Io is sandwiched in the middle of these three larger bodies, meaning that the moon is being pulled in three different directions. The stretching and straining of Io generates the energy which produces dynamic geological activity on the moon.

Callisto is out of synchronicity with the other moons, and is the furthest from Jupiter. As a result, it is not subject to the same tidal forces as Io, meaning it is a much cooler world which has lacked sufficient internal heat to remould its surface following impacts from space debris; thus, Callisto's surface is the most cratered in the solar system.

Both Callisto and Ganymede have a thick ice sheet on their surface, but Ganymede is not nearly as uniform as Callisto. At some point in its history Ganymede probably underwent Earth-like plate tectonics because different areas of the surface are of different ages. There are highlands, but also very old areas that have succumbed to impacts similar to those on Callisto. Ganymede is the largest moon in the solar system; it has its own magnetosphere and is larger than both Mercury and Pluto.

Perhaps the most exciting Galilean moon is Europa,

Comet Shoemaker-Levy 9

In March 1993, Eugene and Carolyn Shoemaker and David Levy identified their ninth comet, Shoemaker-Levy 9, orbiting Jupiter. It was the first comet observed orbiting a planet rather than the sun. When it was discovered, the comet was already in fragments following a break-up when it had approached Jupiter too closely in July 1992. In May 1993 it was realized that the fragmented comet was on a collision course with Jupiter. Such a clash between two major objects in the solar system led to a wealth of interest, not just from astronomers, but the general public as well. The impacts took place between 16 and 22 July 1994. Eager astronomers were disappointed; the collision could not be seen from Earth, but by a fortunate coincidence, the Galileo probe was en route to the planet and managed to capture the event for the world to see. The collision resulted in seismic waves across Jupiter and caused huge plumes to rise from the planet's interior, giving scientists a partial idea as to what was below the clouds – an appetizer before Galileo would probe further.

For many months after the impacts, large dark spots, more vivid than even the Great Red Spot, could be seen where the comet fragments impacted. The episode highlighted how important Jupiter's gravitational pull has been in protecting the inner planets from many impacts during their history, and that Jupiter deserves some of the credit for sustaining the development of life on Earth.

because it may be the most promising place in the solar system in which to find the existence of extra-terrestrial life. Visible streaks across the planet's icy surface bear a resemblance to patterns formed by ice in the salt-water seas of the Earth, and it appears that rafting of the surface ice might have occurred; this is when icebergs are broken up and carried by liquid water. In 1998, NASA announced that data from Galileo indicated there might be a liquid saltwater ocean beneath the Europan ice. Optimists even suggest there might be hydrothermal vents in the ocean, which means that life could be sustained there.

The Non-Galilean Moons

Jupiter's moons are found in clusters, enabling them to be easily divided into six groups, including the Galileans. Each group bears the name of its largest and most dominant member. The moons within each group are clustered into similar orbital radii and it is thought that each group shares a common origin.

Moons nearer to Jupiter than the Galileans, with orbital radii less than 200,000km, are named the Almathea group. As well as Almathea, this group includes Metis, the closest known satellite to Jupiter, and Adrastea and Thebe. All three were only discovered in 1979 when the Voyagers reached Jupiter. This group is located within Jupiter's ring system and material from the four moons is thought to be the source of the rings.

The next group are the Galileans; the innermost, Io, orbits Jupiter at a mean distance of 420,000km and the outermost, Callisto, at a radius of 2 million kilometers.

The remaining four groups are much further out. Leda, the first moon in the Himalia group, is 9 million kilometers beyond Callisto. There are three further groups; the Ananke group containing sixteen moons and the Carme group containing eighteen, each with orbital inclination close to 165 degrees. The outermost group is named Pasiphaë; it is not as clustered as the inner groups. Sinope was long thought to be the outermost member of this group, and as such Jupiter's outermost moon, but three more have been discovered even further away.

Trojans

As well as 63 known moons, Jupiter also has a number of asteroids which share Jupiter's orbit. These so-called "Trojan" asteroids orbit the sun in Jupiter's orbital path, 60 degrees in front and behind Jupiter. The first, 588 Achilles, was discovered by the German astronomer Max Wolf in 1906, and hundreds have been discovered since. Although Trojan asteroids were first observed in Jupiter's orbit, they have subsequently been sighted in the orbits of Mars and Neptune.

Below: Full-disc image of Jupiter's satellite Io made from several frames taken by the Voyager 1 spacecraft on 4 March 1979, from a range of 862,000km. The circular feature at center with a dark spot in the middle is an active volcano, and so are the other features similar to it. Io's volcanic activity appears to be of at least two types: explosive eruptions that hurl material up to 250km into the satellite's sky; and lava that flows across its surface.

Opposite: Voyager 1 image of Jupiter from 25 million miles showing Ganymede.

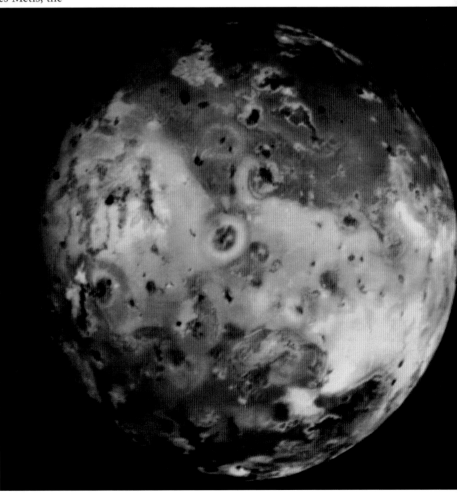

Above: Voyager 2 computer-enhanced photograph of Callisto, the fourth and faintest Galilean satellite of Jupiter. The spacecraft was 2.3 million kilometers from Callisto when the photograph was taken. Callisto is an airless body, where surface temperatures are never higher than -130 Celsius. It is believed that the moon has a large rocky core and a crust that consists of a mixture of water, ice and rocky material. The only surface features evident on Callisto are numerous impact craters formed by meteorites and a number of bright concentric ring systems. Otherwise Callisto is extremely smooth with no mountains or valleys.

Right: Galileo spacecraft image of two volcanic eruptions on Io, a moon of Jupiter. A 120km high plume from the Pillan Patera volcano appears as a gray patch at Io's lower left edge. The second, from the Prometheus volcano, is visible as a plume (gray) and its shadow (black) at center. Prometheus may have been erupting continuously for at least 18 years, whilst this is the first Pillan Patera eruption ever seen. Io's volcanoes are powered by the strong internal tidal forces created because the moon orbits so close to Jupiter. Image taken by Galileo's solid state imaging camera at a range of 600,000km on 28 June 1997. The smallest visible objects are 2km across.

Opposite: Voyager 1 image of clouds in the atmosphere of Jupiter, just to the south-east of the giant planet's Great Red Spot. The view was recorded on 4 March 1979, at a distance of 1.8 million kilometers . Differences in cloud color may indicate relative heights of the cloud layers. The smallest clouds seen in the picture are approximately 30km across.

Jupiter/Earth Comparison

	Jupiter	Earth
Discovered by	Known by the Ancients	-
Date of Discovery	Unknown	-
Distance from the Earth (minimum)	591,000,000 km	-
Average Distance from Sun	778,412,020 km	150,000,000 km
Average Speed in Orbiting Sun	13 km/sec	30 km/sec
Diameter	142,984 km	12,756 km
Circumference	449,197 km	40,075 km
Surface area	62,179,600,600 km^2	510,072,000 km^2
Number of known satellites	63	1
Number of known rings	Up to 3 identified	0
Tilt of Axis	3°	23.5°
Orbital period (length of year)	4330 Earth Days (11.9 Earth years)	365.25 Days
Rotational period (length of day)	9 hours 55 mins Jupiter's rapid rotation causes it to bulge at its equator and flatten at its poles. The planet's diameter is 9,170 kilometers larger at the equator than between the poles	23 hours 56 minutes
Surface gravity	20.9 m/s^2	If you weigh 100 kg on Earth you would weigh 214 kg on Jupiter.
Temperature range	-148° C	-89.6° to 59° C
Atmosphere	Hydrogen, helium, methane, ammonia The southern hemisphere's Great Red Spot (a vast storm) has existed for at least 300 years. Three Earths could fit across the Great Red Spot	Nitrogen, oxygen, carbon dioxide, argon, water vapor
Atmospheric pressure	Varies with depth The pressure inside Jupiter may be 30 million times greater than the pressure at Earth's surface	1.03 kg/cm^2
Mass	1.90×10^{27} kg The most massive in our Solar System – 319 times as massive as the Earth	5.97×10^{24} kg
Volume	1.4×10^{15} km^3 Approximately 1,300 Earths would fit into Jupiter	1.1×10^{12} km^3
Density	1.3 g/cm^3	5.52 g/cm^3
Surface	None – a hot ball of gas and liquid	Water (70%), air, and solid ground. It appears to be the only planet with water

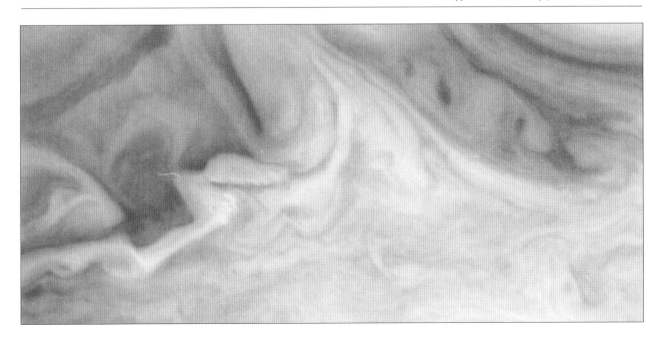

SATURN

Saturn is the second-largest planet in the solar system and until 1781, when Uranus was discovered, it was also the outermost known planet. Even when most people believed in a geocentric universe, Saturn was still considered the outermost planet orbiting the Earth.

Saturn is the furthest planet visible with the naked eye. When it is isolated from areas packed with stars, Saturn shines strikingly, and is arguably the most impressive sight to be viewed through an amateur telescope, especially if its rings are presented towards the Earth. The planet itself is seen as a yellowish disc with bands and zones of clouds, albeit more subtle than those on neighboring Jupiter.

Ancient names

The planet was named Kronos by the Ancient Greeks, and this was changed to Saturn by the Romans in line with their own name for that same god. In Greek mythology, Kronos was the father of Zeus, who was known as Jupiter to the Romans. Therefore, the planet Saturn was cast as the father of the planet Jupiter. The father and son had a rocky relationship. Kronos had a tendency to eat his children so they could not overthrow him, but he was tricked and failed to eat Zeus, who eventually did supplant his father. This dysfunctional family drama might be indicative of how the classical civilizations viewed the relationships between the planets.

Rapid rotation

It takes Saturn 29.5 Earth years to complete one orbit of the sun, making its year almost three times longer than a year on Jupiter. Saturn requires just over ten hours to complete one rotation of its axis because the planet is made up almost entirely of liquids and gases which flow around the axis much faster than solid land masses do. This rapid rotation causes Saturn to flatten at the poles and bulge at the equator, like Jupiter – the equatorial diameter is estimated to be 121,000km which reduces to just

Below: Saturn's moon Iapetus, composite Cassini image. Iapetus is the third largest moon of Saturn, but orbits further out than most of the larger moons, at a distance of 3.5 million kilometers. It was originally discovered by Giovanni Cassini, the 17th-century astronomer after whom the Cassini spacecraft was named. It is primarily composed of water ice and has a mean diameter of 1436km. The light illuminating the moon comes from Saturn, rather than the sun. Consequently a long exposure was used, leading to the smearing of the background stars.

108,000km between the poles. In 2005, the Cassini probe measured an as yet unexplained seven-minute slowdown in Saturn's rotational period.

Saturn has the lowest density of any planet in the solar system, lower than the density of water. It is regularly remarked that if a big enough ocean could be found, Saturn would float.

Hydrogen-based atmosphere

Telescopic observations of Saturn have been made difficult by the rings which often obscure parts of the disc, but it is thought that Saturn's atmosphere is very similar to Jupiter's. It mainly comprises hydrogen with a significant amount – around 5% – of helium, with traces of ammonia and hydrocarbons such as ethane and acetylene. It is thought Saturn's atmosphere contains more sulfur than Jupiter, explaining the planet's yellowish hue.

The cloud decks on Saturn are similar to those on Jupiter. There are thought to be three principal decks: a layer of ammonia clouds in the upper reaches of the atmosphere; a layer of ammonia hydrosulfide clouds sandwiched in the middle; and a layer of water clouds. The different cloud strata result from the varying temperatures at which each of the molecules condenses. Within the cloud decks, it appears that temperature increases with depth, indicating that Saturn has an internal source of heat.

Hazes of smog have been seen on Saturn high in the atmosphere, perhaps a result of seasonal changes on the planet. Saturn's axis is tilted about 27 degrees to the perpendicular of the orbital plane, meaning that Saturn experiences Earth-like seasons, even if they are far less well-defined, as Saturn is much further from the sun.

Like Jupiter, Saturn is banded into zones and belts, albeit much less visibly pronounced. The reason for this is rapid winds which cross the planet at speeds of up to 500 meters per second pushing the air in one direction in a belt and in the opposing direction in a zone either side, giving rise to the banded appearance of the planet's disc.

White spot

A large white spot was detected in the equatorial regions of Saturn's atmosphere in 1990. The arrival of the spot coincided with the launch of the new Hubble Telescope, which monitored its progress. The spot was thought to be a storm caused by convection currents from the planet's interior dragging water, ammonia and other molecules above the cloud tops where the temperature is much cooler, causing them to freeze, forming whitish clouds amidst the surrounding yellow. These clouds, out of place in the upper reaches of the atmosphere, would be moved violently about by the rapid zonal winds. The storm is not a new feature on

Above: True color Cassini spacecraft image of a section of Saturn's rings. The image mainly shows the B ring (beige), the outermost of Saturn's inner rings. Saturn's rings are mostly made of particles of water ice, ranging in size from centimeters to a few meters in diameter. The different colors in the rings reveal the presence of contaminants, such as rock or carbon compounds. This is a composite of images taken by the narrow angle camera on the Cassini spacecraft on 21 June 2004, when Cassini was 6.4 million kilometers from Saturn.

the planet. It has been recorded twice before during the last 125 years, recurring approximately every 57 years. The fact that this time period is nearly two Saturn years, indicates that the White Spot of Saturn might be a recurring feature.

A rocky core

The interior of Saturn is expected to be very similar to that of Jupiter. As atmospheric hydrogen is placed under increasing pressure with depth, it turns into a liquid and then a liquid metallic state, where electrons move freely about different nuclei, transferring an electric current. As the layer of electrically charged liquid metallic hydrogen is churned about as a result of Saturn's rapid rotation, a magnetosphere is generated. Saturn's magnetosphere is the second-largest in the solar system, smaller than only Jupiter's, indicating that the layer of liquid metallic hydrogen on Saturn is much thinner than on Jupiter. This liquid metallic hydrogen envelops a rocky core, which is

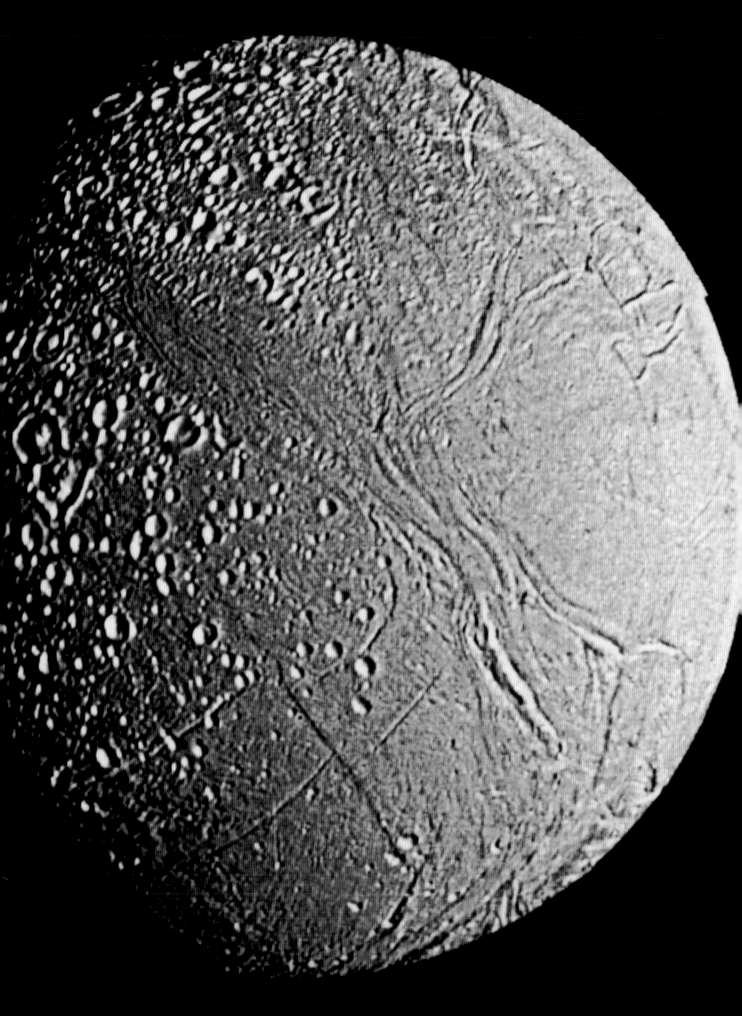

probably larger than Jupiter's because the pressure at the center of Saturn, although intense, is not quite as severe as at the heart of Jupiter.

The rings

One of the greatest fascinations of the solar system is the rings of Saturn. They have often earned Saturn the title of the most attractive planet in the solar system. They are usually visible with an amateur telescope, provided the planet is at the correct angle. The rings are located in the plane of Saturn's equator, and like the equator they are inclined at 27 degrees to the orbital plane, which means that for a short period the rings are facing an Earth-based observer edge-on when they are too thin to be see from Earth. The period when they are not visible recurs once every fifteen years, half the time it takes Saturn to orbit the sun.

The "ears" of Saturn

The first person to see the rings of Saturn was Galileo when he was the first observer to look at the planet through a telescope in 1610. He had no idea what he was looking at. The rings of Uranus and Jupiter were not discovered for centuries, and so Saturn's rings seemed exceptional and inexplicable. Galileo named the rings the "ears" of Saturn, explaining that they might be huge mountain ranges extending high above the planet on both sides, or that they might be two other smaller planets. It was not until 1655, several decades after Galileo's first sighting of the rings, that a Dutch astronomer, Christian Huygens, discovered that these "ears" were in fact rings.

Where did the rings come from?

The rings of Saturn are thought to be the remnants of a moon that strayed too close to the planet and was torn apart by tidal forces. The boundary at which it becomes "too close" for a moon to orbit a planet is called the Roche Limit and was calculated by Edouard Roche in 1849, basing his evidence on Saturn's rings. Another theory is that the rings comprise debris left over from the creation of Saturn, and a third suggestion is that Saturn, or one of its moons, suffered a great impact at some point in history. However, all of Saturn's rings are located within the Roche Limit, indicating that they were most likely created by a moon that wandered too close. Moreover, Roche's explanation accounts for why the small particles in the ring do not gravitationally recombine to create larger particles or a moon. In spite of their impressive appearance, there is actually very little matter in Saturn's rings. If they were to recombine, they would only produce a satellite a mere 100km in diameter.

Above: Saturn from the approaching Cassini spacecraft. This image was taken on 16 May 2004, when Cassini was 24.3 million kilometers and 46 days from Saturn. Enceladus, one of Saturn's 48 known moons, is seen as a tiny speck below Saturn at bottom right. As well as studying the planet from orbit, the Cassini spacecraft dropped the Huygens probe onto Saturn's largest moon, Titan. Saturn is the second largest planet in the solar system. It orbits the sun around ten times further out than Earth, some 1.5 billion kilometers. The yellow color here is due to the filters used.

Opposite: Voyager 2 photograph of Enceladus, a satellite of the planet Saturn. It is 500km across and shows areas that are cratered and others that are criss-crossed with the grooves of canyon-type features.

Icy particles

In the nineteenth century, the physicist James Clerk Maxwell suggested that Saturn's rings comprised many small particles rather than being single solid blocks of rings, as had previously been thought. This theory was supported by evidence of differential rotation; the particles nearest the planet were orbiting at a faster rate than those farther out. The small particles vary in size between several centimeters and several meters. Most of the rocky particles have, at the very least, a surface covering of ice, which is highly reflective, meaning that the particles in Saturn's rings stand out impressively, especially when compared with the rings of Jupiter and Uranus which are dark and not visible from the Earth.

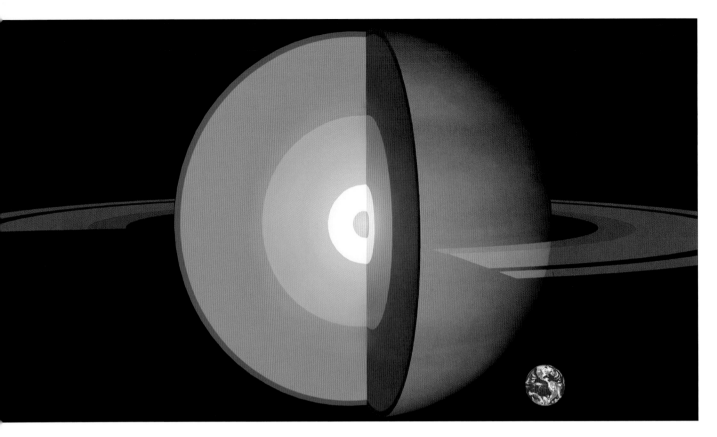

Above: Internal structure of Saturn, cutaway artwork. The Earth is at lower right at the same scale. Saturn is a gas giant, but the name is slightly misleading. It has a core of solid rock (grey) and ice (white). This is overlaid with a layer of liquid metallic hydrogen (light blue). Currents in this layer are responsible for the generation of its magnetic field. Above this layer is a region of normal liquid hydrogen (dark blue), which underlies the gaseous atmosphere. Its ring system, seen at left and right, is formed of millions of small chunks of ice and rock.

Opposite: Voyager 1 photograph of the planet Saturn and one of its moons, Tethys. The shadows of Saturn's three bright rings and of Tethys are cast onto the cloud tops. The large gap in the rings is the 3500km wide Cassini Division, which separates the narrower A-ring (above) from the broad B-ring. The thin gap near the top edge of the A-ring is the Encke Division, beyond which is the faint and narrow C-ring. The picture was taken on 3 November 1980, from a range of 13 million kilometers.

Ring divisions

In 1675, the French astronomer Jean Dominique Cassini was the first to note a gap in the rings. The gap subsequently became known as the Cassini Division and the rings were divided into the A and B rings. Over one hundred and fifty years later, in 1837, the German astronomer Johann Encke discovered another gap in the

rings, now known as the Encke Division. A further three gaps were discovered over the next century, taking the total number of rings to seven. The rings are labeled alphabetically from A to G, in the order in which they were discovered, rather than the order in which they orbit the planet.

The rings vary in size from the E-ring, the furthest from the planet, which is 300,000km in width to the D-ring, closest to the planet, which is just 8500km in width. All the rings are relatively thin, mostly less than one kilometer in thickness and sit in the planet's equatorial plane. In 2005, the Cassini space probe discovered that Saturn's rings have their own atmosphere, comprising molecular oxygen, which is sourced by the water ice found throughout the ring system.

Shepherd moons

Scientists were keen to understand why the ring system remained in place, instead of being pulled towards Saturn or scattering into space. The chief explanation was found in a series of moons, called shepherd moons, which were orbiting within the ring system, using their gravity to maintain the rings' distinct shapes. This theory was proved in 1980 with the discovery, by Voyager 1, of two Saturnian shepherd moons named Prometheus and Pandora. Prometheus guided the inside of F-Ring, while Pandora steered the outside of the same, narrow, ribbon-shaped F-ring. In the same year, another moon, named Atlas, was found to be shepherding the outside of the neighboring A-ring.

Such shepherd moons are located inside the Roche Limit, meaning they are no longer being held together by gravity; instead they have averted collapse because of their own mechanical strength. However, any loose surface particles would be stripped off to form part of the ring system leaving just shells behind.

In 1990, revisiting Voyager 2 photographs, Mark Showalter discovered a moon, Pan, shepherding in the Encke gap. The discovery of this moon indicates that yet undiscovered shepherding moons will likely be found directing other sections of Saturn's ring system. In 2005, the Cassini probe identified a moon shepherding in the Keeler gap in Saturn's A-ring, but no moons have yet been found shepherding rings closer to Saturn than Pan.

Saturn's satellites

Saturn comes second only to Jupiter in the number of natural satellites it possesses. When the Cassini probe set off to Saturn in 1997, only 18 moons were known about. However, during the course of its journey, Earth-based telescopes, and the probe itself, identified more than twice that number. The total of moons currently stands at 48, with more awaiting confirmation. The largest of them, Titan, stands out amongst the planet's satellites – it is much larger and has denser atmosphere.

Saturn has six medium-sized moons: Mimas, Enceladus, Tethys, Dione, Rhea and Iapetus. Although they had all been discovered in the seventeenth and eighteenth centuries, little was known about them until both Voyagers visited in the early 1980s. These moons are all tidally locked with Saturn, so that like Earth's moon, they only ever present one face to the planet.

Iapetus, Rhea, Dione and Tethys were discovered by

Cassini between 1671 and 1684. Tethys has a density similar to water, indicating that it comprises mainly water ice. All of Tethys' surface features are named after characters from the Trojan wars, most notably an immense impact crater, named Odysseus, 400km in diameter, the same size as the moon Mimas. The orbits of all the significant Saturnian moons are in the equatorial plane, except Iapetus, the outermost of the medium-sized moons. This means that while from Iapetus the view of Saturn's rings would be exceptional, the perspective from the other moons is less spectacular because the rings are perpetually viewed edge-on.

Mimas and Enceladus
William Herschel discovered Mimas and Enceladus in 1789, almost twenty years after his discovery of Uranus. They are the innermost of the medium-sized moons. In 2005, the Cassini probe discovered that Enceladus was the source of the microscopic material in Saturn's outermost, diffuse E-ring. Mimas, the closest of the six moons to Saturn, actually lies within the E-ring, with the result that it has been consistently impacted by ring material, leaving it heavily cratered.

When Cassini passed by Enceladus in 2005, the results delighted scientists. An atmosphere was detected on the moon, mainly comprising water vapor and, more interestingly, a hotspot was found at the south pole. The temperature around the pole is warmer than the surrounding planet, indicating an internal heat source on the moon, oddly focused around the pole. This phenomenon could signify another place where scientists might search for sub-surface liquid water in the solar system.

Orbit sharing
In 1966, the small moon, Janus, was discovered inside the orbit of Mimas. Two independent sightings had been made in the same year, but orbital data for both sightings proved difficult to reconcile. In 1978, it was suggested that perhaps there were two moons orbiting on almost the same path. This was proved when Voyager 1 reached Saturn in 1980. The second moon was named Epimetheus. The maximum distance in their orbits is a mere 50km, and although they travel at different speeds, a collision is unlikely. As one moon approaches the other an orbital trade takes place – the gravitational pull from the trailing moon launches it into a slower, outer orbit. Simultaneously, the gravitational pull of the smaller moon drags the leading moon into a faster, inner orbit.

Voyager 1 also identified two smaller moons, Telesto and Calypso, sharing the orbit of Tethys. Telesto always leads 60 degrees ahead of Tethys, while Calypso always trails 60 degrees behind Tethys. Similarly Helene and Polydeuces respectively lead and trail Dione. Polydeuces was discovered in 2004, twenty-four years after Helene, indicating that there may be many co-orbital moons of which we are not yet aware.

Right: Saturn and its moon Dione, Cassini image. The Cassini spacecraft captured this image from a distance of around 600,000km from Dione. Dione is one of the known 48 satellites of Saturn. Image taken on 14 December 2004.

Opposite: Hubble Space Telescope image of the planet Saturn with its rings and two of its moons visible. Here, the planet is viewed at an angle, while its rings are seen edge-on and thus appear as a thin circular band. These rings comprise a sheet of material (rocks coated with ice) orbiting around the equator of Saturn.

Above: Aurora on Saturn. Hubble Space Telescope image of aurora (blue) encircling Saturn's south pole. Aurorae are produced by the interaction of the solar wind with a planet's atmosphere. Charged particles collide with rarefied gases in the atmosphere, causing them to emit light. On Saturn, as on Earth, they occur in polar regions. This is because the magnetic field of the planet channels the charged particles to these regions. This image was taken on 26 January 2004.

Opposite above left: Titan's atmosphere seen from the Cassini space probe. The colors represent infrared (red and green) and ultraviolet (blue) radiation emitted by Titan's atmosphere. Infrared radiation is where methane in Titan's atmosphere has absorbed light. This varies across Titan, and the red color in the northern hemisphere indicates that this area is brighter. Ultraviolet radiation from the upper atmosphere extends hundreds of kilometers above the surface (blue ring). Titan consists of ice and rock with a thick atmosphere of mostly nitrogen. Its diameter is over 120,000km.

Huygens lands on Titan

Opposite above right: Titan's surface as seen by the spaceprobe Huygens on 14 January 2005. The image has been processed to give a suitable indication of the actual color on the surface. The two rock-like objects just below the center of the image are about 15cm (left) and 4cm (center) across at a distance of about 85cm from Huygens. The surface is darker than expected and consists of a mixture of water and hydrocarbon ice. Some evidence of erosion is evident at the base of these objects.

Opposite below: Huygens probe's landing site. Cassini spacecraft image, taken through near-infrared filters, of the Huygens probe's intended landing site on the surface of Saturn's moon Titan. The landing site is indicated by a square in the right-hand image, the left-hand image shows a 400km wide narrow-angle shot of the site. The Huygens probe was released in December 2004 and reached the moon's surface on 14 January 2005. This image was taken during Cassini's flyby on 27 October 2004.

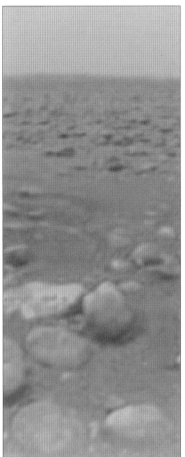

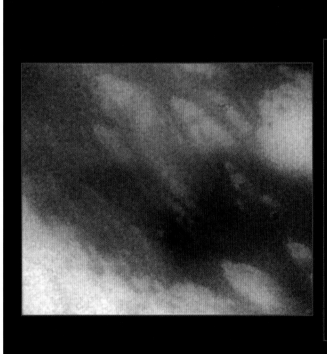

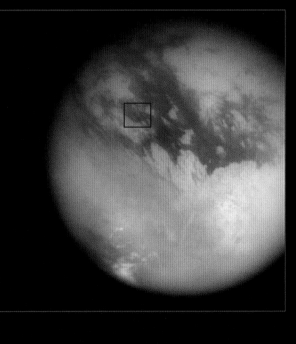

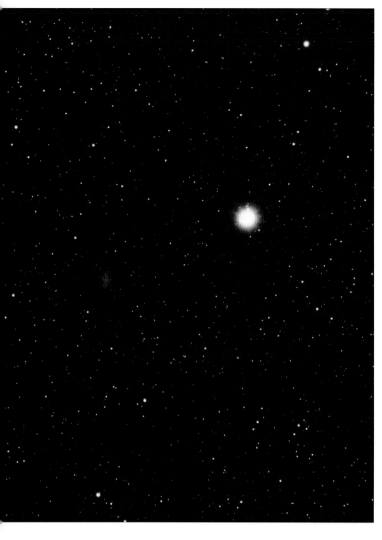

Titan

Titan is much larger than the neighboring Saturnian moons. It is larger than Mercury and Pluto and the second largest moon in the solar system after Jupiter's Ganymede. It was discovered in 1655 by the Dutch astronomer Christian Huygens, the first moon to be detected following Galileo's revolutionary discovery of the four moons orbiting Jupiter. Titan is the only body in the solar system to contain a nitrogen-rich atmosphere like the Earth's, although it is much more dense. The atmosphere has prevented observers from seeing what lies beneath on Titan's surface.

After decades of wondering what lay beneath, the European Space Agency's Huygens lander, which piggybacked on the Cassini mission to Saturn, touched down on the surface of Titan early in 2005. Detailed analysis of the data gathered from the probe is yet to be published, but the immediate indications suggest the moon has many Earth-like qualities, such as changing weather patterns and volcanic activity. Gullies and river beds indicate the presence of methane rain (Titan is so cold that any water present would be frozen). It is speculated that he methane rain feeds methane seas. The Huygens lander has also noted volcanic activity which might be caused by Earth-like plate tectonics. In addition, it has identified organic matter on the surface, materials which are crucial building blocks for life and might help scientist better understand the genesis of life on Earth.

As data from the Huygens mission is analyzed, it may emerge that Titan, not Venus, is our sister planet in the solar system.

Above: Saturn (upper right) in the night sky. The faint blue object (center left) is the Crab Nebula (M1, NGC 1952), a supernova remnant. Saturn is one of the five brightest planets, and can be seen with the naked eye. It shines by reflected sunlight.

Right: Hazy Titan atmosphere, Cassini image. Titan is one of Saturn's moons. This image shows the night-time side of Titan (dark, left) with a thin sliver of light hitting the visible edge. Above this, stretching several hundred kilometers into space, are layers of haze, reflecting the light from the sun.

Opposite: Saturn's rings. Computer artwork of the rings of Saturn. The largest empty region is known as the Cassini Division (best seen at far left), and divides the rings into two main sections.

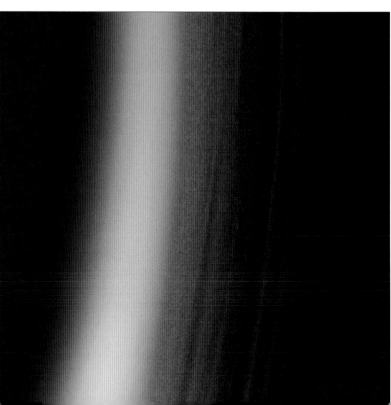

Saturn/Earth Comparison

	Saturn	Earth
Discovered by	Known by the Ancients	-
Date of Discovery	Unknown	-
Distance from the Earth (minimum)	1,277,400,000 km	-
Average Distance from Sun	1,426,725,400 km	150,000,000 km
Average Speed in Orbiting Sun	10 km/sec	30 km/sec
Diameter	120,536 km About 10 times greater than the Earth	12,756 km
Circumference	378,675 km	40,075 km
Surface area	43,466,000,000 km^2	510,072,000 km^2
Number of known satellites	48	1
Number of known rings	7 major rings Saturn's major rings are extremely wide but are so thin that they cannot be seen when they are in direct line with the Earth	0
Tilt of Axis	27°	23.5°
Orbital period (length of year)	10,756 Earth Days (29.4 Earth years)	365.25 Days
Rotational period (length of day)	10 hours 40 mins The rapid rotation of Saturn causes the planet to bulge at its equator and flatten at its poles. The planet's diameter is 13,000 kilometers larger at the equator than between the poles	23 hours 56 minutes
Surface gravity	7.2 m/s^2	If you weigh 100 kg on Earth you would weigh 74 kg on Saturn
Temperature range	-178° C	-89.6° to 59° C
Atmosphere	Hydrogen, helium Winds in the upper atmosphere reach 500 meters per second in the equatorial region	Nitrogen, oxygen, carbon dioxide, argon, water vapor The strongest hurricane-force winds on Earth top out at about 110 meters per second
Atmospheric pressure	Varies with depth	1.03 kg/cm^2
Mass	5.69 x 10^{26} kg Saturn is about 95 times as massive as the earth.	5.97 x 10^{24} kg
Volume	8.3 x 10^{14} km^3 Saturn's volume is 755 times greater than Earth's	1.1 x 10^{12} km^3
Density	0.7 g/c^3 Saturn is only about one-eighth as dense as the earth, and about two-thirds as dense as water. A portion of Saturn would weigh much less than an equal portion of the earth, and would float in water	5.52 g/c^3
Surface	Liquid and gas A dense layer of clouds covers Saturn	Water (70%), air, and solid ground. It appears to be the only planet with water

URANUS

I n 1781 astronomical history was made. After civilizations had, for millennia, believed there to be only five extra-terrestrial planets in the solar system, a sixth disc was discovered. On 13 March a German-born British astronomer, William Herschel, was undertaking a systematic review of the skies when he discovered what he thought to be a comet.

After Herschel had reported his findings to other astronomers, it was realized that what he had seen was not a comet at all, but a planet; the first to be discovered since antiquity, and the first to be revealed by using modern technology, the telescope.

King George's star

As its discoverer, Herschel was given the privilege of naming the planet; he chose Georgium Sidus, George's star,

in honour of his king, George III of Britain. Outside Britain, this name was unpopular. In the rest of Europe, the idea of naming the newest planet in the solar system, one of just seven, after the British king, was looked upon with disfavor. Instead the name "Herschel" went into wide use for the planet in the late eighteenth and early nineteenth centuries.

However, in order to standardize the new planet's nomenclature with its counterparts in the solar system, the desire for a name from classical mythology arose. Astronomers proposed "Minerva", "Neptune" or "Cybele". Yet, in the years following Herschel's death in 1822, it was the astronomer Johann Bode's suggestion of "Uranus" that gained popularity within the astronomical community. Uranus was the father of Kronos, the Greek version of the Roman god Saturn. Saturn had been named after the father of Jupiter by the classical civilizations, so Bode was keeping it in the family when he suggested Uranus as the name for the seventh planet.

Methane clouds

Uranus has perhaps the most featureless exterior of all the known planets in the solar system. Its interior is shrouded by a bluish-greenish blanket, colored by the methane clouds which absorb red light, reflecting blue and green light. Unlike its nearest neighbor, Neptune, Uranus does not appear to have many permanent, noteworthy cloud formations or dark spots. Most of the clouds comprise methane and therefore condense at the same altitude, making the cloud cover relatively uniform across the entire planet. The clouds are moved around the planet by rapid winds which travel at hundreds of kilometers per hour.

High-altitude hazes, comprising ethane and other hydrocarbons, have been observed in Uranus' upper atmosphere. Like all the gas giants, the atmosphere comprises mainly hydrogen and helium.

Iron and silicate core

Temperature and pressure increase with depth on Uranus, with the effect that the methane clouds gradually translate

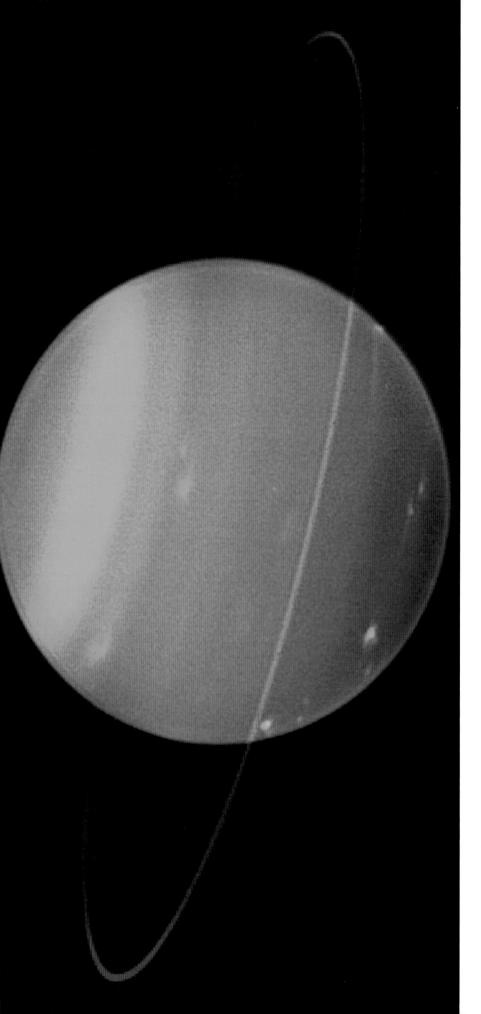

Left: Uranus, infrared image of Uranus. The northern hemisphere (left of rings) is coming out of many decades of darkness. The bright blue spots in the southern hemisphere are clouds above the Uranian atmosphere. Methane in the upper atmosphere absorbs red light, giving the planet its blue-green color. Uranus' tilt is thought to have been caused by a collision with a large body early in the solar system's history. Image gathered by the 10 meter Keck Telescope, Hawaii, on 11-12 July, 2004.

Opposite: German-British astronomer Sir Frederick William Herschel (1738-1822). He discovered the planet Uranus in 1781, resulting in his appointment as private astronomer to King George III of England. He financed the construction of a 50cm telescope with which he discovered two satellites of Uranus (Titania and Oberon) and two of Saturn (Mimas and Enceladus). In 1783 he discovered the intrinsic motion of the sun through space. He recognized the nature of the Milky Way as a galaxy by counting the number of stars in different directions. He found that most lie in the galactic plane and the least at the celestial poles.

from gaseous states into solid ice. Ice crystals begin developing in the atmosphere, and soon become so abundant that the cloud turns into slushy methane ice, and later solid ice. The solid ice layers comprise water and ammonia as well as methane. These layers flow around the planet at an infinitesimal rate, much as glaciers move around the Earth.

At the heart of Uranus is thought to be a rocky core containing silicates and iron. The only probe to have visited Uranus is Voyager 2, when it flew past in 1986 before heading on to Neptune. More probes, destined for Uranus alone, will be required if we are to better understand the structure of the planet's interior and atmosphere.

Tilted axis

Uranus' most noteworthy feature is the highly eccentric tilt of its axis. The planet's axis is tilted over 90 degrees from the perpendicular, probably because Uranus was impacted by a large object at some point in its history.

Such a tilt gives rise to some interesting seasons. The four seasons on Uranus each lasts 21 Earth years, one quarter of the 84 years it takes Uranus to orbit the sun. At the height of summer, the sun shines directly onto the pole facing it. Meanwhile, the other pole experiences a miserable winter, without sunlight for at least 21 years. In 1985 the south pole moved into the sunshine, leaving the north pole entering a long period of darkness. However, the beginning of the twenty-first century heralded the dawn of spring for Uranus' north pole as the sun moved above the equator. Concurrently, the south pole edged closer to its dark winter. The changing of the seasons was accompanied by large storms in the northern hemisphere, as it began to get warmer – by Uranus' standards. The storms were photographed by the Hubble Telescope, and may be a recurrent feature of changing seasons on the planet, undetected before because previous seasonal changes could not be observed through earlier Earth-based instruments

Left: Voyager 2 color composite image of Uranus, as the spacecraft left the planet behind and set off towards Neptune. The thin crescent of Uranus, seen here, shows a pale blue-green color. This results from the presence of methane in the planet's atmosphere, which absorbs red wavelengths of light, leaving a predominantly blueish hue. The crescent tends to become white at its extreme edge due to the presence of a high-altitude haze.

Opposite: Voyager 2 image of the Uranian ring system. The picture reveals a continuous distribution of small particles throughout the ring system. It also shows all the previously known rings, though some of the brightest features in the picture are bright dust lanes which had not been detected before. The long exposure time has resulted in streaks in the photo of trailed stars.

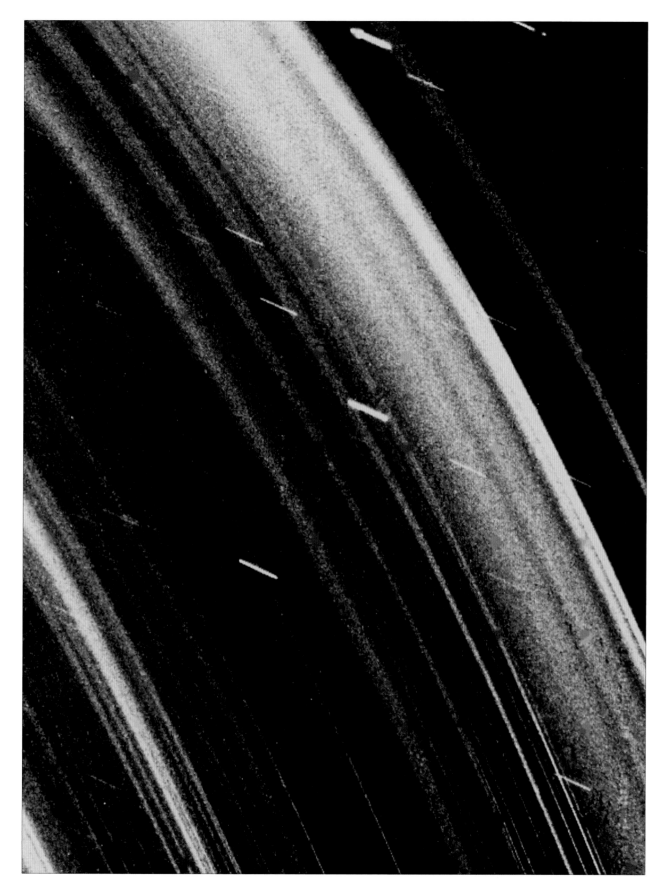

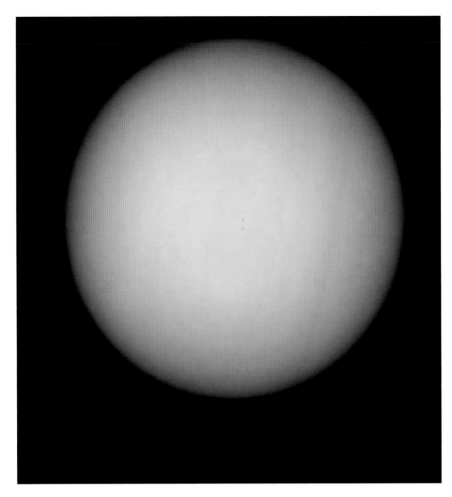

Left: Hubble Space Telescope true-color image of the planet Uranus, orbiting at just under 3 billion kilometers, some 20 times the Earth-sun distance. The cloud bands seen in the filtered image are parallel to its equator. Uranus has an axis of rotation in the same plane as its orbit, so it appears to rotate on its side, unlike the other planets. Images taken in August 2003.

Opposite: Hubble Space Telescope image of the planet Uranus, showing its ring system and five of its moons. Clockwise from the top, they are: Desdemona, Belinda, Portia, Cressida and Puck. Images taken in August 2003.

It is important to note that some scientists believe that astronomers have muddled up their poles for generations. They suggest that the north pole, which is just coming out of winter, is actually the south pole. If this is the case, then Uranus must rotate on its axis in a retrograde direction and the axial inclination would need to be revised to just under 90 degrees.

Rings

In 1977, many astronomers watched Uranus closely as it passed in front of, or occulted, a star. They wished to calculate the diameter of Uranus by seeing how long the star disappeared as Uranus passed in front of it. As Uranus occulted the star, the light from the star blinked five times each side of the planet. The explanation for such an occurrence was that Uranus was surrounded by a ring system comprising five rings. Later that figure was revised to nine rings, and Voyager 2 confirmed the existence of two more, taking the total number of rings to eleven. The rings are much thinner, darker, fainter and comprise smaller material than the rings of Saturn, which explains why they were not detected before 1977.

Literary moons

Not satisfied with having discovered the planet itself, William Herschel also discovered Uranus' first two moons. They were named in 1852 by Herschel's son, John Herschel, who was also an astronomer. He chose Titania and Oberon, after the king and queen of the faeries from William Shakespeare's *A Midsummer Night's Dream*. In 1851, William Lassell discovered two more moons and he requested that John Herschel name them. Herschel chose Ariel and Umbriel, named after characters in Alexander Pope's poem, *The Rape of the Lock*; erroneously but understandably, Ariel is often taken to be named after the "airy spirit" in Shakespeare's *The Tempest*.

The tradition of naming Uranus' moons after characters from English literature has continued, making the planet's satellites exceptional in a solar system named after figures from classical mythology. Only one more moon, Belinda, was named after a character from *The Rape of the Lock*. All the other moons have been named after Shakespearean characters, particularly from his last play, *The Tempest*.

Almost one hundred years after Lassell's discovery of Ariel

and Umbriel, in 1948 Gerald Kuiper discovered a fifth moon, which he named Miranda, after Prospero's daughter in *The Tempest*. Ten moons were discovered by Voyager 2 as it reached the planet in 1986, and an eleventh moon was discovered over a decade later when a scientist revisited pictures from Voyager 2's mission. In the 1990s and early twenty-first century a further 11 moons were discovered, thanks to improved telescope technology and committed astronomers.

Icy cratered worlds

Like most natural satellites, Uranus' moons orbit the planet at right angles to its axis. However, given that Uranus' axis lies horizontal to the plane along which the other planets lie, the Uranian moons appear to be in an unusual, longitudinal orbit of the planet, crossing Uranus' orbital path. Uranus' moons all have similar, eccentric axial tilts as the planet itself.

The largest Uranian moon is Titania, closely followed by Oberon, which has a diameter just 50km smaller. They, like most of Uranus' moons, are icy worlds covered in impact craters. Many of the moons are covered in rift valleys indicating that the rocks may be faulted. But valleys on Ariel suggest formation by the outflow of a liquid, perhaps methane or ammonia.

Cordelia, named after King Lear's youngest daughter, is located within Uranus' ring system and acts as a shepherd for the Epsilon ring, in the same way that several of Saturn's moons shepherd its rings. Cordelia lies within the Roche Limit, and is thought to be close to destruction.

Miranda

Voyager 2 gave the most insight into Miranda. It would not have been scientists' first choice as it is much smaller than Oberon, Titania, Ariel and Umbriel, but the probe needed to fly close by Miranda in order to reach Neptune, its next destination. However, Miranda turned out to be remarkable. Only the southern hemisphere, which was facing the sun, could be seen by the craft when it passed by in January 1986. Miranda looked like a world which had been completely shattered; it was covered all over in steep ice blocks, cliffs and terraces. One cliff measured 20km high, twice the height of Mount Everest.

Initially, scientists believed that Miranda must have been impacted on several occasions by large bodies, which smashed the planet into its current condition. However, more recently, scientists have revised their theories and suggested that many surface features might have been caused by up-welling of warmer ice.

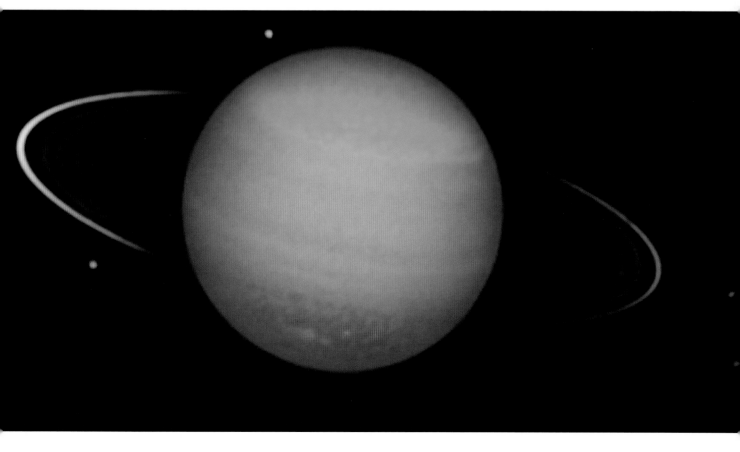

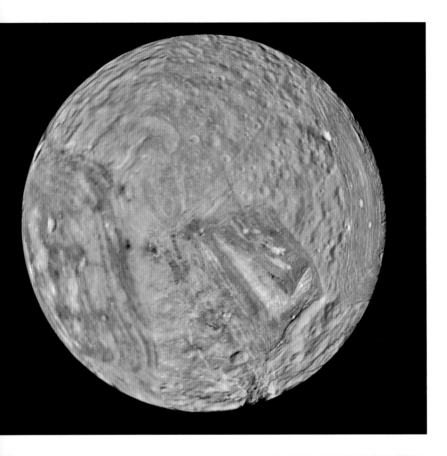

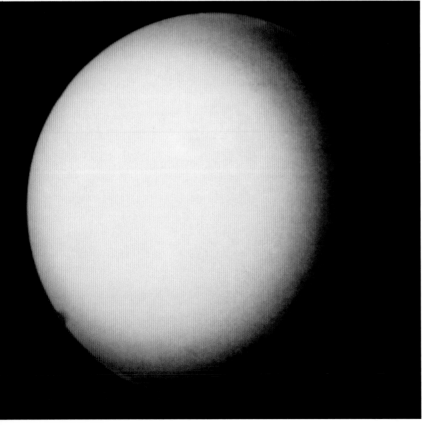

Top: Mosaic of images showing the complex surface of Miranda, a moon of Uranus. Although only 480km across, Miranda displays a bizarre variety of geology. Most obvious are the V-shaped "chevron" just lower right of center and the "ovoids" (concentric rings) at the left limb. There are cliffs near the "chevron" which are twice the height of Mount Everest - about 20km tall. The reason behind this complex surface may be that the moon is seen "frozen" in a partially reformed state following a catastrophic meteor impact in the distant past. The data for this image were gathered by the Voyager 2 spacecraft in January 1986.

Left: Voyager 2 false-color image of Uranus taken on 22 January 1986, when the spacecraft was 2.7 million kilometers from the planet. The picture is a composite of images obtained through orange and methane filters. The pink area centered on the pole is due to the presence of hazes high in the atmosphere that reflect the light before it is absorbed by methane gas in the atmosphere. The bluest regions at mid-latitude represent the most haze-free areas.

Opposite: False-color optical image of the Uranian ring system taken by the Voyager 2 probe at a distance of 4.17 million kilometers.

Uranus/Earth Comparison

	Uranus	Earth
Discovered by	William Herschel	-
Date of Discovery	1781	-
Distance from the Earth (minimum)	2,587,000,000 km	-
Average Distance from Sun	2,870,972,200 km Uranus' orbit extends 19 times farther from the than Earth's orbit	150,000,000 km
Average Speed in Orbiting Sun	7 km per sec	30 km per sec
Diameter	51,118 km Approximately 4 times the diameter of the Earth	12,756 km
Circumference	160,592 km	40,075 km
Surface area	8,115,600,000 km^2	510,072,000 km^2
Number of known satellites	27	1
Number of known rings	11 major rings	0
Tilt of Axis	98° Because Uranus is tipped on its side and spins in the same direction as it travels, it rolls around its orbit. This means that each of Uranus' poles faces away from the sun for half of the planet's orbit and alternates between nights and days that last for 42 years	23.5° The Earth spins around an axis that is perpendicular to its direction of travel
Orbital period (length of year)	30,687 Earth Days (84 Earth years)	365.25 Days
Rotational period (length of day)	17 hours 14 mins (retrograde)	23 hours 56 minutes
Surface gravity	8.4 m/s^2	9.8 m/s^2 If you weigh 100 kg on Earth you would weigh about 86 kg on Uranus
Temperature range	-216° C The temperature on the summer and winter side of the planet hardly differs because Uranus is so far from the sun	-89.6° to 59° C
Atmosphere	Hydrogen, helium, methane It is the methane that absorbs the red light from the sun's ray, giving the planet its distinct blue color	Nitrogen, oxygen, carbon dioxide, argon, water vapor
Atmospheric pressure	Varies with depth	1.03 kg/cm^2
Mass	8.7 x 10^{25} kg. Uranus has a mass about 14.5 times larger than that of Earth	5.97 x 10^{24} kg
Volume	5.9 x 1013 km^3	1.1 x 1012 km^3
Density	1.3 g/c^3 About one quarter of the density of the Earth, and similar to that of Jupiter	5.52 g/c^3
Surface	The surface of Uranus is not solid; it is composed of blue-green clouds made up of tiny crystals of methane. It is thought that Uranus has a core of rock and ice	Water (70%), air, and solid ground. It appears to be the only planet with water

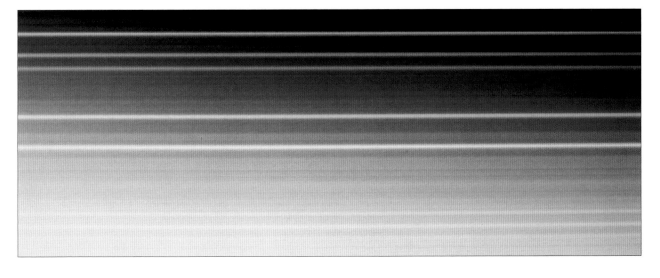

NEPTUNE

Early in the seventeenth century, Galileo recorded an observation of an object in the area of space we now know to be Neptune. However, he took it to be a star and it was to take a further two centuries to discover Neptune as a planet.

During the nineteenth century, Alexis Bouvard calculated the path that Uranus was expected to make around the sun, but it became apparent that it did not follow such a path, indicating that a planet, beyond Uranus, was pulling it off course. Therefore, the discovery of Neptune was principally the result of mathematics and not observation. Based upon the orbit of Uranus two scientists, John Couch Adams and Urbain Le Verrier, independently calculated where Neptune ought to be. However, neither could generate sufficient interest for observatories to check whether Neptune was in the position both said it would be.

Finally, a German astronomer, Johann Gottfried Galle, used Le Verrier's calculations, and sighted the eighth planet of the solar system on 23 September, 1846. It was almost exactly where Le Verrier predicted, and very close to where John Couch Adams had indicated, provoking fierce debate as to who deserved credit for the planet's discovery. Couch Adams was British and Le Verrier was French, and both had the weight of their national communities supporting their accreditation. To break the impasse, credit for the discovery was bestowed upon both, although more recently Le Verrier has increasingly been given the honor alone.

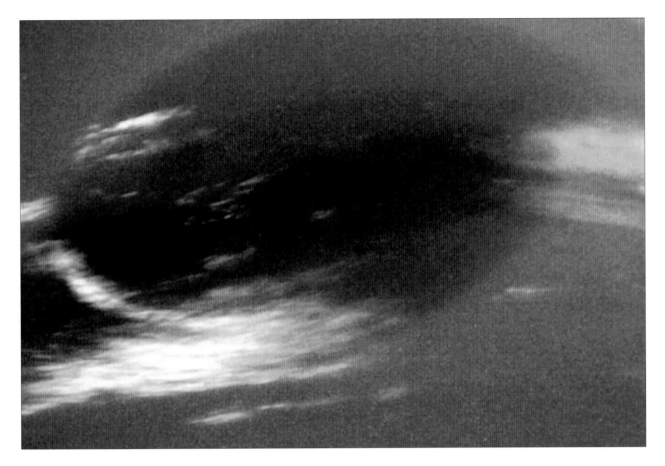

The last planet in the solar system?

It takes Neptune 164.8 years to orbit the sun, which means that since its discovery, in 1846, it has not yet completed one full orbit of the sun, and is not due to have done so until 2011. During its long orbital period, Pluto's highly eccentric orbit takes it inside the orbit of Neptune, making Neptune the last planet in the solar system for a period of twenty years every 248 years. This occurred very recently. Neptune moved outside Pluto's orbit in 1979 and stayed there until 1999. Therefore, when Voyager 2, the only probe ever to have visited the planet, reached it in 1989 Neptune was the ninth and not the eighth planet in our solar system. Of course, it is in contention as to whether Pluto is a planet at all; if Pluto's planetary status is disregarded, then Neptune becomes the last known planet in the solar system for its entire 165-year orbit. The next time Neptune's orbit will go outside that of Pluto's is not until the twenty-third century.

Neptunian seasons

Neptune's axis is tilted to 29.5 degrees from the perpendicular, which is similar to Earth, and as such Neptune experiences seasons, as Earth does. Seasons are much less pronounced than on Earth because Neptune is

Above: Voyager 2 image of the Great Dark Spot on Neptune, photographed on 22 August 1989 from a distance of 2.8 million kilometers. The Spot is a giant storm system as large as Earth. The image shows feathery white clouds that overlie the boundary of the dark blue and light blue regions. The spiral (pinwheel) structure of both the dark boundary and the white cirrus clouds suggest a storm system rotating anti-clockwise. Periodic small-scale patterns in the white cloud, possibly waves, are short-lived and do not persist from one Neptunian rotation to the next. The picture was taken by Voyager 2's narrow-angle camera through the clear and green filters.

Opposite: Voyager 2 image of white, high-altitude, "cirrus" clouds in the atmosphere above Neptune's southern hemisphere. The structure and trails of the clouds, moving from east to west, suggest that waves are present in the Neptunian atmosphere and play a large role in producing the types of clouds that are visible. The image was recorded by Voyager 2's wide-angle camera from a distance of 590,000km on 25 August 1989. It has been processed to obtain true color balance; additional processing was used to suppress the surface brightness of the clouds so that their structure is better seen.

Previous page: Neptune and Triton. Voyager 2 image of the gas giant planet Neptune (upper frame) with its largest moon Triton visible just below center. Triton is a large moon, 2700Km in diameter, which has a surface temperature of -235⁰ Celsius.

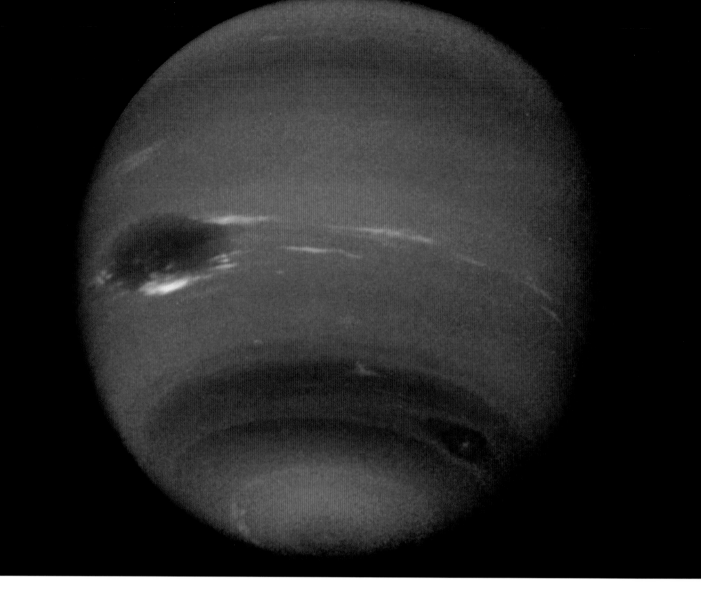

so much farther from the sun than the Earth. Each season lasts much longer than on Earth because of the long period of time it takes Neptune to orbit the sun. At the start of the new millennium, growing bands of clouds on Neptune indicated the start of a Neptunian spring, which will last for several decades.

Whatever the season, Neptune's average surface temperature at minus 220° Celsius is similar to that of Uranus, although it is much further from the sun. This is because Neptune has an internal heat source which compensates for this difference.

Atmosphere and interior

Neptune's atmosphere, like that of all the gas giants, comprises mainly hydrogen and helium gas. However, unlike Jupiter and Saturn, Neptune has noticeable amounts of methane and other hydrocarbons in its atmosphere. Methane clouds, which absorb red light, reflecting green and blue, are thought to be responsible for giving Neptune its blue color. Although initially named a Jovian planet,

Above: Voyager 2 spacecraft image of the planet Neptune, taken as the spacecraft approached to within 5,000km of Neptune's north pole. This virtually true-color image shows two prominent cloud features of Neptune's highly active weather system. At left is the Great Dark Spot, a giant storm system located at a latitude of 22 degrees south that circuits the planet every 18.3 hours. The bright clouds below and to its right were found to change appearance in periods as short as four hours. A second, smaller dark spot (bottom right) circuits the planet every 16.1 hours.

Opposite: Voyager 2 false-color image of Neptune in August 1989. It reveals the presence of a ubiquitous haze that covers the planet in a semi-transparent layer. The picture was made from two images taken through blue and green filters, and a filter that passes light at a wavelength absorbed by methane gas. Regions that appear white or bright red are those that reflect sunlight before it passes through a large quantity of methane. The red edge around the planet is where the haze scatters sunlight; at the center of the disk, sunlight passes through the haze to the methane gas below. The white areas are high-altitude clouds, including one above the center of the Great Dark Spot.

Neptune has more recently been called a Uranian planet, to indicate Neptune's greater similarity to Uranus, which has an atmosphere similarly comprising 2% methane, rather than Jupiter, which only has trace amounts.

Neptune is the third most dense planet in the solar system, despite being the fourth largest planet. The gaseous layers of methane, water and ammonia slowly descend to the mantle, first as liquids under great pressure, then slushy ice crystals and finally solid ice. The mantle, which may be enveloped in a layer of liquid hydrogen, surrounds a dense core made of ice and rock.

Neptune has only been visited once by a probe; no future probes are planned, but one will need to return to the planet if we are to properly understand its interior.

Methane clouds

Neptune has an extremely dynamic weather system, with faster winds than any other planet in the solar system that churn the systems around the planet. Such fast winds may be the result of the temperature difference between Neptune's internal heat source, nearer the planet's center, and the cold cloud tops. The winds might also be accelerated by the Neptunian atmosphere, which is so cold that it presents little friction for the winds, which means they can reach the incredible speed of 2000km per hour measured by Voyager 2 in 1989. The winds usually move westward, retrograde to the rotation of the planet, which is from west to east.

Wispy, white clouds, hundreds of kilometers in length, form at high altitudes and can be seen casting their shadow on the bluish layer of gases below. These clouds are similar in appearance to cirrus clouds on Earth, but, unlike cirrus clouds, Neptune's will not be formed of condensed ice water. Instead, they are likely to comprise crystals of frozen methane. One such "cirrus" cloud formation, known as the Scooter, was discovered by Voyager 2 – named because it "scooted" around the planet in just 16 hours.

As well as methane, Neptune's atmosphere comprises other hydrocarbons such as ethane and acetylene. Just as hydrocarbons form smog on Earth, smog or haze has appeared in Neptune's upper atmosphere.

Great Dark Spot

Neptune's most remarkable feature, a Great Dark Spot in the southern hemisphere, was discovered by Voyager 2 in 1989. It seemed to be similar to the Great Red Spot on

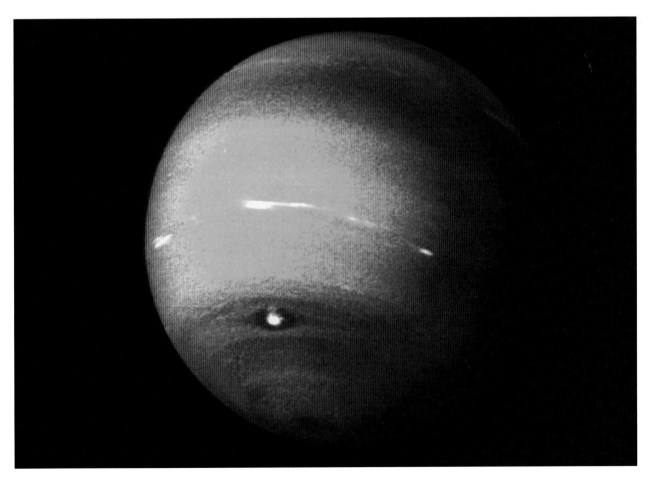

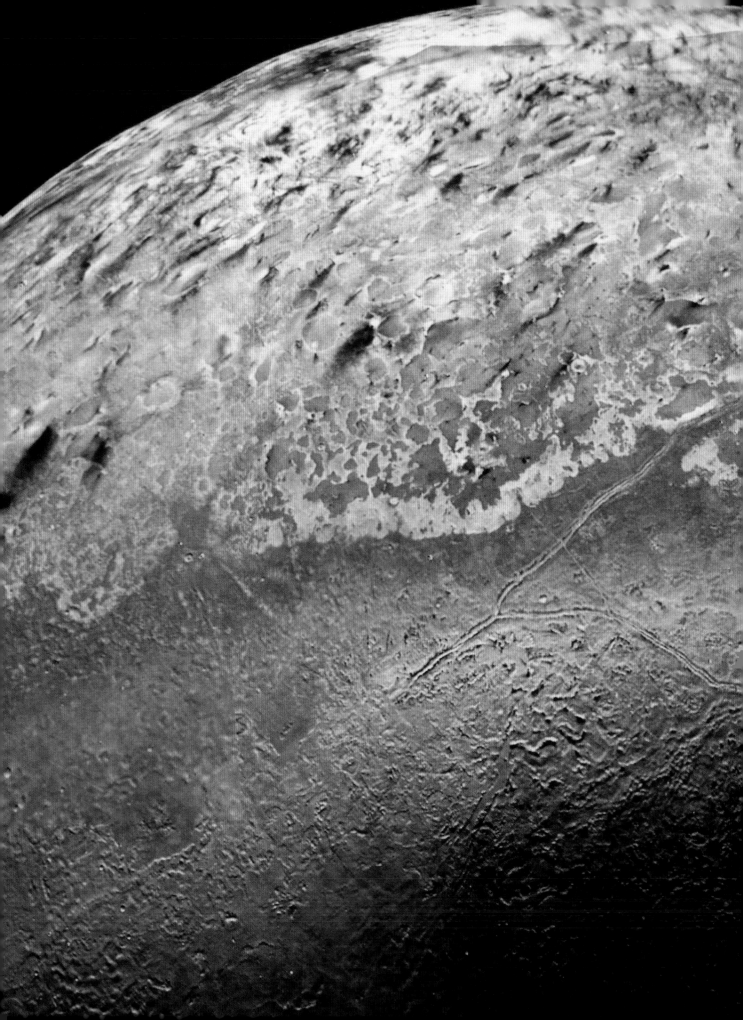

Jupiter; rapid winds of over 2000km per hour were discovered in the vicinity of the spot, which meant it was quickly pushed around the planet in just over 18 hours. However, the Spot is now thought to have been a hole in Neptune's atmosphere, similar to the hole in Earth's ozone layer. In 1994, when the Hubble telescope looked for the Great Dark Spot it seemed to have vanished, only to have been replaced with another spot in the northern hemisphere. To differentiate between the two, the original is known as the Great Dark Spot of 1989, while the more recent one is the Great Dark Spot of 1994. Voyager 2 also discovered a similar, but smaller, dark spot in the southern hemisphere. By 1994, it too had disappeared, a testament to the dynamic nature of Neptune's atmosphere.

Ring system

In the early 1980s, scientists watched eagerly as Neptune passed in front of a star. This process, called an occultation, allows scientists to calculate the planet's size and observe the atmosphere. As Neptune passed in front of the star, it "blinked" at scientists on either side of the planet. This phenomenon is best explained by a ring encircling the planet. However, the existence of a ring system was not confirmed until Voyager 2 arrived in 1989. The reason scientists had not detected it before is because the composite material was much darker than that of Saturn's rings – comprising rock and dust rather than ice, which meant that it did not show up during telescopic observations. The spacecraft identified that the spread of the material was patchy and uneven, which led some scientists to believe that Neptune might be flanked by an arc rather than a ring.

Voyager 2 identified four main rings, but the divisions had not been visible during the occultation exercise because the material in them was too dispersed to cause the starlight to blink. The four main rings are named after the co-discoverers of the planet and its largest moon, Triton – Adams, Le Verrier, Galle and Lassell. Voyager 2, and subsequently the Hubble telescope, have discovered nine rings in total and there may be even more – a new mission to the planet is needed to give us a better understanding of Neptune's ring system.

Left: Mosaic of Voyager 2 images of Triton. The surface shows a great variety of features. The large south polar cap (top) is thought to consist of a slowly-evaporating layer of nitrogen ice, deposited during the previous winter. Below this is a region which has been dubbed the "cantaloupe" terrain. Small dimples with upraised rims and shallow central depressions dot the area. Long fractures cross the region and extend into the polar cap. A band of terrain on the border of the polar cap has a light covering of frost. In the lower left of the image are smooth plains which may indicate recent outflows onto the surface.

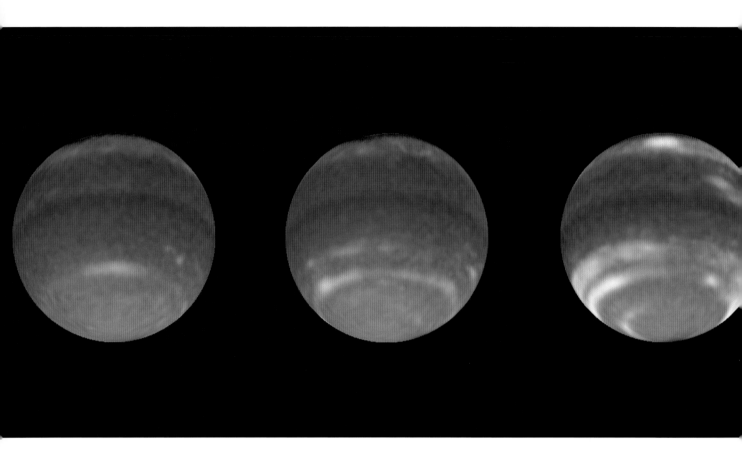

Multiple moons

Neptune is known to have thirteen moons. Triton was the first to be observed, just days after the discovery of Neptune. It was over a century until the next moon, Nereid was discovered by Gerald Kuiper in 1949. Voyager 2 discovered six moons: Despina, Galatea, Larissa, Naiad, Proteus and Thalassa. Larissa had actually been seen by scientists in 1981 when it occulted a star, but it was thought to be a ring, until Voyager showed that it was in fact another moon.

Naiad, Galatea, Despina and Thalassa are located within Neptune's rings; they are extremely close to the Roche Limit – the distance from a celestial body at which its gravitational pull is greater than the gravity holding an orbiting body. When a smaller body enters the Roche Limit, tidal forces from the larger body cause it to break up. If a moon strays too close to Neptune it will either be pulled apart by tidal forces and the debris turned into a ring, or be pulled into Neptune's surface.

Naiad is one of the closest moons in the solar system to its planet's Roche Limit and one day soon will break up, most likely forming another ring before it gets a chance to impact the surface. Even Triton, Proteus and Larissa will one day enter the Roche Limit and break up. Triton is likely to impact the surface, causing unknown

changes to Neptune. However, this will not occur for a billion years or more.

In 2002 and 2003, scientists using telescopes designed to observe trans-Neptunian bodies in the Kuiper Belt around Pluto discovered a further five moons, which are still awaiting names. It is likely that there are more Neptunian moons to be discovered, or that Neptune will acquire more moons. As Neptune is so close to the Kuiper Belt asteroids might well become caught in the planet's gravitational pull. Most of the existing moons, small and irregularly shaped, like asteroids, are from the Kuiper Belt. Only Triton is spherical, although Proteus is believed to be the largest size a body of rock can be, without being forced into a sphere by its own gravity.

Triton

Just 17 days after the discovery of Neptune, a moon was detected in orbit by the British astronomer William Lassell. Lassell did not christen the moon, but the name Triton was floated in astronomical circles. Triton was the son of Poseidon, the Greek version of the Roman god, Neptune. However, the name was not in widespread use until the discovery of a second moon, Nereid in 1949; before that date, it was popularly known simply as Neptune's moon. Triton, unlike the other sizeable satellites of solar system

Opposite: Neptune's seasons. Hubble Space Telescope image of brightening cloud bands in Neptune's southern hemisphere in 1996 (left), 1998 and 2002 (right). This change may be due to the arrival of spring. Seasons on Earth are caused by its axial tilt of 23 degrees, meaning that the hemispheres receive different amounts of light at different times of the year. Neptune has an axial tilt of 29 degrees, so a similar effect could occur. One year on Neptune is 165 Earth years, so the seasonal change is correspondingly slower. Neptune has wild weather despite its distance from the sun, and winds can reach 2000km per hour

Above: Voyager 2 image, tinted pale blue, showing Neptune's two major rings. The rings have radii of 53,000km and 63,000km and are composed of microscopic dust particles. They are narrow and contain clumps and kinks thought to be associated with tiny "shepherd" moonlets, too small to be detected directly. Similar narrow, dusty, braided rings have been detected around Saturn (the F-ring and Enke Gap ringlet) and Uranus (1986U1R). The image was obtained as the Voyager spacecraft was leaving the Neptune system on 26 August 1989, from a distance of 1.1 million kilometers.

planets, orbits Neptune in a retrograde direction, suggesting that the two bodies were not formed together. Before it was captured in Neptune's gravitational field, scientists speculate that Triton would have been much like Pluto, a trans-Neptunian object from the Kuiper Belt. As a relatively large moon which orbits very close to its planet, tidal forces have drawn Triton into an exceptionally uniform, circular orbit. The moon's axis is tilted to such a degree that one pole is usually facing the sun, while the other pole remains in darkness.

When Voyager 2 arrived, summer was just starting at the south pole, which meant that a massive water, nitrogen and methane ice cap, which had built up over the long winter, was beginning to evaporate. The northern hemisphere revealed that beneath the ice, Triton appears similar to a "cantaloupe" melon, with small, shallow depressions dotted across the surface. There is an absence of impact craters, indicating that Triton is still geologically active; massive geysers of ice and dust erupt from beneath the surface, forming plumes of over 7km in height.

The presence of water, combined with geothermal activity, has led scientists to propose Triton as a possible contender to harbor primitive life. A desire to know whether this is the case will undoubtedly see space probes destined specifically for Triton in the future.

Above: Neptune, taken during August 1989, when Voyager passed within 5,000km of Neptune's north pole. This false-color image, obtained using the ultraviolet, violet and green filters of Voyager's wide-angle camera, highlights details of weather systems, revealing clouds located at different altitudes in different colors. The prominent Great Dark Spot (center), a giant storm system the size of Earth, appears surrounded by pink, wispy clouds at high altitudes. Areas of dark, deep-lying cloud appear dark blue in this image.

Opposite: Voyager 2 image of white, high-altitude, "cirrus" clouds in the atmosphere above Neptune's southern hemisphere. The picture clearly shows the vertical relief in Neptune's atmosphere. The linear cloud formations range in width from 50 to 200km, and their shadow widths range from 30 to 50km. Voyager scientists calculated from this that the cirrus clouds are some 50km higher than the surrounding (blue) cloud deck. The picture was recorded two hours before Voyager 2's closest approach to Neptune at midnight on 24 August 1989. The range was 157,000km and the resolution of the image is 11km.

Neptune/Earth Comparison

	Neptune	Earth
Discovered by	Johann Galle, John Couch Adams and Urbain Le Verrier	-
Date of Discovery	1846	-
Distance from the Earth (minimum)	4,310,000,000 km	-
Average Distance from Sun	4,498,252,900 km Neptune is the farthest planet from the sun for a 20 year period every 248 Earth years	149,597,000 km
Average Speed in Orbiting Sun	5 km/sec	30 km/sec
Diameter	49,528 km The smallest diameter of the 4 giant "gas planets"	12,756 km
Circumference	155,597 km	40,075 km
Surface area	7,640,800,000 km^2	510,072,000 km^2
Number of known satellites	13	1
Number of known rings	5 major rings	0
Tilt of Axis	29° Neptune has seasons due to the tilt of the axis which causes the sun to heat the planet's northern and southern halves alternately	23.5°
Orbital period (length of year)	60,190 Earth Days (165 Earth years) This long orbital period means that Neptune has not yet made a full orbit round the sun since its discovery	365.25 Days
Rotational period (length of day)	16 hours 7 mins	23 hours 56 minutes
Surface gravity	10.7 m/s^2	9.8 m/s^2 If you weigh 100 kg on Earth you would weigh 110 kg on Neptune
Temperature range	-214° C	-89.6° to 59° C
Atmosphere	Hydrogen, helium, methane Neptune's atmosphere has the highest wind speeds in the solar system, up to 2000 km per hour	Nitrogen, oxygen, carbon dioxide, argon, water vapor
Mass	1.02 x 10^{26} kg About 17 times the mass of the Earth	5.97 x 10^{24} kg
Volume	6.3 x 1013 km^3 Neptune's volume could hold nearly 60 Earths	1.1 x 10^{12} km^3
Density	1.76 g/c^3	5.5 g/c^3
Surface	Thick clouds cover the surface	The surface of the Earth is divided into dry land and oceans - the dry land occupying c.149,00,000 million km^2, and the oceans c.361,000,000 km^2

PLUTO

I n 1928, an amateur astronomer from Kansas, Clyde Tombaugh, sent detailed observations of planetary movements to the Lowell Observatory in Arizona. Instead of receiving the comments as expected, he was offered a job as a junior astronomer, in which he had to trawl through countless photographs of the space beyond Neptune in search of a ninth planet, called Planet X.

Percival Lowell, the founder of the observatory where Tombaugh worked, had first coined the term "Planet X" for an as yet unknown ninth planet in the solar system. Soon after the discovery of Neptune it was realized that the planet was not massive enough by itself to pull the other gas giants very slightly off their expected courses. Instead the existence of another planet, beyond Neptune, was thought to be responsible. Tombaugh carried out many hours of painstaking research, comparing photos of the same area of space at different times to detect the possible movement of a planet against the background stars. On 18 February 1930, he discovered such a movement and thus the ninth planet was discovered. On 13 March the announcement was made to an excited world and a

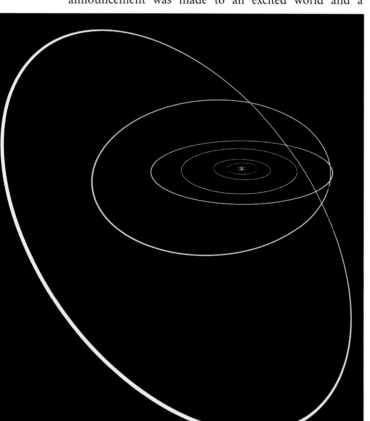

competition was launched for the public to think of a name for the newest member of the solar system. Venetia Burney, an eleven-year-old school girl from Oxfordshire, England, suggested the name Pluto. Such a name was appealing, because in classical mythology, Pluto was the god of the underworld, and this cleverly alluded to the fact that Pluto was so far from the sun. Moreover, it was attractive to the scientists at the Lowell Observatory, because the first two letters were the initials of Percival Lowell.

Planet X?

Initially everybody was satisfied that Pluto was Planet X, the ninth planet in the solar system, and several decades later the size of Pluto was calculated when it occulted its moon, Charon. Pluto was found to be much smaller than earlier estimates had suggested. It was not only the smallest planet in the solar system, it was smaller than several moons: Ganymede, Titan, Callisto, Io, Europa, Triton and even Earth's moon. It also emerged that it was less massive than many of these moons, meaning that it could not have the gravitational effect on the other gas giants that Planet X was supposed to have. However, it was later discovered that the mass of Neptune had been incorrectly calculated. When the new, correct mass for Neptune was factored into the equations, the anomalies in the orbits of the gas giants disappeared.

Nevertheless, it was not the end of controversy about the ninth planet. Given its exceptionally small size, questions began to emerge as to whether Pluto deserved planetary status at all. Its orbit was discovered to be both eccentric and inclined to the plane in which the other planets orbited, rather more like the orbit of a comet, with a distance of 30 AU when it is closest to the sun, 50 AU at its furthest.

Frozen nitrogen

Pluto has never been visited by a probe, so its exact characteristics are unknown, and given its distance from the sun, it is hard to make educated guesses. Pluto reflects quite a lot of sunlight, which has led scientist to predict that

Below: Clyde Tombaugh (1906-1997) with the blink comparator he used to discover Pluto. Tombaugh couldn't afford to study at college, but built his own telescope, and became an assistant at Lowell Observatory. Lowell himself predicted the existence of a ninth planet, and a team was set up to find it. Tombaugh invented the blink comparator to facilitate the search. This device allowed comparison of two photographs of the sky, which showed if any object had altered position. After 7000 hours of work, he found a tiny object outside the orbit of Neptune, which was named Pluto. In the course of his searches, he also discovered some 3000 asteroids.

Left: Pluto on 27 July 1998. Pluto shines at a faint 14.5 magnitude.

Opposite: Computer graphic of the orbit (large oval) of what has been claimed as the tenth planet, 2003 UB313. The orbits of the other nine planets are also shown, the next planet being Pluto. Earth's orbit is shown in red close to the sun, which is at the center of the orbits. 2003 UB313 is a temporary name. It is thought to be larger than Pluto, and takes 560 years to orbit the sun. Its distance from the sun ranges from 38 to 95 times the Earth-sun distance. Like Pluto and Sedna, 2003 UB313 is a large member of the Kuiper Belt of mostly small icy bodies. The discovery was made at the Palomar Observatory, USA, by Mike Brown, Chad Trujillo and David Rabinowitz, and announced in July 2005.

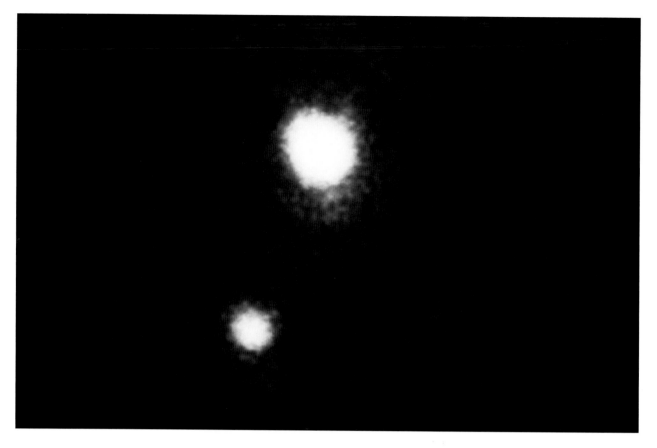

much of the planet's surface is covered in a layer of rock and ice. Scientists think the ice is mostly nitrogen, with some methane and traces of carbon monoxide. As Pluto makes its closest approach to the sun, inside the orbit of Neptune, the ice on the surface begins to melt and evaporate, giving rise to a nitrogen atmosphere. In 2002, when Pluto occulted a star, scientists were surprised to discover that the atmosphere appeared to be getting thicker, despite the fact that it is now moving outside Neptune's orbit and away from the sun. Scientists believe this unexpected activity might be caused by heat that Pluto may have stored during its closest approach to the sun. Like Uranus, Pluto's poles lie close to its orbital path. When the planet was first discovered its south pole was facing observers, but it has subsequently moved so that we are now seeing the equator. Pluto's moon orbits in the path of Pluto's equator meaning that while the equator is facing Earth, eclipses can be seen relatively frequently.

Pluto's moon

In 1978, American astronomer, James Christy discovered that Pluto had a moon when he noticed a small bulge occurring periodically in photographs of the planet. The moon was named Charon, after the boatman, who, in Greek mythology, ferried souls across the river Styx to the underworld, where Pluto was god. Pluto and Charon are perhaps better referred to as a double planet system because both objects are very close to one another and Charon is just under half the size of Pluto, making it the largest moon relative to the size of its parent planet in the solar system. Moreover, not only is Charon tidally locked to Pluto, but Pluto is the only planet, tidally locked to its moon. It takes both bodies 6.4 days to rotate on their axis, meaning that one object keeps the same face presented to the other object and vice versa. The most convenient explanation for the dispropotionte size of Pluto's moon is that Charon formed from the debris of an impact on Pluto early in its history. However, scientists believe that the surface of Charon my be composed of water ice and not nitrogen ice as on Pluto, indicating that the two bodies may have formed separately.

In 2005, the Hubble Space Telescope captured what is thought to be two new moons orbiting Pluto but the International Astronomical Union cannot confirm and name them until Hubble can take further pictures to prove that the two objects are in fact in orbit of the Pluto.

Kuiper Belt

After years as an oddity in the solar system, Pluto found its true place as a member of the Kuiper Belt. The existence of a belt of objects extending beyond the orbit of Neptune, 30 AU to a distance of 50 AU or more was first suggested by the Dutch-born astronomer, Gerard Kuiper. But it is also attributed to the British astronomer Kenneth Edgeworth, and as such is sometimes referred to as the Edgeworth-Kuiper belt. They both believed that beyond Neptune were a series of comet-like objects, which were home to short-period comets, such as Halley's Comet. Evidence began mounting for the existence of the Kuiper Belt in 1992 when the astronomer, David Jewitt discovered a small planetoid beyond the orbit of Pluto. Since then, several hundred trans-Neptunian objects have been discovered, and it is expected that many thousands more remain undiscovered because they are too far from the sun's energy source for us to be able to detect them. The objects in the Kuiper Belt form a band or ring around the ecliptic plane in which the planets orbit, although the orbits of many of these objects, including Pluto, is inclined to that plane.

The Pluto debate

Although the discovery of the Kuiper belt put Pluto's role in the solar system into perspective, it remained the largest known Kuiper Belt object, meaning that it was able to cling on to planetary status. However, the announcement in 2005 that a trans-Neptunian object larger than Pluto had been discovered using photos from 2003, once again called Pluto's planetary status into question. 2003 UB 313 is certainly larger than Pluto, although its exact size is not yet known. It is the most distant known solar system object and it is thought to have an orbital period of over 550 years. Infrared images of 2003 UB313 indicate the presence of methane ice on the surface. Pluto is the only other Kuiper belt object believed to have surface methane ice. The International Astronomical Union needs to decide the fate of Pluto. If Pluto is to remain a planet, 2003 UB313 should also be given that credit, or both should be demoted to the status of minor planets or trans-Neptunian objects. The former option presents difficulty, because as telescopes improve, it is extremely likely that there will be a large increase in the number of Pluto-sized trans-Neptunian objects that are discovered. At the beginning of the twenty-first century, Sedna and Quaoar were discovered. They are both smaller than Pluto, but were large enough to spark the debate on Pluto's planetary status, before 2003 UB313 had even been disovered. The option of demoting Pluto is not feasible either; when such a course of action was first suggested, it met with widespread public outcry. The most likely course of action will be to allow Pluto to keep its planetary status for historical reasons, but not to designate that status to any further trans-Neptunian object unless they are of considerable size.

Opposite: Optical image of the planet Pluto (center) and its large moon Charon (lower left), taken with the Hubble Space Telescope's Faint Object Camera. Pluto is the ninth and smallest planet in the solar system. Discovered in 1930 at Lowell Observatory by Clyde Tombaugh, it has a 248-year orbit around the sun. The moon, Charon, was discovered in 1977. Its 6-day orbit around Pluto is a circle seen almost edge-on from Earth. At the time of the observation, Charon was near its maximum angular separation from Pluto; about 0.9 arc seconds. Both Pluto and Charon are cold, rocky bodies. Pluto is thought to be coated with methane frost, whereas Charon is probably covered with water ice.

Below: Computer-processed image of Pluto, the smallest and outermost planet in the solar system. This image is derived from an observation made using the Hubble Space Telescope, and was processed to bring out the brightness differences on the surface. Twelve bright regions have been identified on the planet, including a large north polar cap. It is thought that the surface of Pluto is largely nitrogen ice, with methane and carbon monoxide ices as impurities. In size and surface composition, Pluto is similar to Triton, a moon of Neptune. No spacecraft has yet visited Pluto.

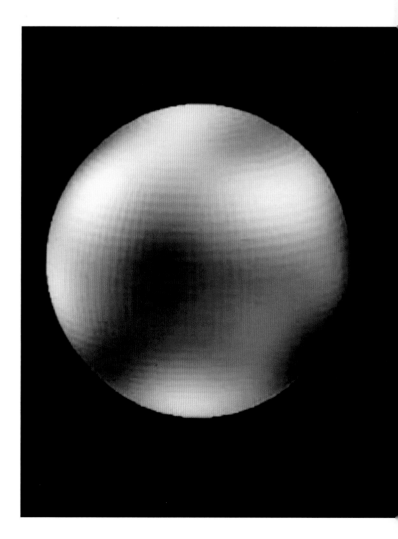

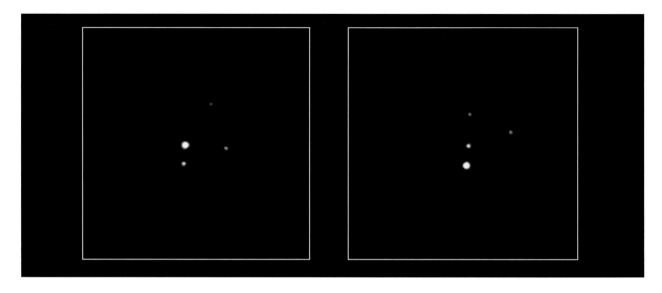

Future

More and more trans-Neptunian objects are discovered every year. This will be a key area of research in the twenty-first century, as scientists endeavor to find other, larger Kuiper Belt members and also understand their compositions. Pluto is the only planet never to have been visited by a probe. The first probe to reach the planet, the New Horizons spacecraft is due for launch in 2006. New Horizons replaced the Pluto-Kuiper Express mission that had been scheduled for launch at the turn of the century, but was eventually scrapped for budgetary reasons. The mission was launched with some haste so that the probe might reach the planet before the atmosphere disappears. The probe will answer many questions presented by Pluto and Charon before moving on to look at other objects in the Kuiper Belt. If the probe detects something of interest, it can be maneuvered to intercept them. This mission will take several years to reach Pluto, after using Jupiter as a slingshot, but hopefully it will be worth the wait, giving us a new insight into this part of the solar system.

New moons of Pluto

Above: Hubble Space Telescope images of Pluto (white) and its large moon Charon (pale blue), and two newly discovered moons (grey). The images were taken on 15 (left) and 18 (right) May 2005. Pluto and Charon have moved significantly with respect to each other in this time, but the outer moons, being more distant, have not moved as much. Pluto and Charon have such similar masses that they orbit a point in between them, rather than a point within the larger body, as is the case with other moons. Pluto has an eccentric orbit; its distance to the sun varies between 4.4 and 7.4 billion kilometers.

Left: Hubble Space Telescope image of Sedna, a large Kuiper Belt object. This image suggests an upper limit on Sedna's size of 1600 kilometers in diameter. Sedna orbits the sun far beyond the ninth planet Pluto. Pluto has a diameter of 2300 kilometers. The Kuiper Belt is a collection of mostly small icy bodies that orbit between and beyond the planets Neptune and Pluto. Sedna was discovered by ground-based telescopes in 2004 and this image was taken by the Advanced Camera for Surveys on 16 March 2004.

Opposite: Illustration of Pluto (the planet in the foreground) and its companion Charon. The sun is visible at right. Pluto, the ninth planet to be discovered, was first seen in 1930. Charon orbits Pluto in 6.4 days, exactly the same as Pluto's rotational period. Pluto is 2300km in diameter, and is thought to consist of a rocky core covered with methane ice. Charon is believed to have a similar structure, although somewhat smaller with a diameter of 1190km. Pluto's unusual orbit occasionally brings it within that of Neptune, as is the case between 1979 and 1999, in the course of its 248 year solar orbit.

Pluto/Earth Comparison

	Pluto	Earth
Discovered by	Clyde Tombaugh	-
Date of Discovery	1930	-
Distance from the Earth (minimum)	4,290,000,000 km	-
Average Distance from Sun	5,906,380,000 km Between 1979 and 1999 Pluto was nearer to the sun than Neptune	149,597,000 km
Average Speed in Orbiting Sun	5 km/sec	30 km/sec
Diameter	2,300 km The smallest of the planets, it has a diameter about two-thirds of the Earth's moons	12,756 km
Circumference	7,232 km	40,075 km
Surface area	16,650,000 km^2	510,065,700 km^2
Number of known satellites	1 (2 more identified in 2005)	1
Number of known rings	0	0
Tilt of Axis	120°	23.5°
Orbital period (length of year)	90,553 Earth Days (248 Earth years)	365.25 Days
Rotational period (length of day)	6 days 9 hours 18 mins	23 hours 56 minutes
Surface gravity	0.8 m/s^2 Low gravity causes atmosphere to be more extended in altitude than the Earth's	9.8 m/s^2 If you weigh 100 kg on Earth you would weigh 8 kg on Pluto
Temperature range	-233 to -223° C	-89.6° to 59° C
Atmosphere	Nitrogen, methane	Nitrogen, oxygen, carbon dioxide, argon, water vapor
Mass	1.3 x 10^{22} kg Due to its low density, Pluto has a mass about 0.17 of the Earth's	5.97 x 10^{24} kg
Volume	6.4 x 10^9 km^3	1.1 x 10^{12} km^3
Density	2 g/cm^3	5.5 g/cm^3
Surface	Believed to have a layer of frozen methane, nitrogen and carbon monoxide on its surface. When Pluto is near to the sun, these ices thaw and create a thin atmosphere	The surface of the Earth is divided into dry land and oceans - the dry land occupying c.149,00,000 million km^2, and the oceans c.361,000,000 km^2

ASTEROIDS · METEORS · COMETS

The key difference between asteroids and meteoroids is size. Meteoroids are fragments of rock and metal less than 50m in diameter, while asteroids are fragments of rock and metal which are greater than 50m in diameter. For humans, this size distinction could mean the difference between life and death.

If a meteoroid strikes the Earth it will burn up in the Earth's atmosphere, presenting a beautiful, and usually harmless, spectacle – a meteor. However, if an asteroid were to strike the Earth, it could devastate eco-systems and even effect the extinction of mankind. Such extinction events are not just theoretical; it is now widely assumed that the asteroid which created a 300km basin in the Yucatan Peninsula in Mexico was responsible for the death of the dinosaurs.

"Star-like"

On New Year's Day 1801 the Italian astronomer, Giuseppe Piazzi, discovered the first asteroid, Ceres, when he was searching for a star. Initially he thought it was a comet, but its orbit was too slow and uniform. Instead, some astronomers suggested it might be a planet between the orbits of Mars and Jupiter. The issue was resolved a year later, in 1802, when the German astronomer, Heinrich Wilhelm Olbers, discovered a second asteroid which he named Pallas. This second find led the discoverer of Uranus, William Herschel, to offer the collective name "asteroid", meaning "star-like". This highlighted the fact that, although asteroids moved like planets across the background stars, from Earth they looked more like stars than planets because they are too small to exhibit a disc shape.

The Asteroid Belt

Many of the asteroids in the solar system are located in a band between Mars and Jupiter called the Asteroid Belt. Thousands of asteroids are known to exist in the Belt, and many thousands more are predicted. It is believed that the Belt is a failed planet – the chunks of metal and rock were unable to group together to form a fifth terrestrial planet because the process was interrupted by the strong gravitational pull of Jupiter. However, most of the asteroids are so small, that even if they had all united, the resulting planet would be even smaller than the moon. The first

asteroid to be discovered, Ceres, was later found to be by far the largest asteroid in the Belt. Ceres is 1000km in diameter. As it is also the most massive asteroid in the Belt, Ceres has ample gravity to compress it into a spherical shape. Pallas, the second asteroid to be discovered is also the second largest; however, it is only half the size of Ceres and much less massive, with the effect that its gravitational force is not sufficient to cause it to form a spheroid, making Pallas the largest irregularly shaped asteroid in the Belt. The third largest asteroid, Vesta, is the only asteroid from the Belt to be visible from Earth with the naked eye.

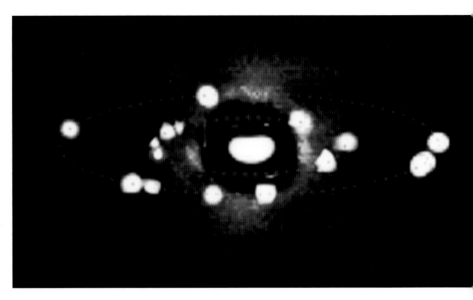

Collision course

The orbits of asteroids are not just confined to the Asteroid Belt, rather they can be found throughout the solar system. Trojan asteroids can be found in the orbital paths of Jupiter, Neptune and Mars, and a number of trans-Neptunian objects in the Kuiper Belt can also be classified as asteroids. However, some follow highly elliptical orbits of the sun – these are often comets which have lost their volatile materials. These asteroids intersect Earth's orbital path during their solar orbit, and are classified as "near-Earth asteroids". If an asteroid and the Earth happened to be at the same point of their orbital paths at the same time, the result would be a collision.

Given that a collision with one of these near-Earth asteroids may seal the fate of humanity, widespread popular interest has developed, and the study of such objects is a keen field for many astronomers. In 1989, the asteroid 4581 Asclepius intersected Earth's orbit at a point where the Earth had been just hours before. Several years later, NASA predicted that the asteroid 2002 NT7 would impact the Earth on 1 February 2019, but later recalculated the data, suggesting it was no longer a hazard. It was feared that another asteroid, 99942 Apophis, could impact with the Earth in 2029, but the date has subsequently been changed to 2036, and the chance of an impact is now considered remote. There are many objects that will be involved in near-Earth misses over the years, and new asteroids will emerge to threaten our planet. The asteroid which currently poses the greatest threat to Earth is 1950DA. Scientists worked out a reasonable probability of impact on 16 March 2880. The chances are favorable that calculations will change or that the asteroid will narrowly miss the Earth. However if the asteroid is on a collision course, it is to be hoped that by then new technologies will exist to move 1950DA off course.

Above: Yepun Telescope image of Asteroid 87 Sylvia and its moons. Moons are shown in various positions around 87 Sylvia (center). 87 Sylvia is around 260km long. Romulus, its outer moon, was discovered in February 2001. It is 18km wide and orbits 1360km from Sylvia. Remus, the inner moon, was discovered in August 2005. It is only seven kilometers wide and orbits just 710km from Sylvia.

Opposite: NEAR (Near-Earth Asteroid Rendezvous) spacecraft image of Asteroid 253 Mathilde. Mathilde is about 59 by 47 kilometers across. It is the commonest type (C-class) of asteroid, its carbonaceous chondritic rocks reflecting only 3.6% of the light that falls on it. Its surface is marked by many large impact craters; the shadowed crater (at center) is about 10km deep. Mathilde orbits the sun in the asteroid belt at distances of 290–500 million kilometers (2–3.5 times the radius of Earth's orbit). Its orbit is 4.3 years long and it rotates about once every 17 days. Image taken on 27 June 1997 at a distance of 2400 km and a resolution of 380 meters.

Probing and mapping

During the Cold War, sending probes to asteroids was not at the forefront of either superpower's space programs, largely because asteroids lacked the prestige element offered by missions to other planets. An asteroid was not visited by a probe until the Galileo probe flew past Gaspra in 1991, and that was a flying visit while en route to Jupiter. Five years later, NASA launched its NEAR (Near-Earth Asteroid Rendezvous) probe which was the first destined exclusively for an asteroid, in this case Eros. Once it reached Eros, NEAR was renamed NEAR-Shoemaker in memory of the American astronomer, Eugene Shoemaker, who died a year after the craft was launched. The probe spent a year mapping Eros, gaining basic understanding of its size,

shape and surface temperatures. The mission ended in a spectacular triumph for NASA, when NEAR successfully soft-landed on the surface of the asteroid, an undertaking which had not been intended before the probe was launched. From the surface, the probe used its gamma-ray spectrometers to assess the composition of the asteroid. For two weeks, data was relayed by the craft from the asteroid's surface.

The Asteroid Belt will also be stepping out of the unknown when NASA's Dawn Mission is launched in summer 2006. The probe is designed to reach Vesta in 2011, where scientists hope to find indications of volcanic activity, before flying on to Ceres in 2015, where some have even suggested that sub-surface water might be discovered. Although the mission is scheduled to end in 2016, if it is possible, NASA might attempt to investigate more of the Asteroid Belt.

Meteoroids

Meteoroids can be found throughout the solar system. They are small fragments of rocks and minerals, usually no larger than boulders in space, and often the size of a grain of sand. Meteoroids are either the chipped-away parts of greater bodies, or are remnants from the creation of the solar system, which stayed in their meteoritic form, rather than coalescing into a larger body as a result of gravity.

Shooting stars

When meteoroids collide with the Earth they burn up in the upper atmosphere, creating a striking spectacle called a meteor. Energy in the form of heat is generated as the meteoroid travels at supersonic speeds, compressing the air beneath it. This energy strips the meteoroid of its electrons in a process is called ionization, which leaves a trail in its wake. This ionization trail glows momentarily as a streak through the sky, earning meteors the common name, "shooting star". Occasionally, a meteor is particularly bright; this means the meteoroid is larger, probably coming from an asteroid, or even the moon or Mars. These meteors are named "fireballs" rather than shooting stars. They are usually accompanied by the sound of a sonic boom and, if they reach the surface, usually result in an impact crater. Small meteoroids collide with the Earth with great frequency. Anyone who watches the sky should be able to observe a shooting star as the meteoroid burns up – all that is required is patience.

Meteor showers

As comets orbit the sun they leave meteoritic debris in their wake. If the comet is a short-period comet, then this debris will, over time, spread evenly throughout the comet's orbital path. When the Earth intersects the orbital path of a comet the debris rains down on Earth as a stream of meteors called a "meteor shower". Meteor showers are a popular event and usually receive advanced media coverage to inform the public of their occurrence. The most famous meteor showers are the Leonids, from the comet Tempel-Tuttle, which occur in mid-November, and the Perseids, associated with the orbit of comet Swift-Tuttle, which peaks on 12 August every year, but is visible during late July and early August. More than fifty meteor showers occur annually; although many are very weak, there are several stronger showers to look out for, such as the Geminids and the Ursids in December, the Orionids in mid-October and the Quadrantids at the start of the New Year.

Outer space reaches Earth

While most meteoroids that collide with the Earth are small and disintegrate in the upper atmosphere, some are able to reach the Earth. When part of a meteoroid reaches the surface it becomes known as a meteorite. Before the Space Age, meteorites were the only way that material from outer space could be handled and analyzed. There are three

Below: Optical time-exposure image of Leonid meteors (streaks) against a starfield containing the Milky Way (band across center). Meteors (shooting stars) are tiny dust particles which enter the Earth's atmosphere at high speeds. They are heated by air resistance, making them visible as streaks of light. The Leonid shower occurs each year for about two days around 17 November when the Earth crosses the debris produced by the comet Tempel-Tuttle.

Opposite: Colored image gathered by the Galileo spacecraft showing Asteroid 243 Ida and its tiny moon (right), provisionally known as 1993(243)1. This picture was the first conclusive evidence that an asteroid can have a satellite. Ida is a member of the Koronis family of asteroids, and is about 56km in length. The moon is about 1.5km in diameter, and is thought to orbit about 100km from Ida's center. This image was taken on 28 August 1993, at a distance of 10,870km from Ida. This was the second asteroid encounter by the Galileo spacecraft on its way to Jupiter.

types of meteorites: aerolites, which comprise stone; siderites, comprising alloys of iron and nickel; and siderolites, comprising both stone and iron. Over 80% of meteorites that fall to the Earth are aerolites called chondrites because they are covered in small, spherical silicates called chondrules. The minority of stony meteorites are achondrites, igneous rocks which have undergone geological processes – the name comes from the fact that no chondrules are present in the rock.

Above: A meteor enters the Earth's atmosphere with a speed of up to 100 kilometers per second. Air resistance heats the particle, making it visible as a streak of light. Another meteor is seen at upper left.

Below left: Image from the Mars exploration rover. This was the first meteorite to be found on another planet. It is about the size of a basketball and is composed mainly of iron and nickel. Photographed on 6 January 2005.

Opposite: Aerial view of Meteor Crater, Arizona. Sometimes called the Barringer Crater, after the mining engineer who first suggested that it was formed by a meteor impact, it is believed to be about 50,000 years old. The crater is in northeastern Arizona, near Winslow, and is about 200 meters deep and 800 meters across. Several attempts to mine the iron-rich material of the meteor were made before a visitor center was built in the 1960s. Two new minerals – coesite and stishovite – were identified here; both are high-pressure forms of silica. In recent years the crater has been used for astronaut training and studies in planet comparison.

Around 25,000 meteorites have been discovered on Earth, but many lie unfound at the bottom of the ocean or in uninhabited parts of the world. There are no records of a meteorite killing a person as it hit the ground, although in 1954 in Alabama, a woman, Ann Hodges, was injured when a meteorite plunged through her roof and clipped her arm after ricocheting off a radio. The only fatality from a falling meteorite is thought to be a dog, which was struck by a meteorite in Egypt in 1911.

Lunar and Martian Meteorites

While most meteorites come from asteroids or comets, rarely they prove to have come from the moon or Mars. When meteorites strike the surface of either of these two bodies, they usually form an impact crater, chipping away at the surface and providing sufficient velocity to escape the body's gravitational pull. Martian meteoroids usually travel into a solar orbit, and impact the Earth millions of years after the meteorite dislodged the meteoroid. Although many lunar meteoroids enter a heliocentric orbit, some do end up in an orbit of the Earth instead, with the consequence that it takes a relatively short period of time for the meteoroid to be transferred from the surface of the moon to the surface of the Earth.

While all meteorites are precious, lunar and Martian meteorites are so rare that they are an exceptional find. Fewer than 100 lunar meteorites have been discovered, and only 34 meteorites of Martian origin have been confirmed. Only as recently as 1982 did scientists realize that some meteorites were from Mars and the moon. The first meteorite to fall to Earth of Martian origin was in Chassingy, France in 1815, but its provenance was not known until the end of the twentieth century. The meteorite Yamato 791197, which fell to Earth in 1979, is the first known lunar meteorite, although it was not identified as such at the time. It was not until two years later when, in 1981, another meteorite, Allan Hills 81005, was identified as of lunar origin, that scientists were able to classify Yamato 791197.

COMETS

I n spite of their sheer beauty, many civilizations throughout history have considered the arrival of a comet as a prophecy of doom. Understandable perhaps, given that comets did not seem to conform to the movements of other objects across the night sky, appearing at what seemed like random occasions.

Their long, streaking tails crowned by what might seem like a white fireball would have looked highly unusual against the backdrop of stars. Consequently, in numerous civilizations, a frequent assumption of the appearance of a comet was that the gods had sent a sign of disapproval. During the Norman invasion of Britain, in 1066, a comet – now known to have been Halley's Comet – appeared. The Bayeux Tapestry, which documented the Battle of Hastings for its victors, placed the comet in the same frame as the defeated King Harold, suggesting that the comet's appearance indicated God's disapproval at his usurpation of the throne and was also a sign of his eventual downfall. Comets have, among many other things, been unfairly charged with causing the Black Death in Europe, earthquakes in various parts of the world, and the defeat of the Incas in South America. Halley's Comet even suffered the indignity of being condemned by the Pope in 1456 as an agent of the devil.

More recently, science has triumphed, and civilization has begun to understand comets as naturally occurring phenomena. Comets are thought to be unchanged remnants from the creation of the solar system.

Snowballs in space

Most of a comet's mass is contained in its nucleus. Located at the heart of the comet's head, the nucleus is an irregular shape, similar to an asteroid. It is significantly smaller than a planet, usually no more than several tens of kilometers in length. The nucleus contains rock, frozen gases and water, meaning that comets are indeed similar to a giant snowball.

The nucleus is obscured by the coma, a region of gas and dust lifted from the nucleus as it nears the sun. The coma may belie the actual size of the comet, because while the nucleus might be only several kilometers long, the coma can be thousands of kilometers across. From Earth, the coma is seen as the giant white fireball at the head of the comet, guiding it across the sky.

As the comet approaches the sun, material in the nucleus begins to evaporate. The evaporated material is streamlined by solar winds, creating the comet's tails; comets usually have two – a dust tail, and an ion tail. The dust tail is composed of the evaporated ice and dust fragments from the comet's nucleus. It appears as an impressive white streak across the sky, extending the debris behind it as far as several million kilometers. The ion tail is

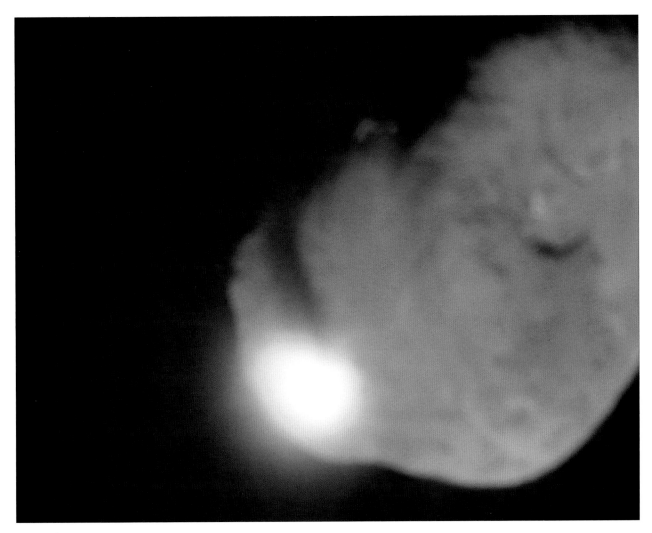

less easily visible in the night sky because of its darker, bluish color. The gases found in the coma react with the sun's rays and undergo a process of ionization; these ionized particles are fanned into a tail by the solar winds. The ion tail is usually even longer than the dust tail, sometimes reaching over one hundred million kilometers from the nucleus.

Deep Impact

In spite of significant increases in our understanding of comets, much remains unknown. In 2005, NASA attempted to remedy that deficiency, by successfully guiding a probe, Deep Impact, within the comet Tempel 1. The intention was to explore beyond the obscuring coma and find out as much about the structure of the comet's nucleus as possible.

It is thought that some of the ice water found on comets might be responsible for water on Earth, following impacts early in the planet's history. Moreover, it is believed that comets contain material that has not been changed

Above: Deep Impact comet strike. Explosion (white) on the surface of the nucleus (gray) of the comet 9P/Tempel 1, after being struck by the Deep Impact impactor. The Deep Impact spacecraft launched a 360-kilogram impactor at the comet, which successfully struck it at over ten kilometers per second on 4 July 2005. The impact caused the ejection of a large amount of interior material. The mission was launched on 12 January 2005. It was designed to study the composition of a comet, as comets are relics from the formation of the solar system. As such, they can provide much information about its history and formation. This image was captured by the Deep Impact spacecraft.

Opposite: Halley's comet, photographed from the Royal Observatory, Cape of Good Hope, 1910.

since the creation of the solar system; a look inside a comet might give us a glimpse back to those days at the dawn of the solar system – Tempel 1 might, in effect, be a 4.6-billion-year-old time capsule.

The probe's impact with the comet caused a long

plume of material similar in consistency to talcum powder to burst out from the comet. It is expected that analysis of the mission's findings will give us a much greater insight into the internal structure of a comet's nucleus.

The results of Deep Impact will be corroborated by a European mission named Rosetta, which blasted off in 2004 on a journey to the comet Churyumov-Gerasimenko. It is due to set down a lander on the comet in 2014. In the same way that the Rosetta Stone unraveled the mysteries of ancient Egypt, so it is hoped that the Rosetta mission will unravel the mysteries of life on Earth, by attempting to reveal the chemical make-up of the comet.

Orbits

The fact that many comets periodically repeat their orbits of the sun was not known until 1705, when Edmond Halley realized that the comet later to be named in his honor was not several different comets appearing randomly, but rather was the same body on a repeat orbit of the sun.

Comets have orbits which are highly eccentric to the plane around which the planets orbit. And, according to type of orbit, three classifications of comet have been identified: the Jupiter family; short-period comets; and long-period comets. Some comets follow a path between the sun and Jupiter, which means that they orbit the sun frequently, taking around five to ten years. These are the Jupiter family, which originated in the Kuiper Belt, beyond Neptune, but were caught by the gravity of Jupiter and

Above: The nucleus of Comet Halley seen by the Giotto spacecraft on the night between the 13 and 14 March 1986. It has a potato shape with dimensions 8.2x8.4x16km and a mass of about 100 billion tons. On the left edge of the nucleus active sites are clearly visible. Here the water ice, heated by sunlight, sublimates to form an atmosphere, also known as the coma. The escaping gases sweep up particles of dust which are carried from the nucleus into the coma. These particles form the comet's tail.

Opposite: The comet Hale-Bopp showing its gas and dust tails. Hale-Bopp was one of the brightest comets of the 20th century. Its gas or "ion" tail (blue) consists of ionized glowing gas blown away from the comet head by the solar wind. The dust tail (white) consists of grains of dust pushed away from the comet head by the radiation of sunlight. Comets have a nucleus of ice and dust. As they approach the sun their surface evaporates, releasing a tail millions of kilometers long. Comet Hale-Bopp was discovered on 23 June 1995. Photographed on 6 April 1997 near Wesel, Germany.

locked in to the short orbit we see today. Short-period comets, such as Halley's Comet, have the Kuiper Belt as their aphelion (their farthest point from the sun). The orbits of long-period comets seem to be parabolic. These comets have such great eccentricities because they are returning to the Oort Cloud at the very edge of the solar system. Most long-period comets are never noticed by humans because they orbit the sun at such a great distance that even our best telescopes can not detect them. The Oort

Cloud is so far away from the sun that it is sometimes influenced by the gravity of other stars, which can knock a comet out of its orbit within the Oort Cloud and send it hurtling into the known solar system, where it can be detected and cataloged.

Hale-Bopp

In June 1995, the comet Hale-Bopp was discovered independently by Alan Hale and Thomas Bopp. It became visible to the naked eye during the latter half of 1996, disappearing as it neared the sun at the end of that year. When it reappeared in early 1997, it was a spectacular sight, lasting the entire year. It was easily visible in the sky, even in areas obscured by light pollution. Its longevity made Hale-Bopp spark global interest among astronomers and the general public alike. Astronomers watching it carefully even detected a third tail, comprising sodium, on Hale-Bopp. The last naked-eye observations of the comet were made in December 1997, after a total of more than eighteen months' visibility, which doubled the record for the longest period that a comet had been visible to the unaided eye.

While Hale-Bopp did a great service in bringing comets into the public consciousness, it also had tragic side-effects. Thirty-nine members of the Heaven's Gate cult committed suicide, in the hope that their souls would be transported to an alien vessel following the comet. The deaths of the cult members demonstrate that even at the end of the twentieth century, superstitious interpretations of comets can still prevail.

STARS

I nterstellar hydrogen gas is not found uniformly throughout the universe; instead, it is found in patches because gravitational attraction pulls it together. These patches are molecular clouds, a cradle in which new stars are formed. After millions of years some, as yet unknown, force disrupts the large cloud causing it to break up into smaller clumps of gas, from which a proto-star is born.

The proto-star is a star's formative phase, during which it strives to gain equilibrium between its internal forces and gravity. Proto-stars are usually difficult to detect optically because they are shrouded by thick layers of gas and dust. Proto-stars can last between 100,000 years and 10 million years. During this period, the proto-star spins very rapidly, generating intense heat and pressure causing the cloud to collapse further, meaning more hydrogen is accumulated in the core of the proto-star. Eventually the temperatures and pressures in the star are sufficient that hydrogen fusion can begin, and the star is born.

Gaining equilibrium

Before fusion begins, the proto-star contracts because of the gravitational pressure exerted upon it. Initially a proto-star can be vast; some are billions of kilometers in diameter. Once fusion begins, the star starts to emit electromagnetic radiation, which counterbalances the force of gravity and

causes the star to begin expanding. When the star becomes too massive, the radiation is unable to overcome the force of gravity, which regains the ascendancy and the star contracts until its surface area is of such a size that the force of the radiation is once again greater than the force of gravity and the process repeats itself. This to-ing and fro-ing continues for many years until the star finally reaches equilibrium, when gravity, the external force, is balanced by internal forces. This unstable period is called the star's T Tauri phase, because the star T Tauri was undergoing this process when it was discovered. It can be detected because the star's output of energy fluctuates significantly over time.

The Main Sequence

Once temperatures inside the core are hot enough, hydrogen fusion begins. In this process, hydrogen nuclei are fused together to make helium atoms. When one such

atom is created, a small amount of energy is released. In a stellar core, this occurs millions of times each second, meaning that incredible amounts of energy are generated. When two scientists, Henry Russell and Ejner Hertzsprung, working independently, put this information on a diagram, plotting temperature against luminosity, it emerged that the stars which produced their energy by hydrogen fusion were all banded together at the center of the graph. This band was called the Main Sequence, and all stars in their hydrogen fusion phase belong to it. Most of the stars we see in the celestial sphere are on the Main Sequence. It is the longest and most stable period of a star's life.

The mass of a star determines how long it will remain on the Main Sequence; the most massive stars tend to live fast and die young, rapidly fusing their hydrogen supply, while less massive stars tend to take a long time to complete their process of hydrogen fusion.

Above: Satellite image of the red dwarf Proxima Centauri (center). Explosive outbursts (flares, red) occur almost continually in the star's upper atmosphere. These flares are caused by the star's low mass, which is a tenth that of the sun's. Nuclear fusion reactions that convert hydrogen to helium proceed very slowly in Proxima Centauri, creating a turbulent, convective motion throughout the star's interior. This motion stores up magnetic energy, which is then released explosively. Image taken on 7 May 2000 by the Advanced CCD Imaging Spectrometer (ACIS) aboard NASA's Chandra X-ray Observatory.

Opposite: Star trails over a lake. These streaks of light are formed on long-exposure photographs due to the apparent motion of the stars caused by the Earth's rotation.

Previous page: Splendid starfield centered on the constellation of the Southern Cross (Crux Australis). It shows an area of our galaxy, the Milky Way, extremely rich in star clusters, dark and bright (pink) nebulae. Four bright stars at upper center identify the familiar cross-shaped asterism in the Southern Cross. The two brightest stars at bottom left are Alpha (closer to the edge) and Beta Centauri. The dark round area seen at lower center is the Coal Sack Nebula. It is a cloud of interstellar gas which absorbs the radiation emitted by the stars in this area.

Red dwarf stars take such a long time to fuse their hydrogen supply that no red dwarf has ever left the Main Sequence because not enough time has elapsed since the Big Bang. The mass of a star has implications for its temperature as well as its life expectancy. While the least massive stars have temperatures less than 3000°C, that of the most massive stars can be in excess of 30,000°C. Our sun has a relatively low mass, with core temperatures around 6000°C. The temperature of a star influences its color. The hottest stars glow blue and white, while the coolest stars appear red. Stars with moderate temperatures, including our sun, are yellow and orange.

Failed stars

Sometimes the proto-star never becomes hot enough to undergo hydrogen fusion. Such stars are called brown dwarfs because of their dull red-brown color. The temperatures and pressures never reached high enough in these stars to initiate the process of nuclear fusion in the core. Brown dwarfs can only be a maximum of 80 times more massive than Jupiter; any greater, and the mass would be such that fusion can occur. While stars do not emit most forms of radiation until the fusion process has begun, infra-red radiation is emitted before this stage, while the star is first contracting under the weight of gravity. It is infra-red radiation that has allowed scientists to discover the existence of brown dwarfs, because they are almost impossible to see optically. The first discovery of a brown dwarf, Gliese 229B, was relatively recent, in 1995. Since then, many more have been found. However, the existence of a brown dwarf is usually difficult to confirm because stars are often found in orbiting pairs, called binaries, and there is some controversy over whether a contender is indeed a brown dwarf or if it is just a very large planet. The key difference is in how each object was formed; stars condense out of the interplanetary nebula, while planets are formed by the accretion of smaller particles which form around those new-born stars.

Constellations

Despite there being many millions of stars in the galaxy, optimistic estimates suggest that no more than ten thousand stars are visible from Earth. This is because interstellar gas and dust obscure our view of stars further away. Looking up at the stars has been a pastime of consecutive generations of humanity. Civilizations that existed many thousands of years ago had a first-rate view of the stars, owing to an outdoor lifestyle and a distinct lack of light pollution, which so often obscures our view nowadays. Therefore, the way we identify stars in the sky today is still influenced by the way the ancients viewed the stars – as constellations. Constellations are configurations of stars as they appear from Earth – but because space is three-dimensional, constellations bear no relation as to where stars are actually located. Throughout history, various civilizations have arbitrarily grouped stars so as to produce a representation. Most of the modern constellations come to us from the Ancient Greeks. Forty-eight constellations still recognized today are acknowledged in Ptolemy's book, *The Almagest*, which

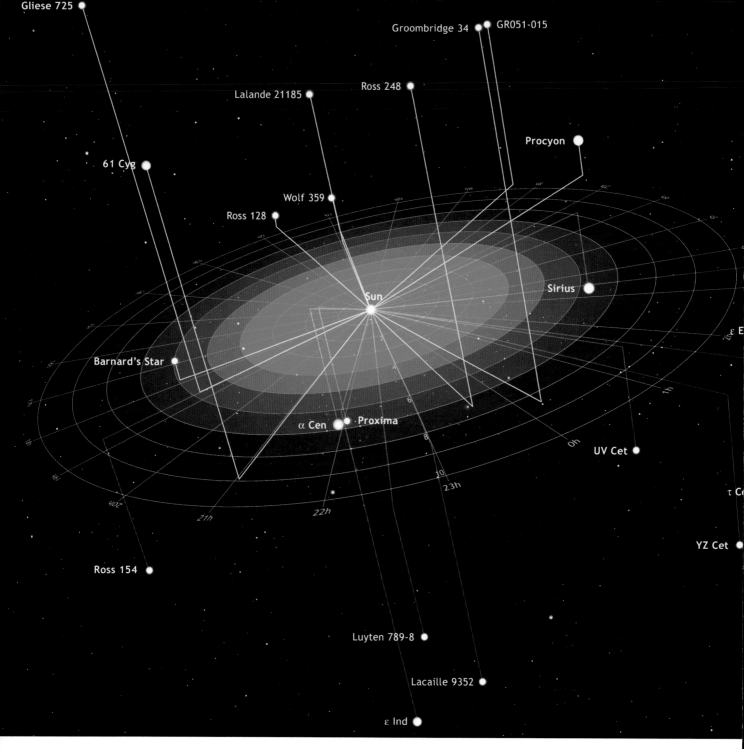

Gliese 725

Groombridge 34   GR051-015

Ross 248

Lalande 21185

Procyon

61 Cyg

Wolf 359

Ross 128

Sun

Sirius

Barnard's Star

α Cen   Proxima

UV Cet

ε E

Ross 154

23h

YZ Cet

21h   22h

Luyten 789-8

Lacaille 9352

ε Ind

contained a summary of the Greek knowledge on astronomy.

One of the most easily recognizable constellations is Orion. According to Greek mythology, Orion was the best hunter in the world. The constellation is probably the most widely recognized of all constellations, because it is visible from most parts of the globe at some point during the year. Several bright stars make up Orion, including two supergiants, Rigel and Betelgeuse, the seventh and tenth brightest stars in the night sky respectively. Orion is most famous for its belt comprising three bright stars; Alnitak,

Alnilam and Mintaka. South of the belt the Orion nebula can also be seen. Orion is flanked by his two hunting dogs – the constellations of Canis Minor and Canis Major. Orion is seen to be fighting the bull, represented by the constellation Taurus. Orion, his hounds and Taurus are not the only mythological figures enshrined in the celestial sphere; Hercules, Cygnus, Andromeda and Cassiopeia are among the 48 listed by Ptolemy.

Twelve of the ancient constellations have a particular importance for astrology. The twelve zodiacal constellations lie close to the ecliptic plane so that all the planets (with the exception of the eccentric Pluto) move across them, leading astrologers to make predictions depending upon which planet is in which constellation.

Today, the International Astronomical Union acknowledges 88 constellations. Most of the additions come from the southern hemisphere, which was not visible to the Ancient Greeks. Fourteen of the new constellations were outlined by the French astronomer Nicolas Louis de Lacaille during a voyage to the Cape of Good Hope in the eighteenth century. Popular star patterns that are not recognized by the International Astronomical Union are named Asterisms. They are an easily recognisable part of a larger constellation, for example Orion's belt is an asterism. The most famous asterism is the Big Dipper, more popularly known as the Plough in Britain. It is part of the constellation Ursa Major (the Great Bear) and only visible in the northern hemisphere.

Neighboring stars

The brightest star in the sky, with the exception of our sun is Sirius, or the Dog Star, in the constellation Canis Major. It is a Main Sequence star more than twice the size of our sun, and the seventh closest to it, at 8.5 light years away; thus, when we look at Sirius, we are seeing light that was generated more than eight years ago. To locate Sirius an observer in the northern hemisphere must look just southwest of Orion's belt.

The nearest star to Earth is Proxima Centauri, part of a triple star system named Alpha Centauri. It is a red dwarf 4.2 light years distant. Although the star is the obvious first destination for a probe, using current technology it would take even the fastest probe 20,000 years to reach it, meaning a mission can be ruled out until our probes can attain much faster speeds. Proxima Centauri is much smaller than the sun, but the other two stars in the Alpha Centauri system, Alpha Centauri A and B, are similar in size, temperature and color to our sun.

Red giants

When a star's core stops fusing hydrogen to make helium, it exits the Main Sequence and enters its death throes. The equilibrium the star fought so arduously to attain at the beginning of its life is upset, as the radiation output ceases and the star begins contracting under gravity. The energy generated by this collapse heats up the stellar atmosphere where hydrogen is still present. The stellar atmosphere becomes so hot and pressurized that fusion of this hydrogen store takes place. This process causes the star to swell in size to become a giant. The increase in surface area of a star causes it to cool, and therefore redden. As such, most giant stars are red giants. The third brightest star in the sky, Arcturus, is a red giant. It is

Below: Galactic Center and Galactic Dark Horse, the Milky Way from Serpens to Scorpius. The Milky Way is the galaxy, made up of some 200 to 400 billion stars and their planets, in which our solar system is positioned. It has a mass of roughly 750 billion to one trillion solar masses and a diameter of about 100,000 light years. Taken near Copper Mountain, Colorado.

Opposite: The 30 stars nearest the sun (center) are found in the 20 star systems shown here. The concentric circles are one light year apart, out to ten light years from the sun, and lines show the positions of the stars above (yellow) or below (red) the celestial equator. The closest stars are part of the Alpha Centauri star system (below sun). The brightest star in the night sky, Sirius, is at center right. The colors of the stars indicate the type of star (sun-like stars are yellow).

expected that our sun will become a red giant in about 5 billion years' time.

Helium fusion

If the temperature in the stellar atmosphere is hot enough to begin hydrogen fusion, the temperature in the core of a giant star is even hotter and under even greater pressure. Core temperatures in giant stars are in excess of 100 million degrees Kelvin. At such temperatures, the nuclear fusion of helium can occur. The conversion of helium into carbon is called a "triple alpha" process, because it requires three helium nuclei. Two helium nuclei are first converted into an unstable beryllium nucleus, which in turn collides with another helium nucleus to form a carbon nucleus. When a further helium nucleus fuses with a new-formed carbon nucleus, oxygen is produced.

Planetary nebulae

The process of helium fusion lasts for several billion years until the helium has run out. Core temperatures in giant stars never get hot enough to fuse the carbon and the oxygen. These stars stop producing energy and instead expel their remaining matter and radiation into space. This process manifests itself across the electromagnetic spectrum. Gamma rays, X-rays, ultra-violet and infrared radiation stream out and can be detected by scientists here on Earth. However, these invisible forms of radiation are not the only way to detect that this process is occurring, because it also manifests itself on the visible portion of the spectrum as a visually stunning planetary nebula. The name "planetary nebula" can be misleading; William Herschel coined the phrase because he thought these spectacles were nebulae resembling the discs of planets. It was only later discovered that these phenomena were dying stars.

White dwarfs

Once the star has ejected its matter, only a core, comprising carbon and oxygen remains. The core continues to shrink under the weight of gravity. The contraction will eventually halt because the atoms are as crushed as they can be; electrons are pushed right up against the nucleus and begin repulsing one another. These relic stars are named white dwarfs. They are exceptionally dense, because so much matter is squeezed into such a small surface area. Any remaining energy and heat is exhausted by the white dwarf so that it reddens in color and will eventually "disappear" – inasmuch as it will no longer be detectable to us; a body of mass will still exist. As the process in which white dwarfs disappear takes billions of years and the universe is a maximum of fifteen billion years old, even the oldest white dwarfs are still detectable.

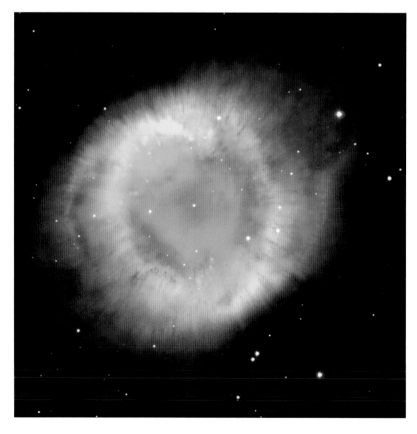

Novas

Most stars in the galaxies are not alone, but they form part of a star system – often in pairs orbiting one another, called binaries – our sun is distinctive in that it does not have a partner star. When a white dwarf forms a part of a two-star system with another, larger star, the gravitational pull of the white dwarf can drag hydrogen from the partner star onto its shell. The gravitational force involved in the process makes the white dwarf once again ripe for hydrogen fusion to occur. All the hydrogen is fused exceptionally rapidly causing a short-lived, extremely bright burst of light. Once all the hydrogen is depleted, the process repeats itself over a number of years; the nova RS Ophiuchi flared five times in the twentieth century. The process repeats until either the white dwarf's companion star runs out of hydrogen or until the star undergoes such a powerful nova that it is destroyed in the process. The term nova from the Latin for "new" was given to the phenomenon because when they were first observed they were thought to be new stars flaring up rather than old ones being given a new lease of life.

Supernova

A supernova is a stellar explosion which is much brighter and more intense than a nova. They are so bright that they are easily visible from Earth. One that appeared in 1572 was said to be as bright as Venus and visible during daylight hours. On average supernovas occur every hundred years or so. The earliest recorded supernovas were observed in the eleventh century; one of those in 1054 was noted by Chinese astronomers in the constellation Cassiopeia, and its remains can still be seen today in the form of the Crab Nebula. As supernovas are so bright it is almost certain that they would have been observed before the eleventh century, but we have no evidence to prove this is the case. In 1572 the Danish astronomer, Tycho Brahe, identified another supernova in Cassiopeia and his colleague, Johannes Kepler, also recorded seeing a supernova in Ophiuchus in 1604. "Kepler's Star", as it became known, was the last supernova to be seen in the Milky Way galaxy. However, at the end of the nineteenth century a supernova could be seen in the Andromeda galaxy. A supernova in the Large Magellanic Cloud in 1987 could be seen with the naked eye in the southern hemisphere, sparking popular interest in supernovas. Unfortunately, this supernova was a few years too early for the Hubble Space Telescope to observe it. Since its launch, Hubble has monitored the after-effects of the supernova, including photographing a large ring of matter which was ejected during the explosion.

Supernovas are formed in two different ways, and therefore they are banded into Type I and Type II categories. Type I supernovas occur in similar circumstances to a nova. When a white dwarf accretes an unsustainable amount of hydrogen gas from its partner star, it begins to collapse and the white dwarf is destroyed in a mighty explosion, a supernova.

When stars exit the Main Sequence, having burned all their hydrogen, we have seen that they turn into red

Above: Death of the sun. Artwork of the sun forming a planetary nebula 5 billion years from now. Ejected gas (purple) is expanding towards the lifeless Earth (lower right) and moon (lower left) from the dying sun (upper center). This stage in the life of the sun follows its expansion during its red giant stage. When its nuclear fuel has been used up, its outer layers are ejected in this way. The remnant cools to forms a white dwarf star.

Opposite: Enhanced optical image of the Helix planetary nebula (NGC 7293). This is the nearest planetary nebula to Earth, lying about 450 light years away in the constellation Aquarius. Planetary nebulae are poorly named, as they have no association with either planets or nebulae. Instead, they consist of shells of gas ejected from the surface of a dying star. This is ionized by radiation from the star, causing it to glow. Their erroneous name arose from their appearance through early telescopes.

giants and undergo the fusion of helium into carbon and oxygen. However, stars which were already giants while they were on the Main Sequence are an exception to this trend. They swell up so greatly that they become supergiants. This means that not only are they able to fuse helium but subsequently also the carbon and oxygen. Oxygen fuses to create neon, which in turn fuses to create magnesium; the process continues and forges silicon from magnesium and then iron from silicon. The fusion process does not create any more energy by the time an iron core has been reached, so the iron is not fused. When the core of a supergiant star turns to iron, it has reached the end of the road. The star collapses under the colossal gravitational forces at play on the heavy iron core. This swift collapse results in an immense explosion: a Type II supernova, as the star ejects its material in a spectacular shockwave. The energy produced during a supernova is so great that fusion of iron can finally begin; thus, it is only because of supernovas that we have all the elements heavier than iron.

The supergiant Betelgeuse in the Orion constellation will inevitably become a Type II supernova. It is the ninth brightest star in the night sky, so the supernova will be a remarkable sight. Some scientists believe that the star may already be in its carbon fusion stage, meaning that the star could become a supernova in less than one thousand years.

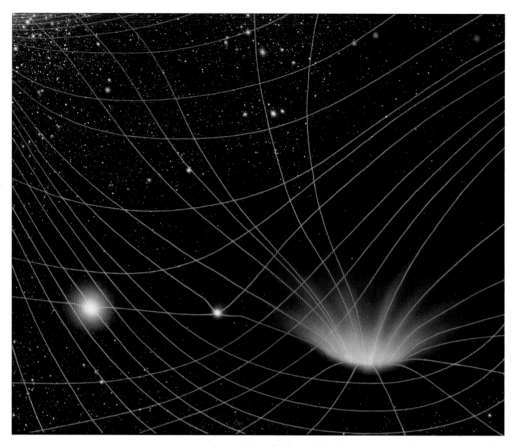

Above: Artwork illustrating the concept of warped space. The fabric of space is represented as a grid in which objects of increasing mass produce increasingly large distortions. Our sun, at bottom left, makes almost no impression. A small, but much denser and more massive neutron star (lower center), creates a slight distortion. The enormous gravitational pull of a black hole (bottom right) creates a yawning chasm, warping the fabric of space for light years around. The idea that space is distorted by gravity is a consequence of Einstein's Theory of Relativity. The grid of space is like a thin rubber sheet on which objects of varying weight produce smaller or larger dents.

Opposite: Hubble space telescope (HST) optical image of quasar PG 0052+251 at the center of a spiral galaxy. The quasar is the bright object at center, surrounded by the outer arms of the galaxy. Quasars are massive black holes at the center of galaxies. The gravitational field of the black hole drags in matter, including interstellar gas and whole stars. This matter releases intense radiation as it falls towards the hole. Quasars are normally several hundred billion times brighter than normal stars. Quasar PG 0052+251 is about 1.4 billion light-years away.

Neutron Star

After a supernova all that remains is the star's core. What becomes of the core depends upon its mass. Cores with a mass of between 1.4 and 3 times that of our sun become neutron stars. The figure of 1.4 solar masses was calculated by the Indian astronomer Subrahmanyan Chandrasekhar in 1930, and is known as the Chandrasekhar Limit. In a white dwarf, the core cannot collapse any further because of the electron repulsion. However, if a star is more than 1.4 times as massive as our sun, gravity would be sufficient to overcome this hurdle. The negatively-charged electrons are pushed into the nucleus where they collide with the positively-charged protons to leave a neutrally-charged core of neutrons. There is insufficient gravity for stars to collapse further, the outward force of the neutrons balances the inward force of gravity. This star, with its neutron core, is unimaginatively named a neutron star. These stars are exceptionally small, averaging just 20km in diameter. A mass at least 1.4 times as great as our sun is condensed into such a small area, making neutron stars the densest objects in the universe.

Pulsars

Even though a neutron star has been through a turbulent supernova, it continues to rotate, just as the original star did. However, because it is much smaller and therefore much denser, it rotates at breakneck speeds. The rotational energy generates electromagnetic radiation which is emitted along the magnetic poles. As the magnetic poles face us we are able to detect this radiation in pulses, like the beam of a lighthouse. The radiation is mostly emitted as radiowaves so they were initially named radio pulsars, but gamma ray and x-ray emission have subsequently been detected. The first pulsar, PSR 1919+21, was discovered by Antony Hewish and Jocelyn Bell Burnell in 1967, but they could not explain what it was. It was labeled LGM-1 meaning Little Green Men, referring to the fact that such pulsating radio waves could have been emitted by extra-terrestrials. However, the matter was cleared up just a year later when it was discovered that the radio signals were emissions from rotating neutron stars. Since 1967 hundreds of pulsars have been discovered. They provide an excellent beacon for astronomers wishing to locate neutron stars. Antony Hewish shared the Nobel Prize for Physics in 1974 for his part in the discovery of pulsars.

Black hole

If the star undergoing a gravitational collapse is three or more times as massive as our own sun, gravity is so strong that the collapse is unstoppable, even the neutrons are crushed. The result is a black hole. The mass of a massive star collapses into a point without any volume, called a singularity. With such a large mass in an infinitely small area, the gravitational force of the black hole is so strong that the escape velocity required for an object to overcome it is greater than the speed of light (300,000,000 meters per second). The speed of light is the maximum attainable speed in the solar system, nothing can exceed it, meaning nothing can escape a black hole. As no light can escape, this phenomenon can not be detected optically (or indeed by any other emissions on the electromagnetic spectrum), leading the American physicist, John Wheeler, to coin the term "black hole" in 1967. Before that time the term "black star" was in wider use, which is perhaps more in keeping

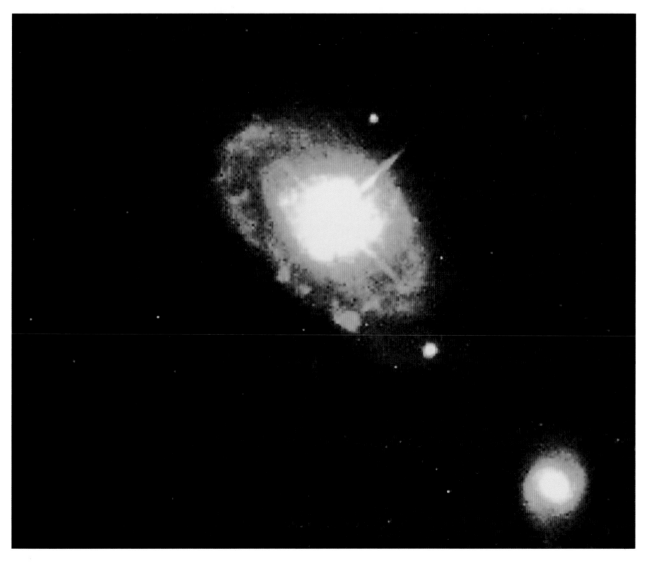

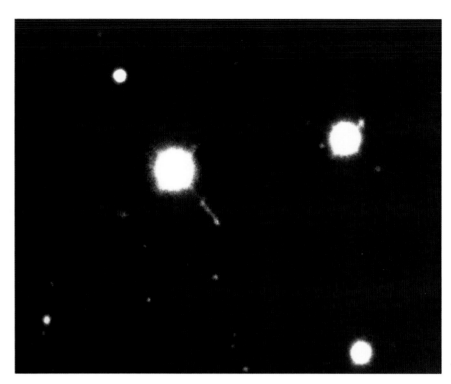

Above: Quasar 3C 273, optical image. The quasar (center) is seen with a jet pointing towards lower right. The jet, some 150,000 light years long, is thought to be ejected material accelerated by the black hole. Quasars are among the most powerful and distant sources of radiation in the universe. 3C 273, 2000 million light years away, is the nearest and brightest of the quasars. In 1962, it was the first quasar to be recognised as a quasar. Photographed by the KPNO 4-meter telescope, Kitt Peak, Arizona, USA.

Opposite above: Colored Chandra telescope X- ray spectrum of the black hole binary system XTE J1118+480. The spectrum (narrow line, top left to bottom right) shows the X-ray energies emitted by the system. The highest energy emissions are nearest to the center of the spectrum. This system is thought to be composed of a sun-like star orbiting a black hole (a star that has collapsed under its own gravity). The spectrum was measured by Chandra's Low-energy X-ray Transmission Grating (LETG), which collects the system's X-rays and then changes their direction by different amounts according to their energies.

Opposite below: Hubble Space Telescope optical image of a massive black hole in the center of the elliptical galaxy NGC 7052. Surrounding the galaxy is a 3,700 light-year (LY) diameter dust disc (brown). The bright spot (white, center) is light from stars crowded around the black hole due to its powerful gravitational pull. This black hole is about 300 million times the mass of our sun. The disc rotates 341,000 miles per hour; the dust may come from an ancient galaxy collision. NGC 7052 in the constellation Vulpecula is 191 million light-years from Earth.

with the naming of other stellar remnants such as neutron stars and white dwarfs.

The Event Horizon

In 1916 the German astronomer, Karl Schwarzschild, calculated the radius to which a given mass would need to shrink if light were no longer to be able to escape. The Schwarzschild Radius for any star can be worked out using his equation: for example, if our sun was to become a black hole, it would need to shrink to a size less than 3km in radius. Schwarzschild died of an illness while fighting for Germany on the Eastern Front against Russia in the same year he calculated the Schwarzschild Radius. His calculations have been influential in the study of black holes. The Schwarzschild Radius is synonomous with the term "Event Horizon" which is the point at which light can no longer escape. The star continues to collapse beyond this point, to a singularity, but it is the Event Horizon which forms the boundary between the detectable and the undetectable universe.

Detecting a Black Hole

As no information can be detected within the Event Horizon, scientists must employ indirect methods to detect a black hole. Most stars form pairs or binaries which orbit one another; if a star can be seen orbiting a point which does not emit any form of radiation, it is assumed that it is a binary star whose partner star has become a black hole. Another clue is accretion discs of material that is being drawn towards the black hole, often from a partner star in a binary system. They can be detected because x-rays are emitted periodically as the material gathers in the disc. Unlike x-rays emitted by pulsars which are regular and substantial, x-ray signals from black hole accretion discs are irregular and extremely short-lived. Such an x-ray source has been detected in the constellation Cygnus (the swan) and is called Cygnus X-1. Analysis of the star nearest the source, HDE 226868, has indicated that it is part of a binary system, but its binary star cannot be detected. Additionally, it has been calculated that the source of the x-rays is massive yet compacted; consequently, a black hole has become the obvious solution.

For a number of reasons, we can never decisively say

that Cygnus X-1 or the 20 other contenders are in fact black holes. Firstly, we can never retrieve information because to do so would require an escape velocity greater than the speed of light, which Einstein has proved impossible to exceed. Secondly, even if a probe were able to return, the gravitational stresses placed upon it as it crosses the Event Horizon would be so great that it would be destroyed by tidal forces, but not before being stretched out like "spaghetti" as the British physicist Stephen Hawking termed it. Thirdly, even if, in some physics-defying miracle, an astronaut and his ship were not destroyed by tidal forces and were able to exceed the necessary escape velocity, the time taken to enter the black hole would seem like an eternity by our standards on Earth. This follows Einstein's General Theory of Relativity which, in part, asserts that time, as observed from one gravitational field, appears to pass differently in another gravitational field. This is known as gravitational "time dilation". In strong gravitational fields time passes more slowly, relative to a weaker gravitational field. If an astronaut in space viewed a clock on Earth, the clock would be moving more slowly than his own clock onboard his ship. Although the passage of time is different, the astronaut would not notice the change. The gravitational field of a black hole is so immense that time passes much quicker on Earth than it does in a black hole, so even if our physics-defying astronaut was able to return home, great swathes of time would have passed on Earth, but the astronaut would not have felt any difference. So even if we could go and retrieve information from inside, it would take too long to get it back to Earth. With all these factors stacked against them, scientists cannot confirm without a shadow of a doubt that black holes exist in reality.

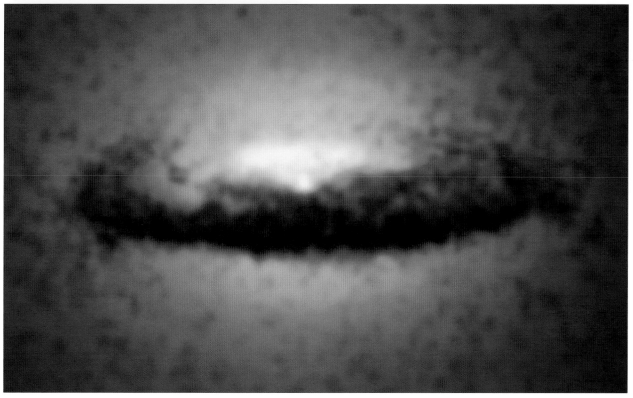

CONSTELLATIONS

For the ancients the importance of observation of the heavens cannot be underestimated. It was the means by which the cycles of the year and longer term phases in time could be measured, calculated and foretold. Astronomers in all early civilizations saw patterns in the stars by which time and place could be fixed. Inevitably perhaps, the eternal and apparently unchanging nature of the skies meant that they became closely associated with, or indeed identified as, these civilizations' gods. Thus stars and star patterns were incorporated into mythologies concerning the exploits of deities and their interactions with humanity, so that many of the constellations we can view today are named after beings and objects in those ancient tales.

The stars' relationship with gods and their unchanging nature lead also to a belief that somehow they controlled the fate of individuals and societies. In the past, many who we would today class as astronomers, and thus scientists, would also practice astrology – trying to divine the future from the positions of stars and constellations. The most well-known astrological symbol is the zodiac, a calendar of constellations which appear in the skies of the northern hemisphere as the year progresses; it was believed (and still is by some people) that the dominant constellation at the the time of birth would determine the character and fate of an individual.

In the west, learning and knowledge developed from Greek and Roman civilizations and this is where many of the internationally acknowledged names for stars and constellations have their origins. What follows here is just a taste of some of those constellations, describing where, and when, they can be located in the night sky. Most are visible from the northern hemisphere, but some, like Crux, or the Southern Cross, can only be seen from the southern hemisphere. It is important to remember when looking at individual stars in a given constellation that, while from the Earth they are in the same region of the sky, they may be millions of light years distant from each other.

Aquarius
The Water Bearer

Above: Aquarius is the eleventh of the twelve constellations of the Zodiac. It is an extensive southern hemisphere constellation. The whole area of the sky in which it lies was associated in ancient times with water. The Babylonians called the area the Sea, and populated it with ocean creatures such as Cetus, Pisces, Capricornus, Delphinus - all controlled by Aquarius. The Egyptian hieroglyph for water is the same as the symbol used for Aquarius.

Aries
The Ram

Below: Aries is the first of the twelve signs of the Zodiac, because in ancient times is was where the sun's path crossed the celestial equator. Since then this point has passed into Pisces due to the Earth's wobble (precession). Aries has been associated with the ram for at least 2000 years. The Greeks associated Aries with the story of the Argonauts and the Golden Fleece. The Chinese called it the Dog, part of a larger figure that included Taurus and Gemini.

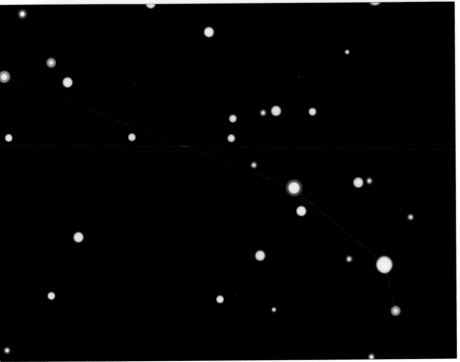

Crux
The Southern Cross

Opposite: The dark patch just below center is called the Coal Sack. It is a nearby dark nebula which obscures the light of the bright Milky Way behind it. The bright star at the left of the cross, just above the Coal Sack, is Mimosa (Beta Crucis). To the right of the Coal Sack, at the foot of the cross, is Acrux (Alpha Crucis). The bright star at far left is Hadar (Beta Centauri) in the neighboring constellation Centaurus, the centaur. Crux is best seen in the fall from the southern hemisphere.

Gemini
The Twins

Left: The twins are the two brightest stars in the lower right of the constellation, with Pollux above and to the right of Castor. In Roman mythology they were the sons of Leda the Swan. Born of the same egg, they were placed in the heavens because of their brotherly love, although they represent the opposing principles of war (Castor) and peace (Pollux). They were also the guardians of Rome and its sailors.

Leo
The Lion

Below: Leo is the fifth of the twelve signs of the zodiac. The stars of Leo form two groups, a triangle forming the Lion's haunches and tail, whilst a sickle-shape forms its head and mane. Leo's brightest star, Regulus, is at the base of the sickle and seems to be more important in mythology than the lion itself. The Egyptians accorded it power because the annual Nile flood came at the time when the sun entered Leo.

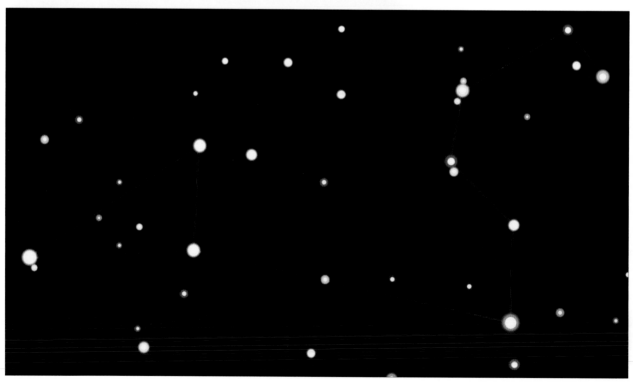

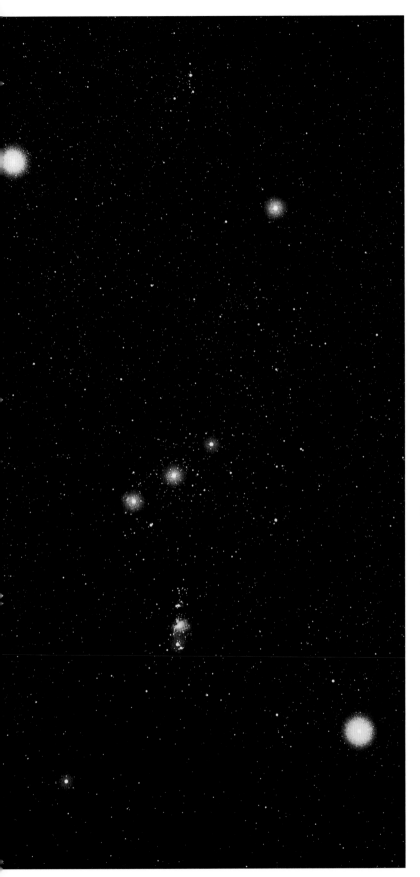

Orion

Left: The most prominent feature of the Orion constellation is Orion's Belt, a row of three bright stars (center left). From left to right, these are Alnitak, Alnilam and Mintaka (Zeta, Epsilon and Delta Orionis respectively). At upper left is the red supergiant star Betelgeuse (Alpha Orionis). The blue supergiant star Rigel (Beta Orionis) is at lower right. Directly below the belt, the Orion Nebula is seen as a pink smudge. Orion's Belt straddles the celestial equator, so the constellation is seen equally well from both hemispheres.

Below: Diagram of stars and other objects in the Orion constellation. This is one of the equatorial constellations visible in both hemispheres of Earth. It is easily recognised by the three stars forming a straight line: Orion's belt. The other object labeled here is McNeil's Nebula (center). This is a variable nebula that was discovered in January 2004. It is variable because the star at its tip varies in brightness. The nebula is the cloud of gas and dust surrounding the star. It is about 1500 light-years from Earth.

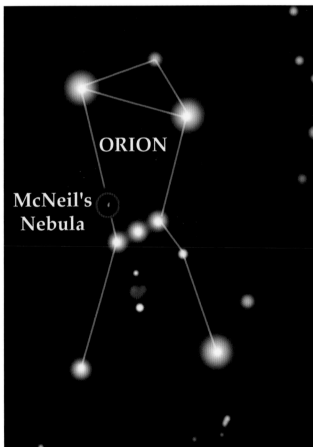

Pisces
The Fish

Left: Pisces, the twelfth of the twelve constellations of the Zodiac, is a large but inconspicuous constellation. It appears as a fish, or two fishes, in several ancient cultures. In Greco-Roman mythology, the two fish represent Venus and her son Cupid, plunging into the Euphrates when the monster Typhon attacked them. They became the fish whose images were raised into the sky.

Sagittarius
The Archer

Center: Sagittarius lies between Scorpius and Capricornus. It is a large southern constellation which contains the star clouds of the central Milky Way (gray), lying in the direction of the center of our galaxy. Sagittarius is depicted as a centaur holding a bow and arrow which is pointed at the star Antares, the heart of Scorpius (the scorpion). In the past, the constellation has been depicted as a human archer, a bow and arrow and, by the ancient Egyptians, as a lion.

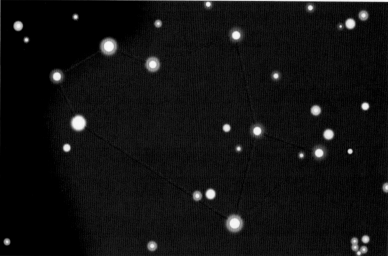

Capricornus
Sea Goat

Below: Capricornus lies just south of the celestial equator, but is still visible to northern observers during early evenings in the fall. It is one of the twelve zodiacal constellations, lying between Aquarius and Sagittarius. In ancient times the whole area surrounding Aquarius was associated with water or rain. The Babylonians called it the Sea and populated it with ocean creatures like Capricornus, Cetus (the Whale), Pisces (the Fishes) and Delphinus (the Dolphin), all under the control of Aquarius.

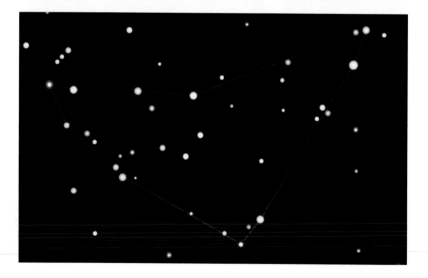

Scorpius
The Scorpion

Left: Scorpius lies between Sagittarius and Libra. It is an important summer constellation for northern hemisphere observers, containing many bright stars, and the star clouds, nebulae and dust lanes of the Milky Way. In mythology, the scorpion was the creature whose sting killed Orion, so the gods placed these constellations on opposite sides of the sky.

Taurus
The Bull

Below: Taurus is the second of the twelve constellations or signs of the Zodiac. The most distinctive feature of Taurus is the v-shape formed by the Hyades star cluster at the base of the constellation's "horns". Taurus is a very ancient constellation, possibly deriving from bull worship in early Mediterranean civilizations. In the mythology of ancient Greece, Taurus was the bull which carried Europa, only to be revealed as Zeus in disguise.

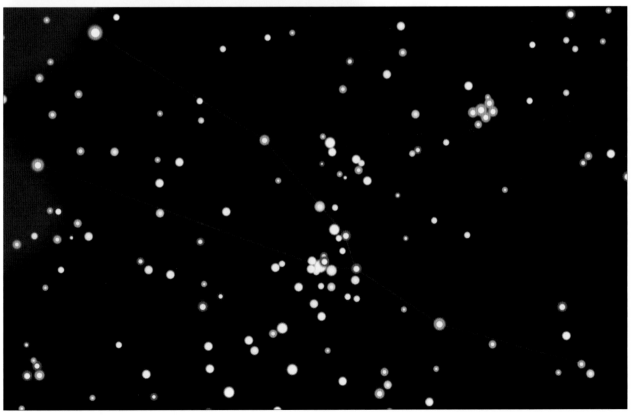

Virgo
The Virgin

Above: The virgin is an old and astrologically important constellation associated with a mother goddess. She was Kanya, mother of Krishna, in India; Ishtar in Babylonia; Isis in Egypt. In Greece and Rome, she was Astreae, daughter of Zeus and Themis.

Libra

The Scales of Balance

Below: Libra is a relatively inconspicuous constellation in the southern hemisphere. Libra was apparently a creation of Roman times; before that it was joined with Scorpius in a double constellation called Scorpius cum chelae, the Scorpion with Claws. Libra was known as the balance beam in India and Middle Eastern cultures before Roman times.

North celestial pole

Opposite below: Optical image of the stars around the north celestial pole. This is marked by the pole star Polaris (Alpha Ursae Minoris, upper center) in the constellation Ursa Minor, the Little Bear. At far right, three of the bright stars in the Plough (part of Ursa Major, the Great Bear) are seen. Surrounding Ursa Minor is the faint constellation Draco, the dragon. The head of the dragon is formed by the quadrilateral of stars at lower left. The brightest of these is the orange star Eltanin (Gamma Draconis), which is just to the left of the white star Rastaban (Beta Draconis), a name meaning "head of the snake".

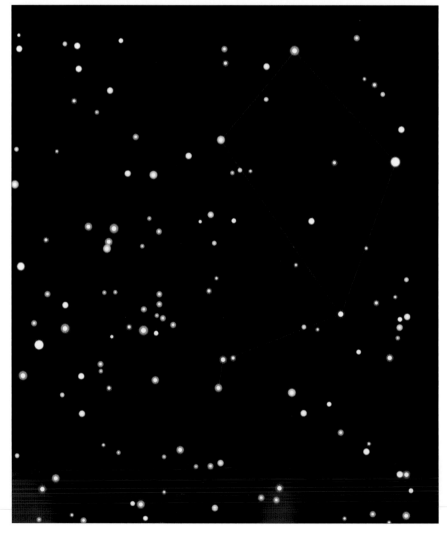

Ursa Major
The Great Bear

The northern constellation of Ursa Major, the Great Bear. The upper left part is also known as the Plough or Big Dipper. This is the third largest constellation in the sky. The Plough forms the back and tail of the bear, with its head and legs being represented by fainter stars at upper right and lower frame respectively.

Canis Major
The Great Dog

At upper right is Sirius (Alpha Canis Majoris), the brightest star in the sky. It is a blue-white star which lies only 8.6 light-years from Earth. At bottom right is the second brightest star in the sky, Canopus (Alpha Carinae), in the constellation Carina, the keel. Canopus lies around 72 light-years from Earth. Canis Major is a winter constellation for northern hemisphere observers.

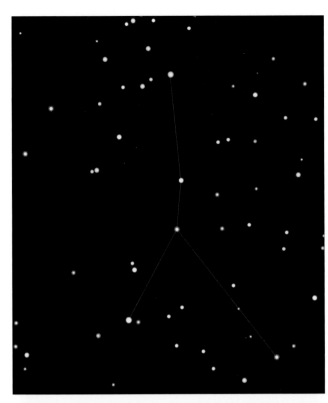

Cancer
The Crab

Left: Cancer is a relatively inconspicuous constellation. In Greek mythology, Cancer was associated with Hercules. The crab was sent by the goddess Hera to bite the hero's foot as he was struggling with the multi-headed Hydra. Hercules killed the crab by treading on it, but Hera placed its image in the heavens.

Pegasus
The Winged Horse

Below: The body of the horse is formed from the square of stars at lower left. Clockwise from the orange star just left of center (Scheat, or Beta Pegasi), these are Markab (Alpha Pegasi), Algenib (Gamma Pegasi) and Alpheratz (Alpha Andromedae). Alpheratz is not actually part of Pegasus, instead lying in neighboring Andromeda. The horse's nose is Enif (Epsilon Pegasi), at lower right. The bright star at upper right is Deneb (Alpha Cygni) in the constellation Cygnus (the swan). To its right is the red North America nebula (NGC 7000).

NEBULAE

The term nebula, meaning "mist" in Latin, was once applied to any fuzzy patch of light in the night sky. In Charles Messier's directory of nebulae and star clusters, he identified 110 objects. Many of the objects originally thought to be nebula were later discovered to be galaxies outside our own.

However, Messier had cataloged a number of genuine nebulae, including the Crab Nebula, which was his Messier Object number 1. He also indexed, among several others, the Eagle, Triffid, Omega, and Orion nebulae.

Nebulae are now known to be interstellar clouds of gas and dust within our own galaxy. This interstellar material is not spread evenly throughout the galaxy; instead vast areas dense in gas and dust can be found, having clumped together as a result of gravity. Nebulae are factories of star formation. Our own planetary system is

thought to have formed from one, the Solar Nebula. There are two different types of interstellar cloud, H I regions and molecular clouds (H II regions). Interstellar clouds are usually exceptionally cold, almost minus 300^0 Celsius, with the result that the atoms join together to form molecules and the cloud is known as a molecular cloud or H II region. The main constituent is molecular hydrogen, but water, ammonia and hydrocarbons are also present. Under different conditions, molecular clouds give rise to three different types of nebulae: emission nebulae and reflection

Above: Horsehead nebula. True-color optical image of the Horsehead nebula in the constellation Orion. North is to the left. The horsehead shape is formed by the intrusion of the dark nebula B33 into the bright emission nebula IC 434. The emission nebula shines red due to the ionization of its hydrogen gas by radiation from hot young stars embedded in it.

Opposite: Optical image of the Crab Nebula, also known as Messier 1. The nebula is the remnant of a supernova explosion observed in 1054 AD, and consists mainly of hydrogen gas. The nebula is 6000 light years from Earth in the constellation Taurus. This image was made using the 8.2-meter Very Large Telescope "Kueyen" at Cerro Paranal Observatory, Chile

Right: Triffid Nebula (M20, NGC 6514), Spitzer Space Telescope infrared image. This nebula is located 5,400 light-years away in the constellation Sagittarius. The infra-red telescope enabled scientists to view the star formation within the nebula. Within each of the four red dust clouds, comprising the lower object, there are embryonic stars. Because particles falling towards these stars get hotter with their increased energy, Spitzer can see them. It is believed that our sun was formed in such a region, but its small size led to it being gravitationally expelled.

nebulae, which are both optically visible, and dark nebulae which can sometimes be detected visibly if the cloud obscures our view of light shining behind it.

Regions of space less dense in interstellar matter are called H I (Hydrogen One) regions. They are composed of atomic hydrogen and are not luminous – they can only be detected by the specific 21cm radio wave that the phenomenon emits. Another way of detecting H I regions is that when they come into contact with an emission nebula they cause greater luminosity of that nebula.

Emission nebulae

Interstellar gas is usually invisible and obscures our view of far-off objects. However, when the interstellar gas is near a powerful star or a tight cluster of stars, it is illuminated to form spectacular emission nebulae. For one star to illuminate the nebula, it needs to be an exceptionally hot star, which emits most of its energy as ultraviolet radiation. Photons from these stars ionize the interstellar gases, and the electrons stripped away during the ionization process

Below: Hubble Space Telescope image showing dark pillars of dense molecular hydrogen and dust in the Eagle Nebula (M16). Ultraviolet light from young stars (out of frame) evaporates gas from the one light-year long pillars, creating the blue halo-like effect. The small protrusions on the pillars contain globules of even denser gas which are embryonic stars; these have been dubbed Evaporating Gaseous Globules, or EGGs. The evaporation of the pillar limits the amount of gas and dust which these embryonic stars can gather. The Eagle Nebula is about 7000 light-years from Earth.

Opposite: Rho Ophiuchi nebula. True-color optical image of nebulosity (IC 4604) surrounding the star Rho Ophiuchi (upper center) in the constellation Ophiuchus. This is an excellent example of a reflection nebula. These clouds of gas and dust do not have any light of their own, but reflect the light of nearby stars. They typically appear blue as blue light is scattered more than red light. Dark dust clouds can be seen blocking the light of background stars at lower left. The reddish star at lower right is Omicron Scorpii, in Scorpius. This image was produced by digitally combining photographs taken by the UK Schmidt Telescope in blue and red light.

try to recombine with the atomic nuclei. This process can be detected on the visible portion of the spectrum, making nebulae among the most striking sights in the galaxy.

Emission nebulae are very often reddish in color, because of the position in the visible spectrum at which hydrogen manifests itself during this process. The reason for the predominance of hydrogen in emission nebulae is not only that hydrogen is simply the most abundant element in the universe but also because less energy is required to ionize hydrogen than other elements. When the ionizing stars are so powerful that they are able to ionize other elements as well, this interrupts the uniform red with other colors.

There are dark patches within emission nebulae where interstellar dust obscures our optical view of parts of the nebula. These areas need to be charted using radio waves, which have longer wavelengths, unobstructed by the interstellar medium.

Reflection nebulae

When the nearby star is not hot enough to cause ionization of a nearby molecular cloud, the light from the star is instead reflected and scattered by the cloud, making it optically visible. Scattering favors the shorter wavelength, blue-colored portion of the visible spectrum meaning that most reflection nebulae appear blue.

Dark nebula

Dark nebulae occur when molecular clouds are not lit up by a nearby star; the particles in the cloud cannot be detected optically. Usually these nebulae go undetected against the dark backdrop of space, but sometimes they block out the view of a cluster of stars or an emission nebula, with the consequence that their impressive silhouettes can clearly be seen. The best views of dark nebulae are in the plane of the Milky Way. The thick profile of stars is frequently broken up by dark patches which are in fact dark nebulae.

Above: The Orion nebula can be seen with the naked eye as a fuzzy patch in the constellation Orion.

Opposite: Rosette nebula, optical image. The nebula is cataloged as NGC 2237-2239. It surrounds the star cluster NGC 2244 (center). This is a vast starbirth region, where coalescence of the nebula's gas led to the formation of the stars in the cluster. The stellar winds of these stars have cleared a hole in the region around them, and their radiation ionizes the hydrogen in the surrounding nebula, causing it to emit pink light. The cluster and nebula are around 5000 light-years from Earth in the constellation Monocero.

MILKY WAY

T he Milky Way is the name given to our own galaxy because, as it is seen from Earth, it appears to be a milky-colored brushstroke sweeping across the night sky. The fact that this whitish band is actually millions of stars was not discovered until Galileo became the first person known to observe the phenomenon through his telescope.

Today, the Milky Way is thought to contain over 200 billion stars, and an immeasurable amount of interstellar gas and dust.

It is impossible to know exactly what the Milky Way looks like because we do not have an objective viewpoint of our galaxy. Nevertheless, observations of other galaxies, as well as the subjective view from Earth and conscientious telescopic studies, have shown the Milky Way to be a large barred-spiral galaxy. At its center is the galactic bulge, a spheroid-shaped body of stars encasing the galactic core. Surrounding the bulge is a much flatter area of spiral arms, named the galactic disc. The disc and bulge are enveloped by a galactic halo, a thin veil of interstellar dust and dark matter broken up by globular clusters of stars. Although the amount of visible matter decreases sharply at the outer edge of the galaxy, this region of space is curiously massive. Scientists claim this mass is something called dark matter – matter which cannot be detected on the electromagnetic spectrum. The dark matter surrounding our galaxy is named the dark halo, but scientists remain unsure of its nature or origin.

Previous page: Milky Way, optical image. The Milky Way is our own galaxy. Because Earth lies in one of its spiral arms, we look into the central mass of stars and see the galaxy as a band of light crossing the sky. There are numerous nebulae (pink) visible here. The brightest, just left of center, is the Lagoon Nebula (M8). Emission nebulae such as these glow red due to ionization of their hydrogen gas by radiation from hot young stars embedded within.

Below: The Milky Way in Scorpius and Ophiucus. The Milky Way is the galaxy, made up of over 200 billion stars and their planets, in which our solar system is positioned. It has a mass of roughly 750 billion to one trillion solar masses and a diameter of about 100,000 light-years. Taken near Copper Mountain, Colorado.

Opposite: The Milky Way from Vulpecula to Scutum.

Origins of our galaxy

Much remains unknown about the formation of our galaxy; it is thought that a great cloud of gas collapsed under the weight of its own gravity between ten and fifteen billion years ago. The first stars produced by the collapsing cloud are those found in the galactic halo, and when we learn more about these stars, we will gain a greater understanding of the origins of the galaxy. The stars in the galactic bulge are similar in age to those in the galactic halo. Unlike our sun, these are Population II stars – small reddish stars that are exceptionally old – as old as the galaxy itself. The disc mostly contains Population I stars, such as our own sun, which are much younger and hotter than stars found in the bulge. Hydrogen and other gases and materials probably ended up here following the gas cloud's collapse, so the process of star formation has persisted in the galactic disc.

Our sun's location

Our solar system is found on the inner rim of the Orion Arm, a minor arm found towards the edge of our galaxy. In

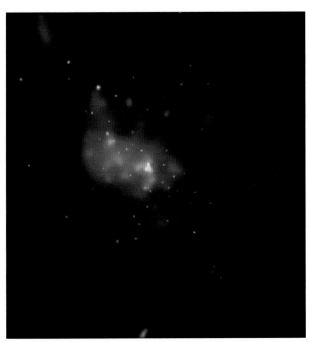

Above: Colored Chandra X-ray telescope image of the center of our galaxy, the Milky Way. The bright white/yellow patch in the center of the image is an X-ray flare released by material falling towards the Sagittarius A radio source. Sagittarius A is believed to be a supermassive black hole, a star that has collapsed under its own gravity. It is thought to have a mass of around 2.6 million times that of the sun. Matter falling towards Sagittarius A is thought to fuel energetic activity at the galactic center.

Opposite: The Milky Way from Scutum to Sagittarius.

the eighteenth century William Herschel stated that the Earth was located in the middle of the disc because the stars seemed similar in abundance in both directions. However, this is, in fact, an optical illusion because light from stars is absorbed by interstellar dust and gas, which meant that our view is equally restricted in both directions, giving the impression that we were in the middle of the disc. It was not until 1918 that Harlow Shapley worked out the Earth's position within our galaxy by observing the distances of globular clusters.

From its position on the outskirts of the Milky Way, it takes the solar system 220 million years to complete one revolution of the core.

Galactic core

The galactic bulge comprises the galactic core – the very center of our galaxy – and a group of tightly packed stars surrounding it. Scientists are still unsure of its exact nature because interstellar dust blinds us from detecting its properties by observations using visible means, ultraviolet or x-ray wavelengths. Analysis of the cores of other galaxies has suggested that massive black holes might be found at their centers. The incredible gravitational pull of a massive black hole would explain why billions of stars are held in orbit of a galaxy's core. Evidence is now available to support the existence of a black hole at the center of the Milky Way; black holes can be indirectly detected by powerful x-ray and radio emissions in the accretion disc produced by material orbiting a black hole. Such x-rays and radio waves are not obscured by the interstellar dust which blinds us from seeing the galactic core optically, so, if there were a black hole at the center of our galaxy, scientists would need to find a radio or x-ray source. Such a source has been found. Emitting from the constellation Sagittarius, in the direction scientists expect the galactic core to be, it is named Sagittarius A. More work is needed, but the evidence in favor of a black hole at the center of the Milky Way is compelling.

Observing the Milky Way

On a clear night, in areas devoid of light pollution, the Milky Way can be observed as a luminous band of stars cutting across the middle of the night sky. What you will actually be seeing is the galactic disc in profile. The Milky Way appears brighter near the constellations of Sagittarius and Scorpio where the stars become densely packed in the galactic bulge where the galactic core is located. However, do not expect to be able to see the core; the interstellar dust which hampers scientist from optically viewing the core, will mask it to the amateur astronomer as well.

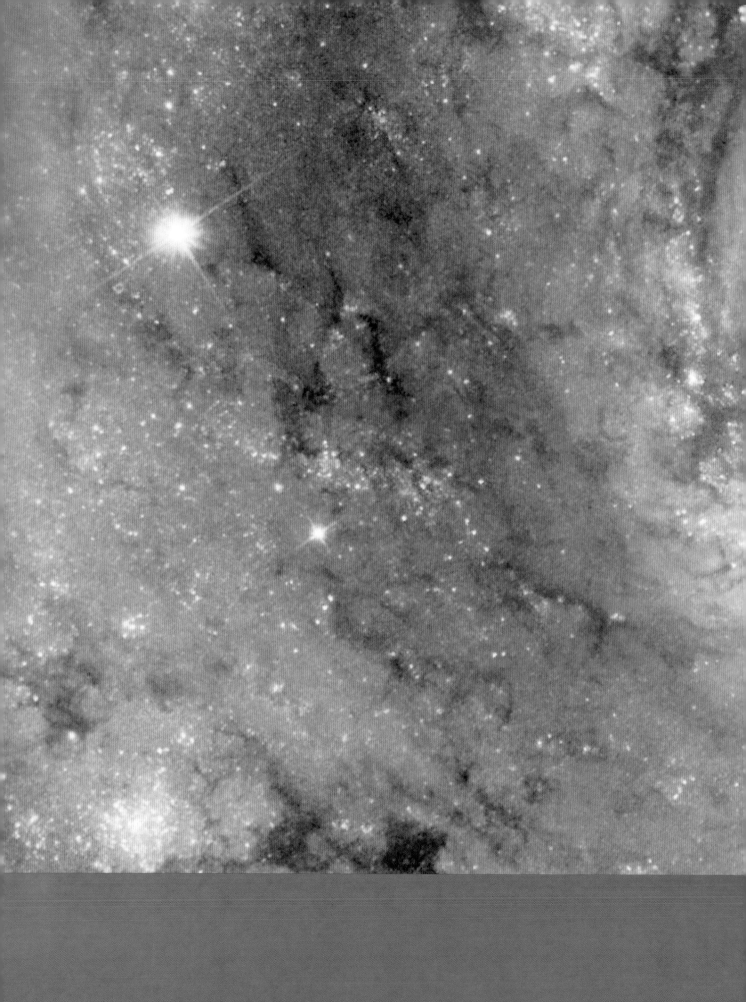

GALAXIES

I n the early 1920s, studies by the renowned American astronomer, Edwin Hubble, showed that our galaxy, the Milky Way, was not the only galaxy in the universe. For a long time it had been believed that the universe and the Milky Way were one and the same thing, but the discovery of other galaxies, outside our own, greatly expanded the size of the known universe.

Within four hundred years Earth had been consecutively demoted from its position as center of the cosmos, to being one of several planets orbiting a star, which turned out to be rather unexceptional and on the periphery of a galaxy, which proved to be just one of countless numbers of galaxies.

Light from other galaxies

Other galaxies had been observed throughout history, but few had imagined that these fuzzy balls of light did not emanate from within our own galaxy. Immanuel Kant

suggested in the mid-eighteenth century that these phenomena might be a group of stars clustered together by gravity, and that what was being observed might be galaxies separate to our own. Nevertheless, these galaxies were named spiral nebulae and were commonly assumed to be within the Milky Way. During the nineteenth century, increasing evidence was gathered to support Kant's theory, but it was not until Hubble provided reliable proof to show how far away these nebulae were, that it became widely understood that these were galaxies in their own right. To measure their distances, Hubble had used the idea of a

Above: Spiral galaxy NGC 6946, Gemini North telescope image. This is a starburst galaxy, one in which stars are born and die at a much greater rate than normal. This can be seen by the abundance of starbirth regions (red) in the galaxy's spiral arms. NGC 6946 was also home to eight supernovas between 1917 and 2004, making it the most prolific source of supernovae in that period. The last supernova in our Milky Way was in 1604. This galaxy lies between 10-20 million light years away on the border between the constellations Cygnus and Cepheus. Image taken on 12 August 2004.

Opposite: Triangulum Galaxy (M33, NGC 598). Also known as the Pinwheel Galaxy, this spiral galaxy is about 2 million light-years away in the constellation Triangulum. It is relatively small, at around 30,000 light years across and is of type Sc, meaning that it has no central bar and has a loosely packed center and arms. It is part of the Local Group of galaxies that includes our Milky Way Galaxy. The galaxy contains star-forming regions that contain ionized hydrogen gas (red).

standard candle; he used the known luminosity of Cepheid stars in these nebulae as a constant and compared it to their observed brightness as a variable in order to work out their distances from Earth.

Spiral galaxies

In 1936 Edwin Hubble continued his investigations beyond the Milky Way by publishing a classification of different types of galaxies. Broadly speaking most galaxies fit into three categories, spiral, elliptical and irregular. Many of the known galaxies are spiral galaxies; they have a bulge at the center surrounded by a flatter disc, separated into spiral arms. The stars in the disc are usually younger stars called Population I stars, while the stars in the bulge are older, Population II stars.

Many spiral galaxies, including our own, are barred-spiral galaxies – their galactic bulges appear bar-shaped. Spiral and barred-spiral galaxies are given an extra

classification to denote the size of their galactic bulges. Each of these type of galaxies is labeled "a", "b" or "c", with "a" denoting a large galactic bulge and "c" denoting a small bulge. When a spiral galaxy has a large bulge it is classified Sa, those with the smallest bulges are labeled Sc. The Milky Way is classified as SBc, to show that it is a barred-spiral galaxy with a small galactic bulge.

It was initially thought that the spiral arms were caused by differential rotation – the stars in the disc closest to the bulge orbiting the galactic core at a faster rate than the stars at the outskirts, but this theory was later dismissed, as this process would quickly result in the spiral arms wrapping themselves around the bulge. Instead, it is now thought that spiral density waves might be giving the galactic disc its spiral shape. A wave would not be affected by the differential rotation, explaining why the arms of spiral galaxies did not wrap themselves around their galactic bulge a long time ago.

Elliptical galaxies

Elliptical galaxies do not have the spiral arms, bright bulges or the flat discs of spiral galaxies, instead they appear to be a block of stars, brighter towards the galaxy's center and slowly fading at the outskirts. Elliptical galaxies which are most elliptical in shape were classified as E7 by Hubble. The roundest of elliptical galaxies were labeled E0; all the other elliptical galaxies fit somewhere between E1 and E6 depending on the degree to which they are elliptical.

Hubble initially believed that elliptical galaxies might evolve into spiral galaxies, but this is not actually the case. Stars in elliptical galaxies are much older than those found in the disc of spiral galaxies and are of similar ages to the stars found in the galactic bulge or halo. These are mainly Population II stars, which are much older than stars like our own sun; additionally, there does not appear to be any star formation occurring in elliptical galaxies, despite the fact that recent observations of elliptical galaxies have revealed younger star clusters inside some elliptical galaxies. This phenomenon seems to be best explained by a galaxy merger in which the gravitational pull of a larger galaxy draws in smaller galaxies and globular clusters.

When galaxies bear resemblance to both elliptical and spiral galaxies, they are called lenticular galaxies. These lens-like galaxies have a similar shape and age as elliptical galaxies but, like spiral galaxies, are surrounded by a disc, although unlike spiral galaxies they do not have arms.

Irregular galaxies

Irregular galaxies do not fit into either elliptical or spiral categories. They do not seem to be organized in any particular fashion. Irregular galaxies comprise younger, Population I, stars and still undergo star formation. Irregular galaxies are the youngest type of galaxy. It is thought that in time these irregular galaxies will evolve into either spiral or elliptical galaxies – meaning that the life cycle of galaxies is either from irregular through spiral to elliptical or directly from irregular to elliptical.

The Local Group

Most galaxies in the observable universe are moving away from us as a result of the great explosion which created the universe, the Big Bang. This movement has been proved because stars traveling away from us emit a longer, redder

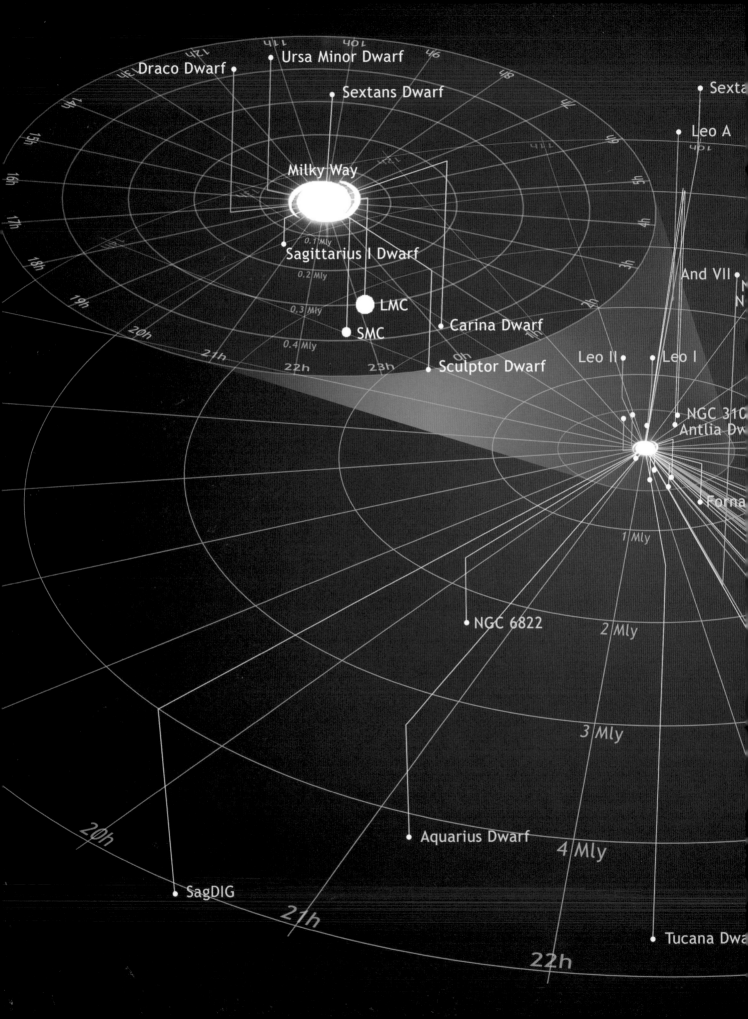

Draco Dwarf

Ursa Minor Dwarf

Sextans Dwarf

Sexta

Leo A

Milky Way

And VII

N

0.1 Mly

Sagittarius I Dwarf

0.2 Mly

0.3 Mly

LMC

Carina Dwarf

0.4 Mly

SMC

Sculptor Dwarf

Leo II

Leo I

NGC 310
Antlia Dw

1 Mly

Forna

NGC 6822

2 Mly

3 Mly

Aquarius Dwarf

4 Mly

20h

SagDIG

21h

Tucana Dwa

22h

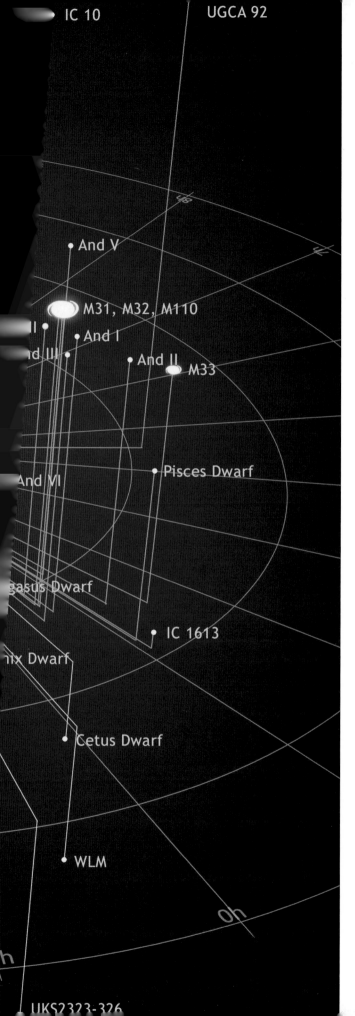

IC 10   UGCA 92

And V

M31, M32, M110

And I

And II

M33

And VI

Pisces Dwarf

gasus Dwarf

IC 1613

ix Dwarf

Cetus Dwarf

WLM

UKS2323-326

wavelength; this phenomenon, known as "red shift", indicates that an object is moving away from the observer. However, the closest galaxies to us emit a shorter wavelength, which appears bluer on the visible spectrum, which indicates that they are moving towards us. This occurs because the force of gravity has overcome the force of the explosion, a process which results in the creation of galaxy clusters.

The galaxy cluster to which the Milky Way belongs is called the Local Group, which consists of around thirty galaxies. The Milky Way is the second largest galaxy in the Local Group, the largest being Andromeda. Together these two galaxies dominate the cluster; twelve smaller galaxies are satellites of the Milky Way and the remainder form the entourage of the Andromeda galaxy. The Local Group's center of gravity is located in between Andromeda and the Milky Way. The third largest galaxy, the Triangulum Galaxy, is the only other spiral galaxy in the Local Group. Although it is a satellite of Andromeda, scientists are trying to work out whether a small, irregular galaxy named LGS 3 is actually a satellite of Triangulum and not Andromeda as previously thought.

The fourth largest galaxy, the Large Magellanic Cloud, together with its near neighbor, the Small Magellanic Cloud, are the closest galaxies to the Milky Way and can be observed with the naked eye from the southern hemisphere in areas unaffected by light pollution. In the northern hemisphere, neither galaxy can be observed, which means they were not officially discovered until Magellan, their namesake, embarked upon his journey around the world in the early sixteenth century.

Left: Local Group galaxy cluster, computer graphic. Some 40 galaxies of the central area of the Local Group are shown relative to our spiral Milky Way Galaxy (center). The concentric circles are 1 million light-years apart, and lines show the positions of galaxies above (green) or below (orange) the celestial equator. The radial lines show the directions in the sky. An inset (upper left) shows the galaxies within 500,000 light-years of the Milky Way. The largest galaxies are the Milky Way and Andromeda (M31, upper right) and M33 (right of Andromeda). The inset includes the two satellite galaxies of the Milky Way, the Large and Small Magellanic Clouds (lower center).

Right: Optical image of the Whirlpool Galaxy (M51, NGC 5194) and its companion NGC 5195 (top). These interacting galaxies are about 20 million light years away in the constellation Canes Venatici. M51 has a diameter of around 65,000 light-years and a mass of about 50,000 million solar masses, about half the mass and size of the Milky Way. The colors show the age of the stars in the galaxies. The nuclei contain mainly older, yellower stars, while the spiral arms have younger, hot, blue stars. The galaxies are linked by a thin bridge of gas and dust which NGC 5195 is pulling from the larger galaxy by gravitational attraction.

Opposite: Optical image of the Andromeda galaxy, the nearest major galaxy to our own Milky Way. It is the largest galaxy in the Local Group, being 150,000 light-years in diameter. It lies 2.2 million light-years away. It is classed as a spiral galaxy (Sb). The Andromeda galaxy has two smaller companion galaxies: M32 (NGC 221, top right corner) and M110 (NGC 205, lower center). Photographed by the 0.9-meter telescope at Kitt Peak National Observatory, Arizona, USA.

Andromeda

Andromeda is the major galaxy of the Local Group. It is one and a half times the mass of the Milky Way and it is currently thought to be about 2.9 million light-years away, making it the most distant object most people would be able to find with the naked eye. The Andromeda galaxy is one of 110 objects visible in the night sky in the northern hemisphere which were cataloged by the French astronomer, Charles Messier. Cataloged as the 31st Messier Object, Andromeda will often be referred to as M31. In 1924, M31 became the first place known to exist outside our own Milky Way, as it was Cepheid stars in the Andromeda "nebula" that first indicated to Hubble that we were dealing with a foreign galaxy. The Andromeda galaxy and the Milky Way are moving towards one another at an incredible pace; it is thought that the two galaxies will impact one another in three billion years' time, which will eventually lead to the creation of one, giant elliptical galaxy.

THE UNIVERSE

Cosmology is the study of the origin, evolution and structure of the universe. It is an ancient field of study, traditionally undertaken by philosophers or religious and spiritual leaders. For centuries, most of the prevailing theories were based upon religious teachings, most of which subscribed to a creationist view, that a god or gods had created the entire universe.

It was not until the twentieth century, with the discovery of the existence of other galaxies, and a dramatic increase in the size of the known universe, that the pursuit gained a scientific foundation.

Knowledge of other galaxies allowed astronomers to observe their behavior and to understand more about the structure and evolution of the universe. Most scientists agreed that red shift, the phenomenon whereby light emitted from stars that are moving away from the observer falls in the red end of the spectrum, had proved that the universe was expanding, giving rise to two contending theories – the Steady State theory and the Big Bang theory.

In spite of these giant leaps in scientific cosmology, religious views on the origin of the universe also remain popular in many areas of the world.

Steady State theory

In 1948, Fred Hoyle, Thomas Gold and Herman Bondi proposed that the universe is eternal and infinite in time and size – it did not have a beginning and it would not have

an end. While this theory appears at first glance to suggest a static universe, these three scientists did not refute the new evidence of an expanding universe, but reconciled it with their idea of a steady state of affairs. Arguing that the universe does not change in its appearance over time, they claimed that when galaxies recede from the Milky Way and disappear from view, new matter creates new galaxies so that the density of the universe remains constant; thus the observable universe appears unchanged.

The Big Bang

Even before the Steady State theory had been proposed, in 1927 a Belgian priest Georges Lemaitre suggested that the universe had begun with the explosion of a "primeval atom". This later became known as the Big Bang, a name which had initially been a derogatory term, coined by Fred Hoyle in order to make the whole idea sound absurd.

Nevertheless, this notion of a single atom from which the universe germinated gained supporters such as George Gamow, who developed the idea much further than

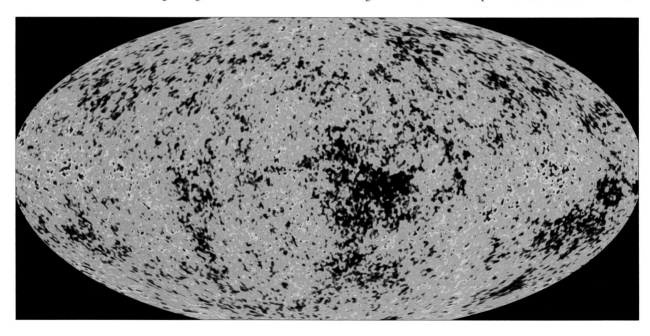

Lemaitre, and is often credited as being the father of the theory. The idea is that if the universe is expanding and the galaxies are moving away from one another, (as had been shown by red shift), then at some stage in the history of the universe, there must have been a point of origin, which was perhaps a gravitational singularity. At this point of origin, there must have been a great explosion, and ever since that moment, the universe has been expanding and cooling.

So, while the Big Bang postulation had been around for a number of years, during the 1950s the Steady State hypothesis was the more popularly accepted theory to explain the creation of the universe; the concept of nothingness before the Big Bang was difficult to fathom and the whole idea seemed too far-fetched.

Radio galaxies and quasars

The Steady State theory enjoyed popularity during the 1950s but it soon came up against a number of challenges which swayed opinion in favor of the "Big Bang" as the more likely explanation of the evolution of the universe. One problem was the discovery of very young galaxies called radio galaxies with their strong radio emissions. The Steady State theory holds that young galaxies are formed throughout the universe while the Big Bang theory maintains that there are no young galaxies because all have aged since the time of the Big Bang, but the furthest galaxies would still appear young because it has taken billions of years for light and other radiation to reach us. Radio galaxies were discovered to be very far from the Earth, seemingly a vindication of the Big Bang.

This blow to the Steady State theory was compounded in 1963 by the discovery of powerful radio sources, later named quasars (quasi-stellar radio objects). Soon after, a number of quasars were discovered emitting strong sources of various types of electromagnetic radiation, not just radio waves. These sources were determined to be billions of light-years from Earth; like radio waves, quasars undermined the Steady State theory which would suggest that galactic phenomena such as quasars should be scattered throughout the galaxy, not just on the farthest reaches of visible space. Quasars were easily reconciled to the Big Bang theory; they would have been part of the universe in its very early stages, and could only be visible at such vast distances because it took so long for light and other radiation from them to reach us.

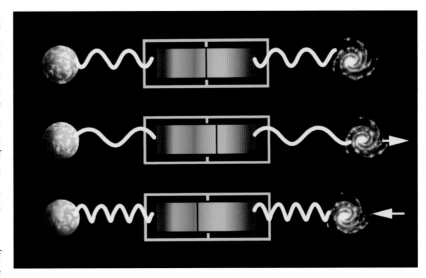

Above: Red shift and blue shift in astronomy. Diagram of the Doppler effect, the change in the wavelength of radiation due to the motion of a source (galaxy at right) relative to the observer (Earth, left). At top, a dark vertical line shows the position of an absorption line when the Earth and the galaxy are relatively at rest. If the galaxy is moving away from Earth (middle), the wavelength of the emitted radiation stretches and the absorption line shifts towards a longer wavelength in the red part of the spectrum (red shift). If the galaxy is moving towards Earth (bottom), the wavelength is compressed and the absorption line is shifted into the blue part of the spectrum (blue shift).

Opposite: Cosmic microwave background. Whole sky image of the cosmic microwave background made by the MAP (Microwave Anisotropy Probe) spacecraft. This map indicates that the age of the universe is around 13.7 billion years. The data also reveal that the universe is expanding at 71 kilometers per second per megaparsec (1 Mpc = 3262 light-years). The colors reveal variations in the temperature of the universe in all directions. This correlates to the density of material at the time when the universe became transparent to radiation, about 380,000 years after its creation. The denser regions (red, yellow) formed the seeds of galaxies and other structures. Data obtained in 2003.

Previous page: Hubble Space Telescope deep-view image of several thousand never-before seen extremely distant galaxies. This is the deepest view yet into the universe. The most distant of these galaxies are around 12 billion light years away, meaning their light has traveled across about three-quarters of the known universe to reach Earth. These galaxies lie in the southern constellation Tucana. This image, the Hubble Deep Field South, was produced by the Hubble Wide Field Planetary Camera 2 (WFPC2) after a ten-day exposure in October 1998.

Cosmic Background Radiation

Although the discovery of distant quasars and radio galaxies discredited the Steady State theory, it did not actively support the Big Bang theory. Advocates of the latter

Above: Hubble Space Telescope view of lensed galaxies (arcs) seen through the galaxy cluster Abell 1689. Abell 1689 lies around 2.2 billion light-years from Earth. It is so massive that it bends the path of the light from galaxies even further away behind it, acting like an enormous lens in space. This means it can be used to study more distant galaxies than would be possible to observe without the cluster. The fine arcs are the distorted images of galaxies from up to 13 billion light-years away, seen as they were when the universe was less than a billion years old.

Opposite: Supercomputer simulation of the distribution of dark matter in the local universe. Dark matter is a form of matter that cannot be detected by telescopes as it emits no radiation. Its presence is inferred by its gravitational action on visible matter. It is thought that visible matter (such as galaxies) occupies halos of dark matter (bright dots). The halos are connected by filaments of cold, invisible dark matter (red). This simulation matches the observed distribution of galaxies well, suggesting current theories about the universe are accurate.

would need to find hard evidence to back up their claim. They believed that after a huge explosion the universe would have emitted radiation, which would have spread evenly throughout space. Essentially, if there had been a big bang, this radiation should be everywhere in space and if the existence of this radiation could be detected, it could support the Big Bang theory.

In 1965, Arno Penzias and Robert Wilson working for Bell Telephone Laboratories in New Jersey were pioneering the development of satellite technology for telephones. To get the signal from the satellite, they needed to remove all interference. However, every time they tried to link up with the satellite, a faint, constant background interference persisted in blocking their attempts. It did not seem to be coming from one specific location, its source was multi-directional, issuing from everywhere in space. Accidentally, they had discovered the radiation the Big Bang theorists had been searching for; it was a microwave, later named cosmic background radiation. This discovery provided the Big Bang theory with some vital supporting evidence, which aided its progress in rapidly replacing the Steady State theory as the main model for describing the evolution of the universe.

COBE

The COBE (Cosmic Background Explorer) satellite was launched in 1989 to analyze the cosmic background radiation to give us a better understanding of the history of the universe. It measured the temperature of the cosmic background radiation at just below 3^0 Kelvin which can tell us a great deal about the universe's evolution.

We know that atoms comprising matter can only form below temperatures of 3000^0 Kelvin; therefore, assuming that the universe has cooled down, we know that the universe has expanded roughly 1000 times in size since atoms first formed and it began taking on the characteristics it displays today. When the temperature was higher than 3000⁰ Kelvin, electrons would have been stripped away as atoms attempted to form, leaving a universe consisting of plasma, an alternative phase of matter to solid, liquids or gases.

How old is the universe?

The universe is thought to be between thirteen and fourteen billion years old – an age calculated by Edwin Hubble, by simply tracing the galaxies back to their point of origin. However, this process assumes that the universe has expanded at a constant rate. There are many who still have concerns with the Big Bang theory; many still find it difficult to imagine a time before the Big Bang, a time of "nothing" could surely not exist, but perhaps that is a problem with the human imagination rather than the theory. Scientists are not troubled by this question, because according to the theory, time started at the Big Bang, so it is pointless to debate what came before. Perhaps it is in this question that philosophers could regain some of their ancient influence over cosmology.

Another criticism is that the Big Bang might just be another scientific paradigm, and the whole theory regarding the evolution of the universe will be transformed by another discovery, just as scientific revolutions have changed conventional thought numerous times throughout history. There is a chance this may well prove to be the case; there is much we do not know about the universe, and discovery of new aspects of its origins and evolution might transform our understanding. In the meantime, with a good body of evidence in support of it, the Big Bang is the best theory thus far promoted to make sense of our current understanding of the universe.

A Big Crunch?

Red shift has shown that our universe is expanding. As an object moves away from an observer, the wavelength of the visible light that it emits is lengthened, and therefore reddened. With this in mind, scientists are faced with the question of whether or not the universe will keep on expanding, or begin contracting. Some of the galaxies closest to the Earth, such as Andromeda, emit a blue shift, rather than a red shift, which implies that they are moving towards us because, when an object approaches an observer, it emits a bluer, shorter wave. The reason these galaxies are moving toward us is because gravity is sufficiently strong to overcome the recession of nearby galaxies.

Some Big Bang theorists have suggested that this blue shift indicates that the universe will end in a Big

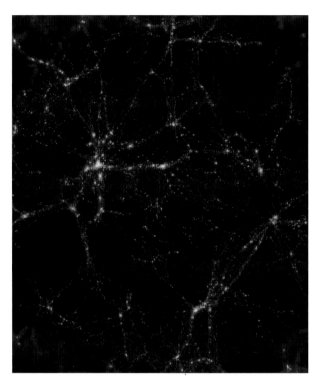

Crunch, when the expansion of the universe is halted and reversed until all matter in the universe contracts back into the gravitational singularity from which it came – at which point time would come to an end.

For the Big Crunch to occur the universe needs a certain density of matter and energy to reverse the expansion; this is called the "critical density". The Big Bang theory holds that matter and energy are not created, the universe was as dense as it was ever going to get at the time of the Big Bang. Cosmologists, therefore, are trying to calculate the density of the universe to see whether it is above or below the critical density.

Recent calculations suggest that the universe might be less dense than the critical density, which would result in the universe expanding for ever. However, scientists have difficulty factoring in dark matter and energy when calculating the density of the universe; thus unbounded expansion or the Big Crunch both remain distinct possibilities.

There are some Big Crunch theorists who think that the whole process might repeat itself as soon as the universe has contracted, in other words there may be a new Big Bang. If that is the case, then this process could have occurred many times already and our universe is only one of a sequence of universes.

APPENDICES

THE SUN

Missions to the sun

Launch date:	Mission	Significant events and findings
1990	Ulysses	Ulysses was launched towards Jupiter from the Space Shuttle Discovery and used Jupiter's gravity to break out of the Ecliptic plane* and fly over the sun's polar regions
1995	SOHO	The international Solar and Heliospheric Observatory (SOHO) is a joint project of the European Space Agency (ESA) and NASA. It keeps the sun under constant observation and has discovered dozens of comets. SOHO's data about solar activity is used to predict solar flares that could potentially damage satellites

* The imaginary plane containing the Earth's orbit around the sun.

Significant dates

1223 B.C.	The oldest eclipse record was found on a clay tablet in the ancient city of Ugarit (now Syria)
c 800 B.C.	The first plausible recorded sunspot observation in China
c400 B.C.	Early people believed that the Earth was flat and that the sun was a god. The Greek philosopher Anaxagoras realized that the sun must be a large body, far from the Earth. He estimated the sun's diameter at 56 kilometers. Anaxagoras' ideas disagreed with the religious beliefs of his time. His life was threatened, and he finally was exiled from Athens
200 B.C.	First mathematically-based attempt at calculating the distance from the Earth to the sun by Aristarchus of Samos
150	The astronomer Ptolemy of Alexandria declared that the Earth was a stationary body in the center of the universe. He believed that the sun, moon, planets, and stars all circled the Earth
1543	Copernicus presented a planetary model with the sun at the center of all planetary motions
1610	Galileo observes sunspots with his telescope
1644	Descartes put forward a theory where the sun is one of many stars
1650-1715	Maunder Sunspot Minimum; a period when there was a dearth of sunspot sightings
1796	French astronomer Pierre de Laplace put forward his nebular hypothesis where the sun and the solar system formed the gravitational collapse of a large, diffuse gas cloud
1845	The first solar image was produced by French physicists Louis Fizeau and Leon Foucault
1852	First connection made between solar activity and geomagnetic activity
1859	First observation of a solar flare by amateur astronomer Richard Carrington
1860	The total solar eclipse was the most thoroughly observed eclipse up to that time and gave rise to the first record of a Coronal Mass Ejection
1908	First measurement of sunspot magnetic fields taken by American astronomer George Ellery Hale
1919	Hale's Polarity Laws helped provide evidence about the sun's magnetic cycle
1942	First radio emission from the sun observed
1946	First observation of solar ultraviolet using a sounding rocket
1946	1,000,000° K temperature of corona discovered via coronal spectra lines
1949	First observation of solar x rays using a sounding rocket
1954	Galactic cosmic rays found to change in intensity with the 11 year sunspot cycle
1956	Largest observed solar flare occurred
1959	First direct observations of solar wind made by Mariner 2
1963	First observations of solar gamma rays made by Orbiting Solar Observatory I (OSO1)
1973-4	Skylab observed the sun and discovered coronal holes
1982	First observations of neutrons from a solar flare by Solar Maximum Mission (SMM)
1994-5	Ulysses flies over polar regions of the sun

MERCURY

Only one spacecraft has ever visited Mercury: **Mariner 10** in 1974-75. NASA has launched a new mission to Mercury called MErcury Surface, Space ENvironment, GEochemistry, and Ranging (MESSENGER) which will orbit Mercury toward the end of this decade.

Significant dates

c385 B.C.	Greek astronomer Heraclides became the first person to suggest that Mercury (and Venus) orbit the sun
1610	Italian astronomer Galileo Galilei made first telescopic observation of Mercury
1631	French astronomer Pierre Gassendi made first telescopic observations of the transit of Mercury across the face of the sun
1639	Italian astronomer Giovanni Zupus discovered Mercury has phases, which is evidence that the planet circles the sun
1889	William Harkness measured the mass of Mercury
1889	Italian astronomer, Giovanni Schiaparelli produced the first map of Mercury's surface features
1962	The first radar contact was established by the radio telescope at Arecibo, Puerto Rico
1965	American radio astronomers Gordon Pettengill and Rolf Dyce measured the rotation period to be about 59 days
1968	Surveyor 7 took the first spacecraft pictures of Mercury from the lunar surface
1974	Mariner 10 made the first flyby within 900 km of Mercury
1975	Third and final flyby of Mercury by Mariner 10

VENUS

Missions to Venus

The first Mission to Venus (Sputnik 7) was in 1961 by the Soviet Union. The probe was successfully launched but did not go further than Earth's orbit. Since then there have been over 40 scheduled missions by the USA and USSR. There are several missions planned for the future, including ESA (European Space Agency) missions, Venus Express and BepiColumbo. This list is a brief timeline of the most memorable and significant of past missions.

Launch dates	Name of Mission	Significant events and findings
1962	Mariner 2	Mariner 2 gathered significant data on the Venusian atmosphere and surface
1966	Venera 2 and 3 (USSR)	Two unmanned Soviet spacecraft "explored" Venus in 1966. Venera 2 passed within 24,000 kilometers of the planet on 27 February, and Venera 3 crashed into Venus on 1 March
1967	Venera 4 (USSR)	In October 1967, the Soviet spacecraft Venera 4 dropped a capsule of instruments into Venus's atmosphere by parachute
1967	Mariner 5	Mariner 5 flew by Venus and revealed new information about Venus's atmosphere, including its composition of 85-99% carbon dioxide
1970	Venera 7 (USSR)	Venera 7 entered the Venusian atmosphere in December 1970. Signals were returned for 35 min. Another 23 min of very weak signals were received after the spacecraft landed on Venus. The capsule was the first man-made object to return data after landing on another planet
1972	Venera 8 (USSR)	Venera 8 was an atmospheric probe and lander. The probe confirmed the earlier data returned by Venera 7, and also measured the light level as being suitable for surface photography
1973	Mariner 10	Mariner 10 was the first spacecraft to encounter two planets (Venus and Mercury) at close range and flew past Venus to within 5,800 km to transmit the first close-up photographs of the planet
1975	Venera 9 and 10 (USSR)	Spacecrafts landed and sent the first surface pictures of the surface of Venus via their orbiters
1978	Pioneer Venus	The Pioneer Venus mission had two components, an orbiter and a multiprobe, to measure and compare the structure and composition of the atmosphere all the way to the surface
1978	Venera 11 and 12 (USSR)	In December 1978 Venera 12 landed on Venus. A second Soviet lander, Venera 11, reached the planet's surface four days later. Both probes sent back data on the lower atmosphere of Venus
1982 - 1983	Veneras 13, 14, 15 and 16 (USSR)	Venera 13 and 14 landed on Venus in 1982 and transmitted photographs and analyzed soil samples. In 1983 Venera 15 and 16 landed and mapped regions of Venus using radar. These two probes provided clear images of features as small as 1.5 kilometers across
1984	Vega 1 and 2 (USSR)	Spacecraft dropped off landers and balloon probes at Venus while en route to Halley's comet
1989	Magellan	Magellan was the first planetary spacecraft to be launched from a space shuttle
1989	Galileo	Galileo used gravity from Venus and Earth to build up enough speed to make the six-year journey to Jupiter
1997	Cassini-Huygens	The spacecraft borrowed a little energy from Earth and Venus to hurl itself into the outer solar system on its way to Saturn. This technique is called gravity assist

Significant dates

c385 B.C.	Greek astronomer Heraclides became the first person to suggest that Venus (and Mercury) orbit the sun
1610	Italian astronomer Galileo Galilei observed that Venus progresses through phases similar to those of the moon
1666	The French astronomer Jean-Dominique Cassini made the first measurements about the rate at which Venus spins on its axis
1691	The English astronomer Edmund Halley presented a method by which the distance scale of the solar system may be determined by using a transit of Venus
1824	The German astronomer Johann Franz Encke calculated the Earth to sun distance using data collected during the 1769 transit of Venus. His figure of 95,000,000 miles was used for several decades
1911	The US astronomer Vesto M Slipher used spectral analysis to show that the rate at which Venus rotates is much longer than one day
1923	First ultra-violet photographs of the cloud features of Venus
1932	Carbon dioxide was discovered in the atmosphere of Venus by the astronomers Dunham and Adams
1962	US astronomer, Carl Sagan became the first to calculate the effect of the Venusian atmosphere on the surface temperature of Venus

MOON

Missions to the moon

More than 70 spacecraft have been sent to the moon; 12 astronauts have walked upon its surface and brought back 382 kg (842 pounds) of lunar rock and soil to Earth.

A timeline of the main missions to the moon:

Launch Date	Mission Name (USA unless otherwise stated)	Significant events and findings	Launch Date	Mission Name (USA unless otherwise stated)	Significant events and findings
1959	Luna 1 (USSR)	Flyby	1967	Surveyor 5	Lander
1959	Pioneer 4	Flyby	1967	Surveyor 6	Lander
1959	Luna 2 (USSR)	Impact	1968	Surveyor 7	Lander
1959	Luna 3 (USSR)	Probe	1968	Luna 14 (USSR)	Orbiter
1961	Ranger 1	Attempted Test Flight	1968	Zond 5 (USSR)	Return Probe
1961	Ranger 2	Attempted Test Flight	1968	Zond 6 (USSR)	Return Probe
1962	Ranger 3	Attempted Impact	1968	Apollo 8	Crewed Orbiter
1962	Ranger 4	Impact	1969	Apollo 10	Orbiter
1962	Ranger 5	Attempted Impact	1969	Luna 15 (USSR)	Orbiter
1963	Luna 4 (USSR)	Flyby	1969	Apollo 11	Crewed Landing
1964	Ranger 6	Impact	1969	Zond 7 (USSR)	Return Probe
1964	Ranger 7	Impact	1969	Apollo 12	Crewed Landing
1965	Ranger 8	Impact	1970	Apollo 13	Crewed Landing (aborted)
1965	Ranger 9	Impact	1970	Luna 16 (USSR)	Sample Return
1965	Luna 5 (USSR)	Impact	1970	Zond 8 (USSR)	Return Probe
1965	Luna 6 (USSR)	Attempted Lander	1970	Luna 17 (USSR)	Rover
1965	Zond 3 (USSR)	Flyby	1971	Apollo 14	Crewed Landing
1965	Luna 7 (USSR)	Impact	1971	Apollo 15	Crewed Landing
1965	Luna 8 (USSR)	Impact	1971	Luna 18 (USSR)	Impact
1966	Luna 9 (USSR)	Lander	1971	Luna 19 (USSR)	Orbiter
1966	Luna 10 (USSR)	Orbiter	1972	Luna 20 (USSR)	Sample Return
1966	Surveyor 1	Lander	1972	Apollo 16	Crewed Landing
1966	Lunar Orbiter 1	Orbiter	1972	Apollo 17	Crewed Landing
1966	Luna 11 (USSR)	Orbiter	1973	Luna 21 (USSR)	Rover
1966	Surveyor 2	Attempted Lander	1974	Luna 22 (USSR)	Orbiter
1966	Luna 12 (USSR)	Orbiter	1974	Luna 23 (USSR)	Lander
1966	Lunar Orbiter 2	Orbiter	1976	Luna 24 (USSR)	Sample Return
1966	Luna 13 (USSR)	Lander	1990	Hiten (Japan)	Flyby and Orbiter
1967	Lunar Orbiter 3	Orbiter	1994	Clementine	Orbiter
1967	Surveyor 3	Lander	1997	AsiaSat 3/HGS-1 (China)	Lunar Flyby
1967	Lunar Orbiter 4	Orbiter	1998	Lunar Prospector	Orbiter
1967	Surveyor 4	Attempted Lander	2003	SMART 1 (ESA)	Lunar Orbiter
1967	Lunar Orbiter 5	Orbiter			

Successful/famous missions to the moon

Launch Date	Mission Name (USA unless otherwise stated)	Significant events and findings
1959	Luna 1 (USSR)	Most of Russia's unmanned moon missions were undertaken by the Luna program which had a number of famous successes as well as some notorious failures. Seventeen of the 45 Luna missions were successful. Luna 1 was the first spacecraft to flyby the moon and the first to go into orbit around our sun
1959	Pioneer 4	The early Pioneer missions marked America's first efforts to reach the moon. All eight Pioneer moon shots provided important information for future space programs but Pioneer 4 was the only one of the series to achieve its goal. It was the first successful mission to the moon, the first US spacecraft to escape Earth's gravity and the first American spacecraft to achieve an orbit around our sun
1959	Luna 2 (USSR)	Luna 2, the first spacecraft to impact the moon, scattered Russian medals on the lunar surface which are still there

1959	Luna 3 (USSR)	Luna 3 was the third spacecraft successfully launched to the moon and the first to return images of the far side of the moon
1964 1965 1965	Ranger 7 Ranger 8 Ranger 9	The Ranger series of spacecraft were designed to take high-quality pictures of the moon and to select landing sites for the Apollo moon missions. The spacecraft were designed to go straight to the moon and send images back to Earth until the moment they crashed into the surface. After a series of malfunctions, Rangers 7, 8 and 9 achieved their objectives and sent back images which were 1000 times better than those taken by Earth-based telescopes
1966	Surveyor 1	Surveyor 1 was the first US spacecraft to make a soft landing on the moon
1966	Lunar Orbiter 1	Designed to photograph the surface of the moon in order to find suitable landing sites for moon landings, Lunar Orbiter 1 also took the first two photographs of the Earth from the moon
1967	Lunar Orbiter 5	The final mission of the Lunar Orbiter missions; by the time the mission was complete the Lunar Orbiters had successfully taken photographs of 99% of the moon's surface
1967	Surveyor 6	The fourth of the Surveyor series to land successfully on the moon, Surveyor 6 was also the first spacecraft to lift off the lunar surface. The lunar "hop" was about 2.5 meters long with a height of 3 – 4 meters
1967	Apollo 1 (AS204)	During a pre-flight test for what was to be the first manned Apollo mission, a fire claimed the lives of three U.S. astronauts; Gus Grissom, Ed White and Roger Chaffee. After the disaster, the mission was officially designated Apollo 1
1968	Apollo 8	Apollo 8 was the first manned spacecraft to go to the moon and back
1969	Apollo 10	Apollo 10 was a "dry-run" for the Apollo 11 mission; all operations except the lunar landing were performed
1969	Apollo 11	"That's one small step for man but one giant leap for mankind". On 20 July 1969 Neil Armstrong and Buzz Aldrin became the first human beings to step on another celestial body
1969	Apollo 12	The second successful manned mission to the moon
1970	Apollo 13	Apollo 13 was intended to be the third mission when men walked on the moon. An explosion in one of the oxygen tanks meant the mission had to be aborted but the crew were returned safely to Earth
1971	Apollo 14	The third successful manned mission to the moon when the astronauts set up scientific experiments, collected lunar samples and took a variety of photographs. Commander Alan Shepard also famously hit 2 golf balls whilst on the lunar surface
1971	Apollo 15	This manned lunar landing was the first to employ the Lunar Roving Vehicle to explore further from the Lunar Module than on previous missions
1972	Apollo 16	Apollo 16 landed in a region of the moon not yet explored
1972	Apollo 17	Commander Eugene Cernan became the last man ever to walk on the moon in this final manned mission
1976	Luna 24	Final launch of the Luna series
1990	Hiten (Japan)	The first Japanese lunar mission, it made a total of 10 lunar orbits before the spacecraft was deliberately crashed into the moon's surface
1994	Clementine	The first US spacecraft launched in over 20 years, Clementine made 297 lunar orbits and successfully provided scientists with their first look at the total lunar landscape, including the polar regions.
1997	AsiaSat 3/HGS-1 (China)	AsiaSat 3 was originally designed as a communications satellite, but after a rocket malfunction failed to put Asiasat 3 into Earth's orbit, pioneering techniques were used to send the spacecraft to the moon in order to stabilise its orbit round the Earth. The satellite was renamed HGS 1
1998	Lunar Prospector	Lunar Prospector was designed to investigate the resources and structure of the moon. After 18 months the spacecraft intentionally impacted the moon near the south pole in a controlled crash to look for evidence of water ice; none was observed. The vehicle also carried the cremated remains of geologist Eugene Shoemaker to the lunar surface
2003	SMART 1 (ESA)	SMART-1 was the European Space Agency's first trip to the moon. The spacecraft's mission was to test new technologies and map and study the moon in great detail

Future Missions

LUNAR –A
Japan's LUNAR-A has been designed to penetrate the lunar surface to study the moon's interior with seismometers and heat-flow probes.

SELENE
SELENE (SELenological and ENgineering Explorer) is a lunar exploration mission to be conducted by the Institute of Space and Astronautical Science (ISAS) and the National Space Development Agency (NASDA) – Japan's two major space agencies. The primary objectives of the mission are to obtain data on the moon's origins and evolution. The program is in development with a scheduled launch date of 2006.

Lunar Reconaissance Orbiter
The proposed Lunar Reconaissance Orbiter is a moon orbiting mission scheduled for launch in 2008. It is designed to study the moon's radiation environment, map the surface of the moon, scan for resources in the polar regions and map the composition of the lunar surface. A primary goal of the mission is to find and identify landing sites for future robotic and human explorers.

MARS

Missions to Mars

More spacecraft have been sent to investigate Mars than any other planet. The first Mission to Mars (Marsnik 1) was initiated in 1960 by the Soviet Union and ended in a launch failure. Since then there have been nearly 40 scheduled missions. Many of these failed to achieve their objectives. However NASA has plans for many future trips into space. The following list is a brief timeline of the most memorable and significant of these missions.

Launch dates	Name of Mission	Significant events and findings
1962 - 1973	Mariner	NASA launched and built 10 spacecraft to explore the inner solar system, visiting Venus, Mars and Mercury
1965	Mariner 4	Mariner 4 was the first space ship to reach Mars and send back close-up pictures
1969	Mariner 6	Mariner 6 and 7 flybys resulted in high resolution images of the equatorial region
1971	Mariner 9	Mariner 9 was the first spacecraft to orbit another planet. It spent nearly 2 years orbiting Mars on a mapping mission, took detailed photos of Phobos and Deimos and sent over 7,000 pictures back to Earth
1971	U.S.S.R. Mars 2	The Mars 2 lander was released from the orbiter in November 1971. It crashed-landed but the orbiter returned data until 1972
1971	U.S.S.R. Mars 3	Mars 3 arrived in December 1971. The lander was released and became the first successful landing on Mars. It failed after relaying 20 seconds of video data to the orbiter. The Mars 3 orbiter returned data until August 1972
1975	Viking 1 and 2	The Viking Mars mission was performed by two spacecraft, Viking 1 and Viking 2. Each spacecraft consisted of an orbiter and a lander. The orbiters took pictures of the Martian surface, from which a landing site was selected. The landers then separated from the orbiters and soft-landed. The orbiters continued taking pictures and, between Viking 1 and Viking 2, imaged the entire planet at what was then high resolution
1988	U.S.S.R. probes Phobos 1 and 2	Contact was lost with Phobos 1 before it reached Mars. Phobos 2 went into orbit around Mars in January 1989. The orbiter moved within 800 km of Phobos, the moon, and then failed. The lander never made it to Phobos
1992	Mars Observer	The spacecraft carried a payload of scientific instruments designed to study the geology, geophysics and climate of Mars but two days prior to planned entry into Mars orbit all contact was lost with the craft
1996	Mars Pathfinder	Inside the lander was a remote-control jeep named Sojourner programmed for rock and soil analysis. Sojourner was the first wheeled vehicle to be used on any other planet of the solar system; it stopped working in September 1997
1996	Mars Global Surveyor	Mars Global Surveyor observed Mars from a low-altitude orbit over the course of one complete Martian year, the equivalent of nearly two Earth years. Surveyor is now on an extended mission and continues to send back images from Mars orbit
1998	Nozomi	Nozomi was intended to be Japan's first Mars orbiter, but a series of mishaps and malfunctions made it impossible for the spacecraft to reach its destination. After more than five years in space, the spacecraft ran out of fuel before it could be put onto the proper trajectory to orbit Mars
1999	Mars Climate Orbiter	This spacecraft was designed to monitor climate conditions, by orbiting Mars, Communications were lost as it prepared to enter orbit. An investigation found the spacecraft burned up in Mars's atmosphere due to a navigation error caused by the failure to translate Imperial units to Metric
1999	Mars Polar Lander	Communications were lost as the lander began its entry into the Martian atmosphere in December 1999
2001	Odyssey	After a 6-month journey Odyssey went into orbit around Mars and continues to provide information to identify landing sites for future mission
2003	Beagle 2 (ESA)	Beagle 2's main mission was to search for signs of life - past or present - in the Martian soil. It touched down on Mars on Christmas Day 2003, but never sent back a radio signal to say that it had survived the landing
2003	Mars Expedition Rovers, Spirit and Opportunity	Spirit and Opportunity landed in January 2004 sending back geological data and many pictures; they are still operating today

Other Significant dates

1604	Johannes Kepler calculated an elliptical orbit for Mars
1609	Galileo first observed Mars
1659	Christiaan Huygens made the first sketch of Mars and arrived at an approximate 24 hour rotational period
1666	Jean-Dominique Cassini (the Italian born French astronomer) calculated the length of a day on Mars to be 24 hours and 40 minutes
1671	Cassini calculated the distance from Earth to Mars
1672	Huygens observed a white spot at the south pole of Mars
1698	Huygens published Cosmotheoros and addressed the question of life on Mars
1704	Italian astronomer Giacomo Filippo Maraldi (Cassini's nephew) observed white spots at the poles
1719	Maraldi suggested that the white spots on Mars could be ice caps
1784	Sir William Herschel observed the seasonal changes to the polar caps and raised the possibility that they might be composed of snow and ice
1840	Wilhelm Beer and Johann Madler created the first global maps of Mars
1862	British astronomer Sir Norman Lockyear agreed with earlier suggestions that there were oceanic areas on Mars
1877	US astronomer Asaph Hall discovered the two moons of Mars – Phobos and Deimos

1911	In Egypt a dog was killed by a meteorite. Tests on this meteorite in 1986 revealed that it had originated from Mars
1927	William Weber Cobblentz and Carl Otto Lampland measured a wide temperature difference between the day and night side of Mars which suggested a very thin atmosphere
1938	When "War of the Worlds" (H.G. Wells) was broadcast it was estimated that over 1 million listeners thought the events were real!
1947	US astronomer Gerard Peter Kuiper detected carbon dioxide on Mars

The two moons of Mars, Phobos and Deimos

	Discovered by	Date of Discovery	Mean distance from Mars	Diameter	Orbital period	Mass	Mean density	Atmosphere	Surface Gravity*
Phobos (fear)	Asaph Hall	1877	9,377 km	21 km	7 hours 39 minutes	1.06×10^{16} kg	$1.90g/cm^3$	None	0.0084 - 0.0019 m/s²
Deimos (panic)	Asaph Hall	1877	23,459km	12 km	30 hours 12 minutes	2.38×10^{15} kg	$2.2g/cm^3$	None	0.0039 m/s²

* The variation in gravitational pull is because of Phobos' ellipsoidal shape

JUPITER

Missions to Jupiter

Flights to Jupiter began in the early 1970s. Many of the later missions were en route to other planets. Future planned missions include the Prometheus initiative to develop nuclear reactor powered spacecraft that can operate in deep space.

Launch dates	Name of Mission	Significant events and findings
1973	Pioneer 10	Pioneer 10 was the first spacecraft to travel through the asteroid belt and reach the outer solar system. After flying past Jupiter it headed out into the solar system through the Milky Way. Pioneer 10 carries a plaque intended to communicate something about its home planet should the spacecraft ever meet up with another intelligent species
1973	Pioneer 11	Pioneer 11 was the second mission to investigate Jupiter and the outer solar system and the first to explore the planet Saturn and its main rings. Pioneer 11, like Pioneer 10, used Jupiter's gravitational field to alter its trajectory radically. It passed close to Saturn and then it followed an escape trajectory from the solar system. The power source for the spacecraft was exhausted in 1995 so we can no longer communicate with it
1977	Voyager 2	Voyager 2 achieved a Grand Tour of our solar system, flying by Jupiter, Saturn, Uranus and Neptune. It returned many images of Jupiter and the 4 largest moons
1977	Voyager 1	Voyager 1 followed Voyager 2 into space within 16 days but arrived at Jupiter 4 months ahead of Voyager 2. Voyager 1 tracked wind speeds and turbulent forms in Jupiter's atmosphere and returned stunning images of the 4 largest moons. Voyager 1 is continuing its journey towards interstellar space and is now farther from Earth than any other spacecraft
1989	Galileo	During its 14 year mission to Jupiter, Galileo discovered a radiation belt above Jupiter's cloud tops, extensive and rapid resurfacing of the moon Io and evidence for liquid water oceans under the moon Europa's icy surface. Galileo was deliberately crashed into Jupiter in September 2003 to avoid an accidental collision with - and possible contamination of - one of Jupiter's moons
1990	Ulysses	Ulysses' main focus is the polar regions of the sun, but since no rocket engines are powerful enough to boost the spacecraft above the Ecliptic Plane (where most planets and spacecraft orbit the sun), Ulysses used Jupiter's gravity to hurl it onto the correct trajectory. During the Jupiter flybys, scientists used Ulysses' instruments to study the giant planet and its influence on the solar system, which is second only to the sun
1997	Cassini-Huygens	Although Saturn was its primary destination, Cassini's fly-by of Jupiter uncovered a lot of new information. Scientists used joint observations from Galileo and Cassini spacecraft to reveal a vast whirling bubble of charged particles surrounding Jupiter

Significant dates

364 BC	The Chinese astronomer Gan De made an observation of a body which is now believed to be Ganymede – 1,974 years before Galileo
1610	Galileo discovered four moons orbiting Jupiter (Io, Europa, Ganymede, and Callisto; the Galilean Satellites)
1664	British chemist and physicist Robert Hooke discovered the Great Red Spot
1665	Cassini measured the rotational rate of Jupiter
1892	Amalthea was discovered by US astronomer Edward Barnard
1904	US astronomer Charles Perrine discovered Himalia
1905	Perrine discovered Elara
1908	Pasiphae was discovered by Melotte
1914	US astronomer Seth Barnes discovered Sinope
1938	Barnes discovered Carme and Lysithea
1951	Barnes discovered Ananke
1955	Radio emissions from Jupiter were detected by US astronomer Kenneth Franklin
1974	Leda was discovered by Charles Kowal (US astronomer)

The moons of Jupiter

Jupiter has 63 identified moons (up to February 2004). 46 of these moons were discovered between 1999 and 2003. Astronomers believe that the moon count of Jupiter could go as high as 100.

They are divided into six main groups (in order of increasing distance from the planet): Amalthea, Galilean, Himalia, Ananke, Carme, and Pasiphae.

The first group (Amalthea) is comprised of the four innermost satellites—Metis, Adrastea, Amalthea, and Thebe.

Io, Europa, Ganymede, and Callisto were discovered by Galileo in 1610, shortly after he invented the telescope, and are known as the Galilean satellite group.

Themisto orbits Jupiter midway between the Galilean and next main group of satellites, the Himalias. The Himalia group consists of five tightly clustered satellites with orbits outside that of Callisto—Leda , Himalia , Lysithea, Elara, and S/2000 J11.

Situated between the Himalia and Ananke groups is Carpo which like Thermisto doesn't seem to fit into any of the main groups. The Ananke group comprises 17 satellites, which share similar orbits S/2003 J12, Euporie, Orthosie, Euanthe, Thyone, Mneme, Harpalyke, Hermippe, Praxidike, Thelexinoe, Iocaste, Ananke, S/2003 J16, S/2003 J3, S/2003 J18, Helike, and S/2003 J15.

The Carme group comprises 17 satellites which share similar orbits: Arche, Pasithee, Chaldene, Kale, Isonoe, Aitne, Erinome, Taygete, Carme Kalyke, Eukelade, Kallichore, S/2003 J17, S/2003 J10, S/2003 J9, S/2003 J5, and S/2003 J19.

The most distant of the groups from the planet is the Pasiphaë which comprises 14 widely dispersed satellites: S/2003 J2, Eurydome, Autonoe, Sponde, Pasiphae, Megaclite, Sinope, Hegemone, Aoede, Callirrhoe, Cyllene, S/2003 J23, S/200 J4, and S/2003 J14.

The moons of Jupiter identified so far

1. Metis	10. Leda	19. Isonoe	28. Sinope	37. Eurydome	46. Helike	55. S/2003 J15
2. Adrastea	11. Himalia	20. Erinome	29. Callirrhoe	38. Aitne	47. Aoede	56. S/2003 J16
3. Amalthea	12. Lysithea	21. Taygete	30. Euporie	39. Sponde	48. Hegemone	57. S/2003 J17
4. Thebe	13. Elara	22. Chaldene	31. Kale	40. Autonoe	49. S/2003 J9	58. S/2003 J18
5. Io	14. S/2000 J11	23. Carme	32. Orthosie	41. Eukelade	50. S/2003 J10	59. S/2003 J19
6. Europa	15. Iocaste	24. Pasiphaë	33. Thyone	42. S/2003 J2	51. Kallichore	60. Carpo
7. Ganymede	16. Praxidike	25. Arche	34. Euanthe	43. S/2003 J3	52. S/2003 J12	61. Mneme
8. Callisto	17. Harpalyke	26. Kalyke	35. Hermippe	44. S/2003 J4	53. Cyllene	62. Thelxinoe
9. Themisto	18. Ananke	27. Megaclite	36. Pasithee	45. S/2003 J5	54. S/2003 J14	63. S/2003 J23

The 17 main moons of Jupiter in order of discovery

Name	Mean distance from Jupiter in km	Diameter of satellite in km	Other characteristics
Ganymede	1,070,000 km	5262 km	The largest moon in our solar system
Io	422,000 km	3632 km	The most volcanically active body in our solar system
Europa	670,900 km	3126 km	May have oceans as deep as 50 km
Callisto	1,883,000 km	4,800 km	Almost the same size as Mercury
Amalthea	181,000 km	189 km	The reddest object in the solar system, even redder than the planet Mars
Himalia	11,480,000km	170 km	The largest member of the group that bears its name
Elara	11,737,000 km	80 km	A member of the Himalia group
Pasiphaë	23,500,000 km	36 km	It gives its name to the Pasiphaë group, irregular retrograde moons orbiting Jupiter
Sinope	23,700,000 km	28 km	The outermost known moon of Jupiter until the discovery of Autonoe in 2001
Lysithea	11,720,000 km	24 km	A member of the Himalia group
Carme	22, 600,000 km	30 km	Gives its name to the Carme group, made up of irregular retrograde moons orbiting Jupiter
Ananke	21,200,000 km	20 km	Gives its name to the Ananke group, made up of irregular retrograde moons orbiting Jupiter
Leda	11,094,000 km	10 km	A member of the Himalia group
Themisto	7,315,786 km	8 km	Discovered then "lost"; re-discovered in 2000
Adrastea	129,000 km	21 km	It is the smallest of the Amalthea group of small inner jovian moons
Thebe	220,000 km	100 km	There appear to be at least three or four very large impact craters on the satellite
Metis	128,000 km	43 km	The innermost member of the Amalthea group of Jupiter's small inner moons. One of the many irregular shaped moons

The Four largest moons of Jupiter

The discovery of the four largest moons of Jupiter is significant because it helped prove that the Earth was not at the center of the Universe.

	Ganymede	Io	Europa	Callisto
Discovered by	Galileo	Galileo	Galileo	Galileo
Date of Discovery	1610	1610	1610	1610
Diameter	5262 km The largest moon in our solar system	3632 km	3126 km	4,800 km Almost the same size as Mercury
Average distance from Jupiter	1,070,000 km	422,000 km The innermost of Jupiter's 4 large moons	670,000 km	1,883,000 km
Density	1.94 g/c³ Its low density indicates that the core takes up about 50% of the satellite's diameter	3.55 g/c³	3.01 g/c³	1.86 g/c³
Mass	1.48 x 10²³ kg The largest of Jupiter's moons	8.93 x 10²² kg Slightly larger than the Earth's moon	4.8 x 10²² kg	1.08 x 10²³ kg
Orbital period	7 days 3 hours 45 mins	1 day 18 hours 30 mins	3 days 13 hours 12 mins	16 days 16 hours 48 mins
Internal composition	Mantle: ice and silicates Crust: thick layer of water ice	Io has a metallic (iron, nickel) core. The core is surrounded by a rock shell. Io's rock or silicate shell extends to the surface	Crust: water and ice	Its interior is probably similar to Ganymede except the inner rocky core is smaller, and this core is surrounded by a large icy mantle
Atmosphere	Probably has a thin tenuous oxygen atmosphere	Sulfur dioxide	Oxygen	Carbon dioxide
Surface	Mountains, valleys, craters, lava flows	Volcanic - the most volcanically active body in our solar system The tidal forces cause Io's surface to bulge up and down (or in and out) by as much as 100 meters	Virtually no craters Europa is the smoothest object in our solar system	Heavily cratered Thought to be the most heavily cratered object in our solar system With a surface age of about 4 billion years, Callisto has the oldest landscape in the solar system

SATURN

Missions to Saturn

Launch date	Mission	Significant events and findings
1973	Pioneer 11	Pioneer 11 was the second spacecraft (following Pioneer 10) to visit the outer solar system and the first spacecraft to visit Saturn. It took close-up pictures and discovered an additional ring.
1977	Voyager 2	Saturn was Voyager 2's second stop in its visit to the outer solar system. It was able to take advantage of a rare planetary alignment to visit the four giant outer planets Jupiter, Saturn, Uranus, and Neptune. Following its encounter with Saturn, Voyager 2 continued on to Uranus and Neptune, and is now continuing its journey toward interstellar space
1977	Voyager 1	Voyager 1 flew 124,000 kilometers above Saturn in 1980, and went on to try to have a close look at Saturn's large moon Titan. However Titan was so heavily covered by its thick atmosphere that Voyager's cameras could not image the moon's surface, although other instruments gathered data about Titan. Voyager 1 returned stunning images of Saturn and its rings, showing that the rings are far more complex than ever imagined
1997	Cassini-Huygens	Cassini is the first spacecraft to orbit Saturn. The NASA orbiter is studying the features of Saturn's system of rings and moons and sent the European Space Agency's Huygens Probe into the atmosphere of Saturn's moon, Titan. It remains in orbit around Saturn, sending back detailed studies of the planet and its rings and satellites

Other Significant dates

1610	Galileo was the first person to observe Saturn's rings
1655	Christiaan Huygens suggested that Saturn was surrounded by a solid ring
1655	Christiaan Huygens discovered Titan – the largest moon of Saturn
1659	Christiaan Huygens discovered that Saturn's rings were separate from the planet
1660	Jean Chapelain suggested that Saturn's rings may be made up of a large number of very small satellites
1671	Cassini discovered Iapetus and correctly surmised that the moon had light and dark sides
1672	Cassini discovered Rhea
1676	Cassini discovered the Cassini division
1684	Cassini discovered 2 more moons of Saturn – Tethys and Dione
1787	Pierre Simon suggested that Saturn had a large number of solid rings
1789	Sir William Herschel discovered two new moons of Saturn – Enceladus and Mimas
1790	Herschel determined the rotational period of Saturn to be 10 hours 32 minutes
1837	The German astronomer Johann Encke observed a dark band in the middle of the A ring which would later be known as Encke's division
1848	William Lassell discovered Hyperion
1856	James Maxwell deduced that Saturn's rings are made up from numerous particles
1876	Asaph Hall observed white spots on Saturn
1883	British astronomer Andrew Ainslee took the first photographs of Saturn's rings
1898	US astronomer William Pickering discovered Phoebe – a moon of Saturn
1967	Walter Feibelman discovered Saturn's E-ring
1969	Pierre Gurin found evidence to suggest the presence of the D-ring
1980	3 more moons of Saturn -Telesto, Calypso, and Helene - were discovered

The moons of Saturn

Christiaan Huygens discovered Saturn's first moon, Titan, in 1655. Since then at least another 47 natural satellites orbiting Saturn have been discovered.

The larger moons with regular circular orbits were named after figures in Greek mythology (Pan, Atlas, Pandora, Calypso, etc.). The smaller moons with irregular orbits were named after Norse (Ymir, Thrym, Skadi, Suttung, Mundilfari), Celtic (Tarvos, Albiorix), and Inuit (Paaliaq, Siarnaq, Kiviuq, Ijiraq) legends.

These are the named moons of Saturn in alphabetical order:

1. Albiorix	2. Atlas	3. Calypso	4. Dione	5. Enceladus	6. Epimetheus	7. Erriapo
8. Helene	9. Hyperion	10. Iapetus	11. Ijiraq	12. Janus	13. Kiviuq	14. Mimas
15. Methone	16. Mundilfari	17. Narvi	18. Paaliaq	19. Pallene	20. Pan	21. Pandora
22. Phoebe	23. Polydeuces	24. Prometheus	25. Rhea	26. Siarnaq	27. Skadi	28. Suttung
29. Tarvos	30. Telesto	31. Tethys	32. Thrym	33. Titan	34. Ymir	

The major moons of Saturn in the order they were discovered:

Name	Mean distance from Saturn in km	Diameter of satellite in km	Other characteristics
Titan	1,221,830	5,150	The second largest moon in our solar system, Titan is enclosed by a thick atmosphere
Iapetus	3,561,300	1,560	Half of Iapetus is 10 times brighter than the other half
Rhea	527,040	1,528	The largest airless moon of Saturn
Dione	377,400	1,120	An icy moon similar to Rhea and Tethys
Tethys	294,660	1,060	Tethys has a very large trench about 40 km wide across its surface
Enceladus	238,020	496	One of the shiniest objects in our solar system. It is covered with ice and extremely cold (about -201° C)
Mimas	185,520	392	Mimas has a giant crater which is one-third as wide as the moon itself
Hyperion	1,481,100	288	One of the smaller moons of Saturn, but also one of the largest irregularly shaped natural satellites ever observed
Phoebe	12,952,000	220	A very dark moon with a retrograde orbit
Janus	151,472	180	Epithemus and Janus share the same orbit and are only separated by about 50 km. They trade orbits about once every 4 years
Epimetheus	151,422	120	Has an irregular shape with several large craters (>30km wide)
Helene	377,400	37	A very small, faint moon
Telesto	294,660	23	Telesto and Calypso are referred to as Trojan moons
Calypso	294,660	21	
Pandora	141,700	87	Pandora is the outer shepherd moon* for Saturn's F ring
Prometheus	139,353	105	Prometheus acts as a shepherd moon* for the inner edge of Saturn's F ring
Atlas	137,670	33	Atlas is about 40x20km in size. Believed to be a shepherd moon* for Saturn's A ring
Pan	133,583	19	The innermost known satellite. Acts as a shepherd moon*

* A "shepherd moon" is one that herds Saturn's orbiting particles into one of its distinct rings.

URANUS

The Rings of Uranus

The first rings of Uranus were discovered by chance in 1977 and confirmed when the Voyager 2 probe passed Uranus in 1986. There are now 11 known rings encircling Uranus.

Ring Name (working outward from the planet)	The distance from the planet center to the start of the ring	Width of ring	Thickness
1986U2R	38,000 km	2,500 km	
6	41,837 km	1 km – 3 km	0.1 km
5	42,235 km	2 km – 3 km	0.1 km
4	42,572 km	2 km – 3 km	0.1 km
Alpha	44,718 km	4 km – 13 km	0.1 km
Beta	45,661 km	7 km – 12 km	0.1 km
Eta	47,176 km	1 km – 2 km	0.1 km
Gamma	47,627 km	1 km – 4 km	0.1 km
Delta	48,300 km	3 km – 7 km	0.1 km
Lambda	50,024 km	2 km – 3 km	0.1 km
Epsilon	51,149 km	20 km – 95 km	<15 km

Missions to Uranus

Only one spacecraft has observed Uranus at close range –Voyager 2. In 1986 Voyager 2 flew by Uranus at distance of 107,000 kilometers from the center of the planet. Voyager took pictures of 10 new moons in addition to the 5 moons already identified and measured the length of a Uranian day. Following its visit to Uranus, Voyager 2 continued on to Neptune and is now continuing its journey towards interstellar space.

The moons of Uranus

There are 27 moons of Uranus identified so far. Prior to 1986, only five of Uranus's natural satellites were known: Titania, Oberon, Ariel, Umbriel, and Miranda. When Voyager 2 flew by Uranus in 1986, it discovered 10 more natural satellites. Two additional satellites were discovered in 1997, and three more, were found in 1999. Trinculo, a small irregular satellite, was discovered in 2001 followed by the discovery of several smaller, irregularly shaped satellites in 2003.

These are the 21 named moons of Uranus in order of their discovery.
The moons are all named after characters of William Shakespeare or Alexander Pope.

1. Titania	2. Oberon	3. Ariel	4. Umbriel	5. Miranda	6. Puck	7. Juliet
8. Portia	9. Cressida	10. Desdemona	11. Rosalind	12. Belinda	13. Cordelia	14. Ophelia
15. Bianca	16. Caliban	17. Sycorax	18. Setebos	19. Stephano	20. Prospero	21. Trinculo

The 5 largest moons of Uranus:

	Titania	Oberon	Ariel	Umbriel	Miranda
Discovered by	Herschel	Herschel	Lassell	Lassell	Kuiper
Date of Discovery	1787	1787	1851	1851	1948
Diameter	1578 km	1522 km	1157 km	1170 km	472 km
Average distance from Uranus	436,298 km	583,519	190,945	265,998 km	129,872 km
Density	1.7 g/c^3	1.6 g/c^3	1.7 g/c^3	1.4 g/c^3	1.2 g/c^3
Mass	3.5 x 10^{21}	3.0 x 10^{21}	1.4 x 10^{21}	1.2 x 10^{21}	6.6 x 10^{19}
Orbital period	8 days 16 hours 48 mins	13 days 11 hours	2 days 12 hours	4 days 3 hours 20 mins	1 day 9 hours 50 mins
Composition /Surface	Roughly 50% water ice, 30% silicate rock, and 20% methane-related organic compounds. Has a huge canyon that dwarfs the Grand Canyon	Roughly 50% water ice, 30% silicate rock, and 20% methane-related carbon/nitrogen compounds. It has an old, heavily cratered, icy surface	Roughly 50% water ice, 30% silicate rock, and 20% methane ice. Long rift valleys stretch across the surface with a network of canyons	The darkest of the Uranian moons; mostly composed of water ice, with the balance made up of silicate rock and methane ice	Possibly mostly water ice, with silicate rock and methane-related organic compounds. Surface is criss-crossed by huge canyons up to 20 kms deep

Significant dates

1781	Sir William Herschel discovered Uranus
1787	Sir William Herschel discovered Uranian moons Titan and Oberon
1845	Mathematicians, John Adams (British) and Jean Leverrier (French) predict the existence of Neptune based on orbital motion of Uranus
1851	William Lassell discovered Uranian moons Ariel and Umbriel
1948	Dutch-born astronomer Gerard Kuiper discovered Uranian moon Miranda
1977	James Elliot, Edward Dunham and Doug Mink discovered the rings of Uranus
1985	US astronomer Stephen Synott discovered Puck from images taken by Voyager 2
1986	Voyager 2 discovered 9 small moons (Portia, Rosalind, Juliet, Belinda, Cressida, Desdemona, Cordelia, Ophelia and Bianca), detected the magnetic period, and measured the length of the Uranian day
1997	Caliban and Sycorax (2 new moons) were discovered using the 200-inch Hale telescope
1999	3 new moons - Setebos, Stephano and Prospero – were discovered
2001	Holman et al discovered the moon, Trinculo
2003	6 new satellites of Uranus were discovered

NEPTUNE

The Rings of Neptune

Neptune has a faint planetary ring system of unknown composition. Recent Earth-based observations announced in 2005 appeared to show that Neptune's rings are much more unstable than previously thought.

Ring Name (working outward from the planet)

Ring Name (working outward from the planet)	The distance from the planet center to the start of the ring	Width of ring	Other characteristics
Galle	41,900 km	2,000 km	
Le Verrier	53,200 km	110 km	
Lassell	53,200km	4,000 km	
Arago	57,200 km	<100 km	
Adams	62,930 km	<50 km	Contains 3 prominent arcs named Liberty, Equality and Eternity

Missions to Neptune

Voyager 2 is the only spacecraft to have visited Neptune (1989) following its flybys of Jupiter and Saturn . Voyager 2 passed over the north pole of Neptune at a height of 4,800 kilometers and returned information about the basic characteristics of Neptune and its largest moon, Triton.

The moons of Neptune

Neptune has 13 known moons. The largest by far is Triton, discovered by William Lassell just 17 days after the discovery of Neptune itself. Five new irregular moons were announced in 2004.

These are the 8 named moons of Netune in order of their discovery. Since Neptune was named after the Roman god of the sea, its moons were named for various lesser sea gods and nymphs in Roman mythology.

1. Triton	2. Nereid	3. Proteus	4. Larissa
5. Despina	6. Galetea	7. Thalassa	8. Naiad

The 8 named moons of Neptune:

	Discovered by	Date of Discovery	Diameter	Average distance from Neptune	Density *estimated	Mass	Orbital period	Composition/Surface
Triton	Lassell	1846	2704 km	354,760 km	2.1 g/c³	2.1×10^{22}	6 Earth days (retrograde)	Colder than any other object in the Solar System – surface temperature of -235°C
Nereid	Kuiper	1949	340 km	5,513,400 km	unknown	2×10^{19}	360 Earth days	Orbit is one of the most eccentric of any moon in the Solar system
Proteus	Synott, Voyager 2	1989	418 km	117,650 km	*1.3 g/c³	5×10^{19}	1 Earth day	Was not discovered by Earth-based telescopes because it is so close to the planet that it is lost in the glare of reflected sunligh
Larissa	Reitsema	1982	193 km	73,550 km	*1.3 g/c³	4.9×10^{18}	13 hours	Irregular (non-spherical) in shape and appears to be heavily cratered
Despina	Synott, Voyager 2	1989	148 km	52,530 km	*1.2 g/c³	21×10^{18}	8 hours	Another irregularly shaped moon
Galetea	Synott, Voyager 2	1989	180 km	61,950 km	*1.3 g/c³	3.7×10^{18}	10 hours 18 minutes	Slowly decaying due to tidal forces and will one day break up into a planetary ring or impact Neptune
Thalassa	Terrile, Voyager 2	1989	80 km	50,070 km	*1.3 g/c³	3.7×10^{17}	7 hours 30 minutes	Irregular shape with no sign of geological modification
Naiad	Voyager 2	1989	54 km	48,230 km	*1.2 g/c³	1.9×10^{17}	7 hours 6 minutes	Circles the planet in the same direction as Neptune rotates

Significant dates

1613	Galileo observed Neptune when it was near Jupiter, but mistook it for a fixed star
1845	Mathematicians, John Adams (British) and Jean Leverrier (French) predict the existence of Neptune based on orbital motion of Uranus
1846	German astronomer Johann Galle discovered Neptune using predicted location provided by Adams and Leverrier
1846	British Astronomer William Lassell discovers Neptune's largest satellite, Triton
1949	American astronomer Gerard Kuiper discovered Nereid
1985	Rings of Neptune discovered by astronomers based on star occultations
1989	Scientists with Voyager 2 discovered six small satellites: Naiad, Thalassa, Despina, Galatea, Larissa, and Proteus
1989	US space probe Voyager 2 flew within 4950 km of the cloud tops of Uranus
1994	Hubble Space Telescope observes changes in Neptune's atmosphere
2002	3 new satellites of Neptune were discovered by Holman *et al*
2003	2 more satellites of Neptune were discovered

PLUTO

Pluto's moon

Charon, the only known moon of Pluto, was discovered by astronomers in 1978. However, the Hubble Space Telescope has recently identified two possible new moons around Pluto. The candidate moons have been given the provisional names S/2005 P1 and S/2005 P2 and are between 45 and 160km in diameter.

	Charon
Discovered by	Christy
Date of Discovery	1978
Mean distance from Pluto	19,600 km
Diameter	1186 km
Orbital period	6 days 9 hours 18 mins This is the same period as Pluto's rotation. The two objects are gravitationally locked so they each keep the same face towards the other
Rotation period	6 days 9 hours 18 mins synchronous with Pluto
Mass	1.6×10^{21} kg one-seventh the mass of Pluto
Mean density	2.2 g/cm^3
Atmosphere	None
Surface gravity	0.4 m/s^2

Missions to Pluto

No spacecraft have ever visited Pluto. It is possible NASA will initiate a mission called New Horizons in the future to explore Pluto and the Kuiper belt region.

Historical Timeline for Pluto

1930	Pluto is discovered by William Tombaugh
1954/5	Pluto's day rotation period is determined
1976	Methane on Pluto's surface is discovered
1978	US astronomer James Christy discovered Charon
1985	Onset of Pluto-Charon eclipses (lasted 1985-1991)
1988	Pluto's atmosphere is discovered
1992	Nitrogen and carbon monoxide on Pluto's surface is discovered
1994	First Hubble Space Telescope maps of Pluto

INDEX

Abell 1689   234
Adams Ring   159
Adrastea   123, 125
Aino Planitia   67
Aitken Crater   91
Alan Hills 81005   179
Albor Tholus   114
Aldrin, 'Buzz' Edwin E   23, 87, 96
Algenib   205
ALH84001   104, 107, 108
Alnilam   188,199
Alnitak   188,199
Alpha Andromedae   205
Alpha Canis Majoris   204
Alpha Centauri   189
Alpha Crucis   197
Alpha Cygni   205
Alpha Pegasi   205
Alpha Ursae Minoris   202
Alpheratz   205
Amalthea   123, 124, 125
Ananke   125
Ancient Greek   10, 187
Anders, William   88
Andromeda   188, 191, 205, 227,
                              228, 235
Antoniadi Dorsum   53
Aphelia   34
Aphrodite Terra   62, 67, 68
Apollo 4   75
Apollo 8   88, 96
Apollo 11   23, 27, 82, 87, 88, 89, 96
Apollo 12   41, 76, 96
Apollo 13   97, 98
Apollo 14   87, 97
Apollo 15   82, 97
Apollo 16   97
Apollo 17   97
Apollo 18   98
Apollo 19   98
Apollo 20   98
Apollo/Saturn V   75
Aquarius   197, 200
Arcturus   190
Ariel   148, 149
Aries   197
Aristarchus   15

Aristotle   14
Armstrong, Neil   23, 87, 88, 96
Arsia Mons   109
Artemis   87
Artemis Chasma   62
Ascraeus Mons   109
Asterisms   189
Asteroid 243 Ida   177
Asteroid Belt   174, 175, 176
Asteroids   32
Astraea   202
Astrology   13
Atlantis   26
Atlas   135
Aurora/ Aurorae   81, 138
Aurora Australis   48, 81
Aurora Borealis   48, 81
Aztecs   87
Babylonians   10, 13
Bailey's Beads   43
Barringer Crater   178
Beagle 2   107
Belinda   148
Bell Burnell, Jocelyn   193
BepiColombo   57, 70
Beta Centauri   197
Beta Crucis   197
Beta Pegasi   205
Beta Regio   68
Betelgeuse   188, 192, 199
Big Bang   187, 225, 232, 233, 234
Big Crunch   235
Big Dipper   189, 203
Bode, Johann   144
Bondi, Herman   232
Bopp, Thomas   183
Borman, Frank   88
Bouvard, Alexis   154
Brahe, Tycho   15, 17, 90, 191
Braun, Werner Von   22
Burney, Venetia   166
Bush, George W   98, 115
Callisto   16, 124, 125, 126, 166
Caloris Basin   54
Calypso   137
Camelot Crater   97, 98

Cancer   75
Candor Chasma   103
Canes Venatici   228
Canis Major   188, 189, 205
Canis Minor   188
Canopus   204
Capricornus   197, 200
Carina   205
Carme   125
Carrington, Richard   44
Cassini   70, 121, 123, 130, 133, 135,
                              137, 138
Cassini Division   134, 140
Cassini, Jean Dominique   134
Cassini-Huygens   121
Cassiopeia   188, 191
Castor   187, 198
Centaurus   197
Centaurus A   224
Cepheid   223, 239, 223
Ceres   174, 175, 176,
Cerro Paranal Observatory   209
Cetus   197, 200
Challenger   26, 98,
Chandra   194, 219
Chandra X-ray Observatory   187
Chandrasekhar Limit   192
Chandrasekhar, Subrahmanyan   192
Charon   33, 166, 168, 169, 170
Christy, James   168
Churyumov- Gerasimenko   182
Clementine (probe)   91
Coal Sack Nebula   197
COBE (Cosmic Background Explorer) 234
Collins, Michael   23, 96
Colombia   28, 96
Columbia Hills   114
Columbia Space Shuttle   78
Command Module   82
Copernicus   15, 54, 63, 90
Cordelia   149
Coriolis   81
Couch Adams, John   154
Crab Nebula   140, 191, 208, 209
Crescent Earth   82
Crescent Moon   90
Cressida   148

Crux 197

Cupid 200

Cybele 144

Cygnus 188, 194, 205, 223

Cygnus X-1 194, 195

Dawn Mission 176

De Lacaille, Nicolas Louis 189

Deep Impact 181, 182

Deimos 108

Delphinus 197, 200

Deneb 205

Desdemona 148

Despina 160

Diana 87

Dione 135, 137

Discovery 26, 28

DMSP 75

Dog Star 189

Doppler 233

Draco 202

Eagle 96, 208

Eagle Nebula 211

Earth 40, 46, 57, 58, 62, 63, 64, 65, 67, 68, 73-84, 86, 88, 89, 91, 95, 96, 98, 103, 105, 120, 121, 123, 124, 130, 131, 133, 134, 150, 166, 174, 187, 199, 205, 216, 219, 233, 235

Edgeworth, Kenneth 169

EGG (Evaporating Gas Globules) 211

Egyptians 12

Einstein, Albert 17, 18, 19, 40, 195

Eisenhower 23

Eistla Regio 70

Eltanin (Gamma Draconis) 202

Elysium Planitia 116

Enceladus 133, 135, 145

Encke Division 134

Encke, Johann 134

Endeavor 23

Enif 205

Enke Gap 161

Epsilon 149, 199

Epsilon Pegasi 205

Eratosthenes 11

Euphrates 200

Europa 16, 124, 166

European Space Agency 36, 57, 68, 115, 140

Event Horizon 195

Explorer 1 22, 81

F-ring 161

Gagarin, Yuri 23, 25

Galactic Center 189

Galactic Dark Horse 189

Galatea 160

Galilei, Galileo 16, 17, 18, 48, 63, 124, 133, 154, 216

Galileo (probe) 70, 91, 120, 123, 124, 125, 126, 175

Galle, Johann Gottfried 154, 159

Gamma Pegasi 205

Gamow, George 232

Ganymede 16, 124, 125, 140, 166

Gaspra 175

Gemini 187, 198

Gemini North Telescope 223

Geminids 177

General Theory of Relativity 18

George's Star 144

Georgium Sidus 144

Giza, pyramids 11

Gliese 229B 187

Gold, Thomas 232

Gossamer Ring 123

Great Bear 189

Great Dark Spot 121, 155, 156, 157, 159, 162

Great Dark Spot of 1989 159

Great Dark Spot of 1994 159

Great Red Spot 121, 123, 124, 126, 157

Great Star 63

Gusev Crater 107

Hadar 197

Hadley 68

Hadley-Apennine 82

Hale, Alan 183

Hale-Bopp 182, 183

Hall, Asaph 108

Halley, Edmond 182

Halley's Comet 169, 180, 181, 182

Halo Ring 123

Hawking, Stephen 195

HDE 226868 194

Helene 137

Helix 191

Hellas Basin 107, 108

Hera 205

Hercules 188

Herschel, John 89, 148

Herschel, William 137, 144, 145, 148, 174, 190, 219

Hertzsprung, Ejner 186

Hewish, Anthony 193

Himalia 125

Hipparchus 11

Hodges, Ann 179

Hooke, Robert 121

Horatio 98

Hoyle, Fred 232

HRSC (High Resolution Stereo Camera) 103, 108, 114

Hubble Space Telescope 107, 131, 137, 138, 146, 148, 161, 168, 169, 170, 191, 192, 194, 211, 224, 233, 234

Hubble, Edwin 222, 223

Huygens (probe) 138. 140

Huygens, Christian 133, 140

Hyades Star 201

Hydra 205

Iapetus 135

International Astronmical Union 168,169,189

Io 16, 123, 124, 125, 126, 166

Irwin, James B 82

Ishtar 68,202

Ishtar Terra 64,67,68

Isis 202

Janus 137

Jewitt, David 169

Johnson Space Center 104

Jovian Planets 32

Jupiter 19, 32, 58, 70, 91, 118-128, 130, 131, 150, 156, 170, 174, 175, 182, 187

Kant, Immanuel 222

Kanya 202

Kennedy Space Center 28, 96

Kennedy, President 95

Kepler, Johannes 15,17,191

Kepler's Star 191

Khrushchev, Nikita 23

Kitt Peak National Observatory 194, 224, 228

Korolev, Sergei 22

KPNO 194

Krishna 202

Kronis 177

Kronos 130, 144

Kueyen 209

Kuiper Belt 32, 33, 160, 161, 167, 168, 169, 170, 175, 182

Kuiper, Gerald 54, 148, 160, 169

Lagoon Nebula 216

Laika 23

Lander Missions 110

Large Megallanic Cloud 13, 191, 227

Larissa 160

Lascaux Caves 11

Lassell, William 148, 160

Le Verrier, Urbain 154, 159

Leda 125

Lemaitre, Georges 232, 233

Leo	198
Leonids	177
Levy, David	124
Libra	201, 202
Little Green Men	193
Lovell, James	88
Lowell Observatory	166, 167
LRV (Lunar Roving Vehicle)	82
Luna	87
Luna 2	23, 95
Luna 3	86, 95
Luna 10	95
Lunar Orbiter 1	96
Lunar Prospector	91
Lycus Suici	116
Maat Mons	70
Magellan (probe)	62, 63, 64, 67, 68, 70
Magellan, Ferdinand	13
Main Sequence	186, 187, 189, 191
Mare Crisium	92
Mare Fecunditatis	92
Mare Nectaris	92
Mare Tranquillitatis	92
Mariner 2	65, 67
Mariner 3	109
Mariner 4	104, 109
Mariner 6	109
Mariner 7	109
Mariner 9	109, 110
Mariner 10	53, 54, 55, 57, 58
Markab	205
Mars	32, 55, 58, 78, 100-117, 125, 150, 174, 175, 178
Mars 1	109
Mars 2	109, 110
Mars 3	109, 110
Mars 4	111
Mars 5	111
Mars 6	111
Mars 7	111
Mars 96	113
Mars Climate Orbiter	114
Mars Exploration Rover Spirit	107, 115
Mars Express	103, 108, 114, 115, 116,
Mars Odyssey Spacecraft	103
Mars Polar Lander	114
Mars Reconnaissance Orbiter	115
Mars Science Laboratory	108
Mars Surveyor Program	113, 114
Maxwell, James Clerk	68, 133
Maya	12
McAuliffe, Christa	26
McNeil's Nebula	199
Melas Chasma	103
Mesopotamia	87
Mercury	10, 18, 19, 32, 50-59, 63, 64, 70, 150
MESSENGER	57, 70
Messier, Charles	208
Meteor Crater	178
Metis	123, 125
Michelson Doppler Imager	45
Midnight Sun	75
Milky Way	145, 197, 200, 201, 214-219, 222, 227, 228
Mimas	135, 137, 145
Mimosa	197
Minerva	144
Minkowski, Hermann	18
Mintaka	188, 199,
Mir Space Station	28
Miranda	148
Mitchell, Edgar	87
MODIS	80
Monocero	213
Montes, Maxwell	64, 67, 68
Moon	41, 43, 63, 76, 85-99, 125
Mount Everest	68
Naiad	160
NASA	22, 23, 33, 36, 65, 65, 67, 68, 70, 80, 89, 91, 97, 98, 103, 104, 107, 108, 111, 113, 114, 115, 121, 125, 175, 176, 181
NEAR (Near Earth Asteroid Rendezvous)	175, 176
NEAR-Shoemaker	175
Nebulae	206
Neireid	160
Neptune	18, 32, 33, 58, 125, 144, 149, 150, 15-163, 166, 169, 175, 182
Neutron	192, 193
New Horizons Spacecraft	170
Newton, Isaac	17, 18, 19
Nimbus 7	75
Niobe Planitia	67
Nixon, President	96
Northern Lights	81
Nozomi (probe)	114
Oberon	125, 148, 149
Ocean of Storms	96
Odysseus	137
Odyssey	105, 115
Olbers, Heinrich Wilhelm	174
Olympus Mons	103, 109, 113, 116
Omega	208
Oort Cloud	33, 182, 183
Ophir Chasma	103
Ophiuchus	191, 216
Opportunity	104, 115
Orion	188, 199, 208, 213, 219
Orion Nebula	199
Orion's Belt	12, 189, 199,
Orionis Beta	199
Orionis Delta	199
Pallas	174, 175
Palomar Observatory	167
Pandora	134
Pangaea	76
Pasiphaë	125
Pathfinder	113
Pavonis Mons	109
Penzias, Arno	234
Perihelia	34
Perseids	177
Phobos	108
Phobos 2	111, 113
Phoebe	87
Phoebe Regio	68
Phoenix (probe)	104, 108, 115
Piazzi, Guiseppe	174
Pinwheel Galaxy	223
Pioneer Venus	62, 67, 68
Pioneer Venus Programme	67
Pisces	197, 200
Planet X	166
Planet-C (probe)	70
Plough	189, 202, 203
Pluto	32, 33, 58, 150, 155, 164-171
Pluto-Kuiper Express	170
Polaris	202
Pollux	187, 198
Polydeuces	137
Pope, Alexander	148
Population I Stars	219, 223
Population II Stars	219, 223, 225
Portia	148
Poseidon	160
Prometheus	134
Proteus	160
Proxima Centauri	187
Ptolemy	14, 17, 188
Puck	148
Pulsars	193
Pythagoras	11
Quaoar	33, 169
Quasar	192
Ranger 7	23, 95
Rastaban (Beta Draconis)	202
Red Planet	105
Regulus	198
Relativity	18, 19
Rhea	135
Rigel	188

Roche Limit 108, 133, 135, 160
Roche, Edouard 133
Romans 54, 62
Rosetta 182
Royal Observatory 181
RS Ophiuchi 190
Russell, Henry 186
Russian Venera 62
Saggitarius 200, 201, 209
Saggitarius A 219
Saturn 32, 58, 123, 129-142, 144, 145, 150, 156, 161
Saturn V 27
Scheat 205
Schiaparelli, Giovanni 54, 105, 106, 110
Schwarzschild, Karl 194
Scorpius 200,201,202,216
Scott, David R 82
Scutum 216, 219
Sea of Tranquillity 27, 90, 96
Sedna 33, 169,
Selene 87
Shapley, Harlow 219
Shepard, Alan 23, 97
Shoemaker, Eugene 124, 175
Shoemaker, Carolyn 124
Shoemaker-Levy 9 124
Showalter, Mark 135
Sif Mons 70
Sinope 125
Sirius 189, 199, 205
Skylab 1 46
Small Magellanic Cloud 227
SOHO (Solar and Heliospheric Observatory) 44, 45
Solar System 31-37, 133, 170, 189, 216
Sombrero Galaxy 224
South Massif 98
Soviet (probes) 65
Soviet Union 22
Space Shuttle 26
Spicules 41
Spitzer Space Telescope 209
Sputnik 1 22,23
Sputnik 2 22
Stanford University 104
Steady State Theory 233
Stickney Crater 108
Stonehenge 11,12
Sun 12, 17, 19, 38-49, 63, 76, 86, 133, 168, 191, 198, 219
Sunspots 41, 43, 45
Surveyor 3 96
Swan 198

Swift-Tuttle 177
Taurus 188, 201, 209
Taurus-Littrow 97, 98
Telesto 137
Tempel 1 181
Tempel-Tuttle 177, 178
Terra Meridiani 115
Tethys 134, 135, 137
Thalassa 160
Tharsis Ridge 113
Thebe 123, 125
Themis 202
Themis Regio 68
Theophilus 92
Thoth 87
Titan 133, 135, 138, 140, 166
Titania 145, 148, 149
Tombaugh, Clyde 166, 167, 169
Trapezium 213
Triangulum Galaxy 223, 227
Triffid Nebula 208, 209
Triton 155, 159, 160, 161, 166, 169
Trojan 125
Tsiolkovsky Crater 88
Tsukuyomi 87
Tycho, Brahe 90
Type II (supernova) 192
Typhon 200
Umbriel 148
Unity 23
Uranus 17, 32, 58, 133, 143-151, 157, 168
Ursa Major 189, 202, 203
Ursa Minor 202
V-2 rockets 22
Valles Marineris 103, 110
Vallis, Ares 104, 113
Vallis, Ruell 108
Van Allen Belt 22, 81
Van Allen, James 81
Venera 68
Venera 7 67
Venera 9 67
Venera10 67
Venus 12, 16, 32, 36, 36, 58, 60-69, 103, 150, 191
Venus Express 68
Viking 1 107, 111
Viking 2 111
Viking missions 104
Virgo 202, 224
Voss, James S 27
Voyager 1 36, 121, 123, 125, 126, 134, 137

Voyager 2 36, 121, 126, 133, 135, 146, 148, 150, 155, 159, 161, 162
Vulpecula 216, 194
Waldenburg, Germany 64
Welles, Orson 106
Wells, H G 106
Wheeler, John 193
Whirlpool Galaxy 228
White Nights 75
White Spot 131
Williams, Jeffrey N. 27
Wilson, Robert 234
Wolf, Max 125
Wolszczan, Aleksander 36
Worden, Alfred M 82
Yamamoto 791197 179
Yepun Telescope 175
Zarya 23
Zeta 199
Zeus 130, 201
Zodiac 201

Dedication

In memory of my Grandfather, Ronald James Good.

Acknowledgements
This book would not have been possible without the help of the following people:
Jane Benn, Mathlida Hoyle, Hayden Wood, Richard Betts, Kevin Davis,
Cliff Salter, Melanie Cox, Christopher Chillingford.
Design by John Dunne.

All images are courtesy Science Photo Library

American Institute of Physics (19); David P. Anderson SMU/NASA (64t);
Julian Baum (141,192,198,197,201,202,200,205t); Wesley Bocxe (78); Chris Butler (140t,164,171);
California Association For Research in Astronomy (142,145); Celestial Image Co. (210);
Chandra X-Ray Observatory (195t,219); John Chumack (167t,172,189,216,217,218); Tony Craddock (38,49);
Luke Dodd (184); Dr Fred Espenak (52,177,186); European Southern Observatory (175,208);
European Space Agency (109,115,139tr,182); European Space Agency/DLRFU Berlin/G. Neukum (100,108,116);
John Foster (99); Mark Galick (33,34,57,65,111,134,188,226); Robert Gendler (206,212,213);
Pascal Goetgheluck (8) Francois Gohier (179) Dr Leon Golub (48) Tony & Daphne Hallas (214,222);
David A. Hardy (14,15); Roger Harris (80,203); Mehau Kulyk (40,151); Larry Landolfi (36,90,95);
M. Ledlow Et Al NRAO/AUI/NSF (55); Jon Lomberg (199r); Jerry Lodriguss (42,43,178t,183); John Mead (11);
G. Antonio Milani (96); Mount Stromlo & Siding Spring Observatories (190,209);
NASA(4,20,24,26,27,29,41,47,50,53,59,60,62,66,67,68,69,70,75,76,79,81,84,86,87,88,89,97,98,103,
105,112,113,114,118,120,121,122,123,124,125,126l,126r,127,128,130,131,132,133,135,137,139b,140b,146,147,152,154,
155,156,157,158,161,162,163,168,174,176,178b,187,232,237,240,246);
NASA/ESA/STScl (2,3,6,106,136,138,139tl,148,149,160,169,170,193,195b,211,220,225,230,234);
NASA/KSC (128l); NASA JPL-Caltech/UMD (181); NASA JPLCornell (107);
National Optical Astronomy Observatories (229); Adam Nieman (166); NOAO (224); NOAO/AURA/NSF (194,223);
Novosti (22,25); David Nunuk (37); David Parker (233); Max Planck Ins. For Astrophysics (235);
Planetry Visions Ltd (72,74,77); Royal Greenwich Observatory (180); Royal Observatory, Edinburgh (18);
John Sanford (93); Science, Industry & Business Library, New York Public Library (16);
Eckhard Slawik (12,64b,92,94,196,199l,204,205b); SOHO/ESA/NASA (44,45); Space Imaging Europe (10);
Ulli Steltzer, US Geological Survey (56,150); Sheila Terry (144); Joe Tucciarone (104,191,243);
Detlev Van Ravenswaay (23,46,54,5863,102,110,117); Jason Ware (228); Frank Zullo (32).